Immersive T
and Activ.

Immersive Theater and Activism

Scripts and Strategies for Directors and Playwrights

NANDITA DINESH

McFarland & Company, Inc., Publishers
Jefferson, North Carolina

ISBN (print) 978-1-4766-7204-5
ISBN (ebook) 978-1-4766-3411-1

LIBRARY OF CONGRESS CATALOGUING DATA ARE AVAILABLE

BRITISH LIBRARY CATALOGUING DATA ARE AVAILABLE

Front cover photographs by People Images/IStock

Printed in the United States of America

*McFarland & Company, Inc., Publishers
Box 611, Jefferson, North Carolina 28640
www.mcfarlandpub.com*

To Nikhil Dinesh,
for always having my back

Table of Contents

Introduction

You walk into a space. You have been told, or maybe you've intentionally not been told, that this theatrical experience will require your participation.

You walk into this space and as soon as you do, you are told that you must become someone else. You, the audience member, are given a character and asked to stay true to that character for the duration of your time in the theatrical experience.

You, the audience-member-character, enter this space and over the course of the following minutes/hours/days, you embody an Other. And through this vicarious embodiment, it is hoped that you will encounter a glimpse into someone else's experience of the world.

You, the audience member, become a character.

You, the audience member, become an Other.

You, the audience member, become a participant.

You, the audience member, become an actor.

You, the audience member, become—to borrow from Augusto Boal (1985)—a "spect-actor."[1]

You become a spect-actor and, in so doing, experience what many of us call immersive theater.

Immersive theater is far from being an uncontested term. What is "immersive theater" to me, is "role-playing" to someone else; the "spect-actor" to me, is a "participant" to someone else. But my fascination with the aesthetic choices described above is not semantic in nature. Rather, my explorations around immersive aesthetics stem from a position of practice. What does this aesthetic "do" differently than another? How can this form of vicarious, theatrical experience of an Other become more ethical? How might writers and directors for the theatre have to re-conceptualize our approaches in the creation of immersive theater? It is this last question that inspired this book.

Although recent years have seen a number of academic and theoretical analyses about immersive environments that place audience members in multi-sensory settings and invite spectators to co-execute a performance/ performance-like event (Machon, 2013; White, 2013; Hill & Paris, 2014;

1

Magelssen, 2014; Alston, 2016; Frieze, 2016; Harpin & Nicholson, 2016), dramatic scripts that utilize participatory aesthetics are difficult to find—possibly because the process of scripting for a form that is hinged on audience immersion and/or participation requires different tools; tools that await some definition in the burgeoning field of immersive theater. What elements of "traditional"[2] playwriting have to shift so as to accommodate the spirit of improvisation that lies at the heart of such immersive forms? How can this book address the current lack of immersive theater scripts by generating texts and theories—specifically for playwriting, and direction—that might be utilized by a range of researchers and practitioners?

While the abovementioned questions frame one part of this writing project, another dimension to this book is brought in through a meditation on the concept of "gray zones"; a term that I borrow from Primo Levi (1988) in its being used to speak to narratives and lived experiences that exist between the more easily identifiable voices of the "victim" and the "perpetrator" in a context of conflict. I highlight this concept of the gray zones since applied theatre interventions that ask spect-actors to become an Other seem to be predicated on the creation of binaries. Spect-actors either step into the shoes of an "oppressor," as can be seen in the immersive aesthetics that are used by social psychologists like Stanley Milgram (1963) and Philip Zimbardo (1971) in their obedience and prison experiments, respectively. Or, when spect-actors are not characterized as "oppressors," they are generally asked to step into the shoes of the "oppressed"—as in *Un Voyage pas comme les autres sur les chemins de l'exil (Chemins)*[3]—the piece that initially catalyzed my interest in this form.

Perhaps unsurprisingly then, the creation of these binaries catalyzes important questions that have to do with voyeurism and ethics: don't we stand the risk of essentializing complex social situations when we perpetuate problematic binaries between "oppressor" and "oppressed," or "victim" and "perpetrator"? Don't we over-simplify the prison and the process of immigration when we do not present the multiple positions that inhabit the spaces between prisoner and guard; between asylum seeker and immigration official? As Jill Bennet (in Shaughnessy, 2012:6–7) says, the empathy that is derived through immersive experiences might ultimately manifest in a crude empathy in which "another's experience" is seen as being "assimilated to the self in the most simplistic and sentimental way." Furthermore, such a "conjunction of affect and critical awareness may be understood to constitute the basis of an empathy grounded not in affinity (feeling for another insofar as we can imagine being that other) but on a feeling for another that entails an encounter with something irreducible and different, often inaccessible" (Shaughnessy, 2012:6–7).

So, how might participatory texts be crafted so as to invite spect-actors to step in the shoes of an Other in the gray zones, i.e., where they do not become the prisoner or the guard; where they do not become the asylum seeker or the immigration official; they become, instead, an Other who occupies a space between the positions of "most" and "least" power within a particular conflicted context? Could the writing of the spect-actors into these gray zones assuage some of the ethical risks that come with embodying an "oppressed" or "oppressor" Other within a theatrical scenario? With these questions in mind, the chapters in this book are not only framed around addressing a lack of immersive theater scripts. Rather, they also seek to explore if such works might be less ethically fraught by inviting spect-actors to embody voices from the gray zones of a particular conflict.

Before moving on to a discussion about existing attempts to give written form to participatory environments though, I would like to clarify my approach to audience immersion in this book as being composed of two important characteristics. First, my work is inspired by the principles of applied theater and as such, hinges on "some component of pedagogy or social change—whether or not they bear witness in some manner to past experiences and/or injustices, or as Augusto Boal puts it, 'rehearse' their participants for 'real life'" (Magelssen, 2014:5). Second, in my approach to participation/immersion—there are many ways in which the term is understood—the spect-actor is invited to physically embody an Other, akin to the realm of social psychology experiments of the past: the spect-actor *becomes* the asylum seeker in *Chemins* just as she *becomes* the prisoner in Zimbardo's (1971; 2007) Stanford Prison Experiment and the torturer-teacher in Milgram's (1971; Perry, 2012) obedience experiments. With this framework in mind, therefore, the first step in writing this book involved looking at what material does exist, that I could draw on to develop scripts for such a participatory theatrical aesthetic; a process of investigation that led to the study of a range of examples[4]: from tabletop role playing games in war studies to drills from language learning; from simulations in nursing education to training in outdoor education; from refugee simulations designed by the Red Cross to, ultimately, the Live Action Role Plays[5] (LARPs) that became most pertinent for the scripts in this book.

This is both a book of plays and a book about writing plays for an immersive theater. Having clarified my approach to immersive theater early on, I do *not* seek to enter into further discussions about terminology, and use terms like "participatory" and "immersive" freely. Additionally, I do *not* seek for this book to present "formulas," which present one way to write and direct an immersive theater text. Instead, I see this writing project as inhabiting a space between theory and practice and as speaking to some of the complex mechanics of composing/executing a participatory/immersive theatrical experience. Therefore, although the scripts in this book have not been "tested" on stage—like most published play scripts are required to be—the strategies that surround the texts' creation and implementation have been explored often in my own practice. My experiments with immersive aesthetics are ongoing and I see this writing project as one more step in a long-term effort to understand a form that both amazes and terrifies me—for its potential to theatrically unlock the experience of an Other; for its risks of oversimplifying the experiences of that Other.

From Tabletop Role-Playing Games to In Exile for a While

I began my process of investigation by looking at role-playing games that take place around a table (Bowman, 2010; Cover, 2010; Tresca, 2011) and in so doing, encountered Philip Sabin's (2012) work that shares his "scripting" process for tabletop role-playing games about historical wars. While Sabin sometimes uses different section names in different games, for elements that essentially have the same function, combing through his various "scripts" suggests that his game scripts include the following:

- **Introduction:** An overview of the events that are set to take place in a particular game and the objectives of what is to be studied through it
- **Map:** A physical map of the real-life terrain on which the conflict took place
- **Scenario Overview:** A description of the particular events that are included within the scope of the game
- **Actions That Are Possible:** A list that describes the potential actions that participants can utilize within the world of the game
- **Sequence of Play:** A timeline of events that occur in the game
- **Example of Play:** A detailed description of how one scenario in the game might play out, with regards to player turns and possibilities
- **Notes for Facilitators:** Guidance for the individuals conducting such tabletop role-playing war games

There is, immediately, a clear difference between such an approach that works around a table, and the simulation of multi-sensorial environments like those I seek to craft in my own immersive theatrical aesthetics. And yet, the similarity of intention behind Sabin's work and my own—of using particular kinds of immersive environments to better understand conflict—warranted a consideration of the potential applicability of the framework above.

While a majority of the elements that Sabin uses might be adapted quite easily to an immersive theater script, there are two elements that would need reframing: the "map" and the "sequence of play." Now, the former (the map) is more easily adaptable to a theatrical context: the concept being useful to give readers/directors/performers a pictorial representation of the spatial dynamics of the piece in question. The sequence of play, however, is not as visibly applicable. Although the potential utility of a sequence of play in a dramatic script is evident, the primary difference between the sequence, as described by Sabin, and the needs of a theatrical effort that works with actors and spect-actors (as compared to every participant being more similarly positioned in tabletop role-playing games) is the absence of dialogue: how does the structure of the "game" guide characters/participants in how to speak to each other? Since looking at tabletop simulations of conflict did not address this question of dialogue, I then turned to the use of simulation drills in language learning, nursing education, and outdoor leadership to understand the ways in which dialogue might be crafted in a participatory environment.

Drills and dialogues are among the most traditional materials used by language teachers and these requisites have been put forth for the execution meaningful drills:

- that they should "look like real language"
- that the interchanges "should not be totally predictable"
- that they should be centered on topics that are relevant to the students that there should be some element of control so that the teacher can evaluate the degree of learning that is taking place (Epstein & Ormiston, 2007:1–3)

Language-learning drills take a variety of forms:

- repetitions that are used to familiarize students "with a specific structure or formulaic expression" (Epstein & Ormiston, 2007:3)
- substitution drills that more improvisational and give students the chance to change words/phrases when responding within the context of the drill
- transformational drills that allows students more freedom in the responses that they craft.

With the particular intentions of language learning, therefore, and their repetitive/substitution/transformational styles, a combination of the following strategies are used to craft drills (Epstein & Ormiston, 2007:20–23):

- **Introduction:** An identification of the aims and objectives for the drill
- **The Context:** An articulation of the physical/spatial environment of the drill
- **Scenario Overview**: An outline of the event

- **Preparation:** A list of the necessary linguistic tools that students will need to navigate the context/scenario
- **Role Information**: A description of participants' characters for the duration of the drill
- **Modeling the Role-Play:** A familiarization process where students are informed about possible activities they might have to undertake. For example, "You can do this using a sequence of pictures and audio recordings, or model a scripted role-play with another student"
- **Doing the Role-play:** A strategy/strategies for dialogue creation among participants. Options include:
  - controlled dialogue with fill in the blanks
  - open dialogue where students have handouts only with their character's dialogue
  - choice from a list of available expressions
  - free practice that goes beyond the script and allows students to go outside the confines of a pre-determined text
  - cue card dialogues with cues given to each student, including information that could be used to generate dialogue
  - situation cards with explicit instructions for how the scene should unfold (describing actions, not dialogue)
  - discourse chains, where diagrammatic representations of how the conversation might unfold are handed out to participants
- **Processing the Role-play:** A follow-up activity in which the participants are debriefed about their experience in the drill by asking them to, for homework, "write-up their role play as a narrative or a script," and/or fill in a worksheet "based on the role play"

I initially looked at literature surrounding second language learning drills to think about how dialogue might be crafted for performers in an immersive theatrical experience. However, what I came away thinking about was the potential of creating dialogue "hints" for spect-actors and thus addressing some of the vulnerability that immersive theater environments are likely to cause for those who are new to it. If the goal of an immersive theatrical environment is pedagogical in nature, as is the case with my work, would it behoove spect-actors to have "cues" that indicate to them how they might engage with the piece? Is it the presence of such "cues" that leads to the general success of Augusto Boal's (1985) Forum Theater—in that the Joker (facilitator) walks audiences through exactly how spect-actors should interact with the performance in question? While immersive pieces that do *not* seek a pedagogical outcome might well desire the vulnerability that is caused when spect-actors are not given any rules of engagement, can the risks of the immersive form in an applied theater context (dealing with "real" people and "real" issues) be mitigated through the use of cue cards/dialogue cards/discourse chains/situation cards as in the examples above, which would serve as a "crutch" for spect-actors during their immersive journeys?

With these questions in mind, in looking for other pedagogical, immersive environments that share language learning drills' focus on skills acquisition, I encountered the use of simulations in nursing education. By consulting an array of nursing simulation "scripts" that seem to be more widely available than texts for other types of immersive/participatory/simulated environments, I discovered that these events—like their language learning counterparts—almost always involve a pre-simulation briefing that then feeds in to a similarly structured simulation that focuses on the transference of particular skills to the nursing student (Montgomery College Simulation Library, 2016):

- **Briefing:** A session that includes a welcome and introduction in which the purpose of the simulation is shared in the context of a safe learning environment. Participants are informed about the preparatory work that they need to undertake before the simulation. Furthermore, they are asked to ensure confidentiality through a "fiction contract" in which the participants agree to maintain the reality of the simulated world through the fictional content. Finally, the participants are oriented to the space and equipment, introduced to their roles, and informed about the logistics surrounding time, place, and before/after sessions
- **Cognitive/Psychomotor Skills Required Prior to Simulation:** An outline of skills that are required by participants *before* their participation in the simulation
- **Scenario/Simulation Focused Objectives:** A list of information that is provided to the participants and facilitators vis-à-vis the expected outcomes of the training simulations
- **Requirements of Actor/Mannequins:** A section of the "script" that includes information about the context of the patient within the framework of the scenario (the human or mannequin on whom the student-participants will be learning specific nursing skills)
- **Fidelity of the Simulation:** An outline that includes descriptions of,
  - Setting/Environment
  - Props needed
  - Documentation forms/information required from participants in the simulation
- **Scenario Progression Outline:** A timeline for the scenario that includes,

⊚ details about the actions performed by a mannequin or human patient/actor

⊚ descriptions of the interventions to be performed by the participant/nursing student

⊚ cues for the scenario's progression

This information is represented in a table, through the use of a flowchart, or in the form of more "conventional" script with dialogue

- **Debriefing/Guided Questions for Reflections:** A final section that includes questions that are designed to help students discover the thinking behind their doing

In addition to the simulations/drills that are used in language learning and in nursing education, another example skill-building oriented immersive structures can be found in the simulations used by the National Outdoor Leadership School (NOLS). These documented structures seem to include:

- a description of desired outcomes
- a summary of what is to be expected within the simulation scenario in question
- ground rules that frame the simulation (similar to the "fiction contract" that was mentioned in the nursing education material above) preparation that the simulation leader will need to undertake prior to its execution, and the script itself.

In these NOLS scripts, within each documented stage of the simulation, the leader is required to have a checklist of events that should happen during that stage; a checklist that is based on each specific training location's Emergency Response Plan. This checklist is used by the simulation leader in conjunction with a detailed, time-based breakdown of events as below (Vermeal, n.d.):

9:00 a.m.: Incident simulation begins
9:15 a.m.: Event #1
9:25 a.m.: Event #2
9:35 a.m.: Event #3
9:50 a.m.: Event #4

   and so on

12:45 p.m.: End of simulation
1 p.m.: Debrief led by the simulation leader

In comparison with the structure provided for a less "embodied" simulation, the three structures that follow a consideration of Sabin's work—from language learning drills, nursing simulations, and NOLS—provide noteworthy distinctions. The first distinction lies in the pre-role-play preparatory sessions that are required, that seem to be more extensive than the simpler introductions that occur in tabletop role-playing games. Such pre-session briefings are also complemented, in nursing education and in NOLS, by a post-role-play debrief during which the students/participants are asked to reflect upon the learning that has occurred for them. That said, while Sabin's tabletop war simulations do not overtly require a debrief as part of the written structure of the game, given the simulations' pedagogic goals, it would not surprise me if post-session debriefs are indeed an unscripted part of tabletop role-playing games as well.

In addition to the distinctions between preparatory/debrief mechanisms, differences are evident in how dialogue is scripted (or not) in the abovementioned scenarios as compared to the simulations of war that are constructed by Sabin:

- variations that are more structured in the case of language learning drills
- the scenario progression outline/flowchart/script structure options that are put forward by the simulations for training nurses
- a more detailed timeline that is provided by NOLS, which when accompanied by constant references back to a "central text" (the Emergency Response Plan of the location in which the simulation is being conducted) functions as a tool to control the quality and content of improvisation-heavy scenarios.

Now, the simplicity behind the variations of dialogue structure in the language learning drills is, of course, attributable to the fact that the participants are second-language learners, making improvisation more difficult for this particular target audience. Similarly, the particular structures that govern the execution of the nursing simulations and the NOLS example are geared toward the particular, very focused, training objectives of those particular curricula.

With these context specific reasons in mind, however, can we extrapolate from language learning drills, to make an argument that the form of theater itself might function as a "second language" for spect-actors—especially when they are invited to participate in a fashion that they might not be accustomed to? Furthermore, could the use of progression outlines, flowcharts, and timelines in an immersive script, inspired by the nursing education simulations, allow for an easier transference and replication of the text amongst its performers and directors? Could the potential reference back to a "central text"—

like the use of the Emergency Response Plan in the NOLS simulation—allow for performers in immersive aesthetics to improvise more cohesively when met with unpredictable responses from spect-actors? And finally, what might be said about the pedagogical potential that arises through the creation of pre/post-performance spaces? While I hope to more rigorously explore preparatory and debrief spaces in my theater practice in the near future, the ubiquitous presence of these two elements within the examples showcased in this Introduction does seem to point toward an already acknowledged benefit vis-à-vis the inclusion of such processes in immersive environments.

Ultimately, although the language learning drills, nursing education, and outdoor leadership drills provided me with many interesting elements to consider adding to the theatrical, immersive scripts in this book, I was still left with questions surrounding nuance and complexity in these texts. Since the drills and simulations described above are designed with a certain simplicity of narrative/plot because of their particular intentions and target audiences, how could I craft a structure that might allow for more complexity? This is to say, how could I write a participatory script that could be about more than one transactional scenario (as in the case of the language learning drills), or that could interweave more than one kind of setting (as in the case of nursing education), or that could be focused on more than one particular type of situation (as in the outdoor leadership example)? It is in looking for ways of scripting complexity that I came across one particular use of role-plays in a social science classroom.

David Sherrin (2016) proposes the following elements as being necessary when creating complex, dynamic, simulations that are based on a historical event:

- **Selecting and researching** the story
- **Creating (or determining) the characters**: Students are asked to choose characters, choose three skills (from a pre-provided list), and two possessions (also from a predetermined list)
- **Determining the scenes**
- **Writing the background narratives**
- **Deciding on conflicts and choice moments:** Choice moments are when one or more individuals in the role-play make a key decision, often ethical, that will drive the subsequent acting and action
- **Creating action and speaking cards:** Action and speaking cards that seek to help strike the balance between providing students freedom of choice, and guiding them toward specific conflicts and actions that are historically accurate
- **Gathering props**
- **Determining homework assignments**

- **Pivotal decision debates (PDD):** These are moments in which members of the participating community gather to discuss a question whose resolution will have great bearing on their future. This is distinct from "choice moments" which are often individual in nature and usually require coming to a quick decision. These PDDs add additional skill-building elements to the role-playing toolbox by incorporating students' growing knowledge, their perspective of their roles, and their use of evidence from homework texts into a debate
- **Creating an assessment:** Similar in function to a debrief, this assessment seeks to test knowledge gained by students during these simulations

The dynamism allowed by the Choice Moments, PDDs, and Options in Sherrin's work is an element that I find particularly interesting in thinking about how immersive, theatrical scripts with more complex narratives might be framed. The challenge, of course, lies in the strong presence of the teacher within the execution of such simulations in the classroom: the individual educator performs many tasks within the context of a role-play like the one above, unlike a theatrical environment in which multiple performers facilitate a single immersive event. And with this significant difference in play, would Sherrin's ideas work within an immersive theater script?

In light of this emergent query, I began to seek examples for simulations/immersive environments/role-playing games that would allow for multiplicity and complexity, i.e., texts that could be layered beyond the simplicity of language learning drills, but that could still function *without* the central presence of one teacher/facilitator. It is in thinking about this question that I decided to revisit the well-known Red Cross simulation (n.d.), *In Exile for a While,* that uses complex immersive environments toward a very specific pedagogic objective: the spect-actor's acquisition of an affective, embodied awareness about the experiences of refugees and asylum seekers:

- **Introduction:** An outline of objectives and goals of the simulation
- **The Event:** An itinerary that has a detailed time-based breakdown of how the events are to unfold during the course of the event. A detailed timeline is provided for the entire time frame of the event and organizers are encouraged to use a duration that works best for their particular context
- **Debriefing:** A description of the general themes that might guide an articulation of what participants can do after the simulation i.e., "in real life," to engage with programs promoting the rights of refugees and asylum seekers
- **Actors' Roles:** A list of characters in the simulation

- **Logistics:** A list of necessary personnel and infrastructure. For instance: describing the responsibilities of an individual who takes on a managerial role, specifying the specific spatial requirements as being a farm or a site in a provincial park, creating lists of food needed by participants; detailing information vis-à-vis sponsorship for the event
- **Forms:** An extensive array of documentation including registration forms for participants, consent forms, and information/fact sheets about themes that are central to the event (i.e. data about existing refugee camps, globally and locally; the intersection between gender and refugee status; health issues being faced in refugee camps). These information/fact sheets are intended both for organizers to inform themselves, and to better facilitate the debriefing sessions. Given the pedagogic objectives of this particular simulation, these are also documents that can be shared with the participants as handouts during the debriefing at the end of the simulation

Given the heightened relevance of an initiative like *In Exile for a While* for the kind of immersive work that frames this book, I then undertook more investigation into large-scale immersive environments that were *not* tied to a particular discipline like language learning, nursing education, outdoor education, or social science. Intentionally deciding *not* to reinvent the wheel, encountering different structural possibilities forced me to dig deeper; to see if there was "something" that came closer to my approach to immersive theater; "something" that had a practical repertoire of scripted materials that would allow me to make more informed choices about points of departure for the scripts in this book. After much scavenging then, after meandering through the worlds of tabletop role-playing games, language learning drills, nursing education simulations, outdoor education training, social science role-plays, and initiatives like *In Exile for a While,* I came across the genre of Live Action Role Plays—a form whose practice and research came to most influence my decisions vis-à-vis the scripting process in this book.

Live Action Role Plays (LARPs)

Not only is it complex to track "a" history of LARP but also, the terminology that is used for these events seems to change based on the setting of their execution: "from Knutepunkt (Norway) to Knutpunk (Sweden), Knudepunkt (Denmark) and Solmukohta (Finland)" (Stenros & Montola, 2010:10). "The established Nordic larp cultures trace their roots back to the 1980s" and the combined influences of activities like "Dungeons & Dragons," "tabletop role-playing games," "the anti-role-playing film Mazes and Monsters (1982)," "Tolkien societies, historical re-enactment[s], scouting, assassination games, community theater et cetera" are all said to be integral in understanding how LARPs exist today in the Nordic countries and beyond (Stenros & Montola, 2010:15).

LARPs are created for "a first person audience, for players relating to the fictional world from the first person perspective of a fictional character" (Stenros & Montola, 2010:20). It has been called "a medium, an art form, a social art form, a new performance art that creates a social body, and a subjective form of art" (Stenros & Montola, 2010: 305) and has been particularly compared to diverse theatrical forms:

> Commedia dell'Arte (usually without obvious masks), a particularly obscure Theater Game, untherapeutic psychodrama, a sort of Invisible Theater, or amateur improvisational theater. Indeed, from a spectator's point of view the closest relative to larp might very well be a long, uninterrupted impro rehearsal. But this is the key distinction: Larp is not designed to have an audience [Stenros & Montola, 2010:301].

Despite the concept of "audience" being one that is used to differentiate LARPs from theater, LARP literature does seem to acknowledge that such a distinction might not be entirely sufficient either. The role of the audience in the theater is constantly being reinvented: from the use of Viola Spolin's (1999) *Theater Games* for the *Classroom*, in which the difference between actor and audience vanishes; to experimental genres like performance art (or "happenings" or "actions" as they are sometimes called) where a piece does not need to have any spectators; from ritualistic forms of theater making in which the performers themselves form a first-person audience (akin to the work of Jerzy Grotwoski, 2002), to the "spect-actor" in Augusto Boal's (1985) "Theater of the Oppressed" who intervenes directly within the action on stage. For instance, in particular immersive theater projects that I have undertaken (see Dinesh, 2015a) the experience is constructed around individual spect-actors' engagement in self-contained spaces, in intimate—in terms of actor-audience ratios—interactions with performers. This individual spect-actor then, is both audience and actor; there is no non-performer in the mix, who would fit the traditional understanding of an audience member that watches and listens to a staged work.

LARPs and particular forms of theater making have long been recognized as containing resonances with each other, requiring a more careful articulation of how these particular genres/aesthetics might be differentiated—at least superficially—from each other. Brian David Phillips (in Stenros & Montola, 2006:301), for example, considers LARP "to be a part of a wider group of playful forms of pretence," like "Interactive Drama" (Back, 2014:108), where more conventional theatrical strategies are done away with and where traditional boundaries between performers and spectators are challenged. While embarking on such a comparative analysis is fascinating, I must clarify that I do *not* seek to find a prescriptive answer to what makes immersive theater different from LARP in this book. Rather I hope to encounter some points of departure from which I might better understand how lessons from the world of LARP could be put to use in the immersive, theatrical arena.

In order to develop such points of departure, I draw (in Table 1, below) from ideas put forth by Jamie MacDonald (2012), where she delineates the differences between a staged aesthetic—a term that she uses to refer to a theatrical experience in which the audience watches and listens to performers on a stage—and what MacDonald refers to as an immersed aesthetic that is put to use in LARPs. As such, Table 1 summarizes the differences that MacDonald, a self proclaimed theater artist turned LARPer, articulates. However, I also add a third (middle) column, which considers the very same aspects as Macdonald does, but in reference to the immersive aesthetic that underpins the scripts in this book.

Table 1: Aesthetic Comparisons

Stage Aesthetic (as per MacDonald)	Immersive Theater Aesthetic (as per the approach in this book)	Immersed Aesthetic in LARPs (as per MacDonald)
Beautiful to watch, i.e., the aesthetic focus lies in the visual and auditory components of the performance that takes place on a stage.	Beautiful to watch and do. While a central part of the focus in this book's scripts lies in the construction of spectator participation, the texts also consider aesthetic elements that are integral to "conventional" theatrical environments. Elements such as set design, lighting design, costumes, make-up, props, and the use of audiovisual materials.	Beautiful to do, i.e., the aesthetic focus in LARPs are said to lie in their "playability." "Conventional" theatrical design elements are not of particular concern (though they might be an important by-product, precisely to promote playability).
Directed story in which the playwright, or the director, controls how the narratives unfold. In certain kinds of devised/collaborative performances, actors direct the performance as	An experience that is directed by creators and developed by spect-actors. This is to say that there are particular parts of the immersive theater scenario that are always scripted and static; while	MacDonald contends that, in contrast to a "developed," staged aesthetic, LARPs are considered to be "developing." This does not imply that these environments have *no* direction, just that the

Stage Aesthetic (as per MacDonald)	Immersive Theater Aesthetic (as per the approach in this book)	Immersed Aesthetic in LARPs (as per MacDonald)
well. The important point of note here is not who has the power in a given theatrical framework. Rather, what is significant is who does *not* have any power to control a particular theatrical experience; usually, the spectator.	other parts of the narrative shift and evolve in situ, with spect-actors' contributions.	story is not directed in one particular way. While the organizers might have particular checks and balances in place to help guide the story, the narratives' development is (more often than not) entirely in the hands of the participants.
The performed work, that takes place on the stage, is ultimately designed to elicit responses from the spectators. That said, although Mac-Donald does not mention this, there are also staged aesthetics that are actor-centered, where audience response is invited (or sometimes, actively dis-invited). In such experiences, the point of focus is enabling particular kinds of learning for the performers/creators.	Occupying a space between what MacDonald suggests as the objectives of staged versus LARP immersed aesthetic, in my approach to immersive theater, each script has two objectives. The first is a desire to elicit a particular response: heightens both actors' and spect-actors' understanding of a particular situation of social or political injustice. The second objective is to allow for interpersonal negotiations and individualized affects that might emerge from the participants' lived experience of a theatrical situation.	MacDonald suggests that LARPs are not about eliciting responses from "spectators." Rather, they are all about crafting effectively negotiated situations between all the participants in that experience.
Performative excellence is the barometer that is typically used to judge the quality of a staged performance.	In my immersive work, the actors' execution of performative excellence is integral. However, what is also important as a marker of "success" is the affect that is sparked toward the particular socio-political issue that lies at the heart of each	Quality of engagement (with Self & Others) is the barometer that is used to assess the quality of a LARP experience.

Stage Aesthetic (as per MacDonald)	Immersive Theater Aesthetic (as per the approach in this book)	Immersed Aesthetic in LARPs (as per MacDonald)
	script. Consequently, the prioritization of this affective emphasis warrants placing importance on the "quality of immersion" within the world of the theatrical effort.	
MacDonald suggests that there is a "low" demand from audience members in these aesthetics. I place "low" in quotation marks though, because I am not in favor of the qualitative judgment that is implied in the use of this term. That said, the "low" demand that MacDonald refers to might be understood in terms of the expectations that are placed on audience members—where apart from having to turn off cell phones and not disturbing fellow audience members, no more behavioral requirements are placed on spectators.	Spect-actors are invited to use more than two senses. Because spectators become "performers" themselves, there is more demand placed that is placed on their behavior—behavior that is regulated by the rules of that theatrical world.	Participants are asked to use all five senses and there is a demand for direct involvement in the construction of the LARP itself (the creation of their own costumes, for instance).
The integration of a more cohesive message, which has to do with the narrative being shared. Clearly, MacDonald does not take into account Postmodern or Experimental/Avant-garde forms of theater making. Rather, she focuses on a Realism[6]–influenced approach where theater	My approach to the scripts in this book prizes spect-actors' individualized message perceptions of the piece in question, i.e., there is not *one* "thing" that I want spect-actor to take away from the performance. And yet, there is cohesion in that there is a tar-	LARPs are said to contain scattered messages, where the goal is more about the situation/scenarios being experienced in an embodied way, rather than any particular outcome that every single participant must take away.

Stage Aesthetic (as per MacDonald)	Immersive Theater Aesthetic (as per the approach in this book)	Immersed Aesthetic in LARPs (as per MacDonald)
shows a "slice of life," as it were. Extending MacDonald's argument though, we might say that even a Postmodern, staged piece is more cohesive in what is witnessed by all spectators—in that they see the same visual/auditory images on that stage; their interpretations being completely individual, of course.	geted, socially conscious empathy that is desired.	
Two hours is the average length of such experiences, MacDonald suggests, though there are multiple instances of practitioners experimenting with this staged work of shorter/longer durations.	More similar to LARPs in this particular characteristic, the scripts in this book have been crafted for different lengths of time. Ultimately, the choice of duration was made based on what worked best for the particular script's sociopolitical focus; the time I thought each script needed to increase the likelihood of particular affective responses to occur for spect-actors (and, less so, for the performers).	Forty-eight hours is the time frame that MacDonald puts forth as being typical for LARPs, though I have encountered examples in my research that speak to shorter/longer durations—based both on the context being explored and the desires of the organizing team.
Audience members to a staged performance, usually, walk in off the street and are expected to engage with the codes that govern that theatrical environment. As a result, there is an assumption of "informed consent," that audience	I consider different levels and types of immersion as requiring different kinds of preparation. As such, each script in this book puts forward a different approach to spectator-participant preparation, based on the specific goals and needs	LARPs often require some form of preparation so that participants are best positioned to take on the rules of that world. Some LARPs have multiple preparatory sessions at different time periods ahead of the experience; others incorporate prepa-

Stage Aesthetic (as per MacDonald)	Immersive Theater Aesthetic (as per the approach in this book)	Immersed Aesthetic in LARPs (as per MacDonald)
members know what they are in for—that they will need to seat themselves in empty chairs and keep silent. It is because of this assumed understanding of what theatrical spectatorship requires that ethical questions arise when less known forms are put to use in otherwise conventional theatrical spaces.	in each text. More analyses of particular preparatory choices are included in the Preludes and Interludes that precede and follow each script. It is important to highlight also, that given each script's focus on a current socio-political issue, I do not take the piece's ethical minefields lightly. As a result, I see preparation as a way to allow "informed consent" to occur for spect-actors in an immersive theater experience.	ration into a session right before the main LARP event; others use email/alternate modes of communication as a form of preparation. Whichever method is adopted, LARP participants are made aware, even before the preparatory session, of how the event will work. As a result, akin to the expectations that audiences to staged performances come in with, there is an assumption of informed consent amongst LARP participants.

There is one more difference that LARP literature espouses, although Macdonald does not explicitly refer to this, and that is the place for out-of-character knowledge. In more conventional, staged performances, audience members do *not* have a character and as such, out-of-character knowledge—as a concept—is not relevant. In LARPs, however, this concept is especially important and is centered on participants *not* bringing out-of-character knowledge into the personas that they take on for the duration of the LARP experience. This is to say that I will not rely on my lived experience in the "real world" in the portrayal of my character in a LARP. Rather, that LARP character will know only what s/he can know within the bounds of that experience.

Inhabiting a space between irrelevance and relevance though, the concept of out of character knowledge is more complex within the scripts in this book. Since, unlike LARP participants, spect-actors in immersive theater do not always provide prior informed consent, there is an in-between quality to the characters that they take on. Yes, they are given a character in each of the scripts in this book and consequently, are expected to step into that character's shoes for the duration of the performance. And yet, these spect-actors are *not* asked to leave their prior selves behind; they are welcomed to use out of character knowledge to compensate for the discomfort that may emerge from the novelty of the form.

That said, although the elimination/limitation of out of character knowledge is important to LARP experiences, recent research seems to suggested an increasing interest "in creating [LARP] situations in which exactly this kind of emotional bleed [...] this intense spilling over of effect from one's out-of-game life into the game and vice versa, is central to the community's LARP" (Simkins, 2015:158). Certain stakeholders in the LARP community seem to present arguments *against* an emotional bleed between participant, character, LARP setting, and the real world for its potential to become "amateur therapy," "irresponsible confusion," and potential triggers for trauma (Simkins, 2015:158). The stakeholders who argue *for* emotional bleed, however, suggest that through an intentional application/evocation of this person-character identification, the LARP participants' potential to learn about themselves is magnified (Simkins, 2015:158).

This intentionality, it is further suggested, might manifest through a careful framing of events, the inclusions of workshops "to prepare players to deal with intense in-character emotion and simulated real world social connection," the inclusion of debriefs that go beyond a "report of what happened and act as a sort of group meeting to discuss and unwind from the events of the LARP," and, when needed, the use of "out of game follow up counseling services with non-game affiliated counselors, to help players deal with the emotions elicited by the game" (Simkins, 2015:158). In their desire to create emotional bleeds therefore, and in their objectives of provoking empathy toward a particular Other, the scripts in this book are closest to what might be considered "educational" LARPs where "live-action roleplaying [is] used to impart pre-determined pedagogical or didactic content" (Kurz & Balzer, 2015) and to catalyze—to varying degrees—mental, emotional, and physical objectives (Bowman & Vanek, 2012:121):

- Mental objectives (of Mind): Cognitive, educational objectives [that are] aimed at improvement; development and correction of cognitive processes; analytical skills; and intellectual virtues
- Emotional objectives (of Heart): Affective education objectives [that are] aimed at improvement; development and correction of emotional processes; self-awareness; will management; imagination; creativity; moral conflict resolution; and other virtues of character
- Physical objectives (of Body): Psychosocial education objectives [that are] aimed at improvement; development and correction of behavioral processes; mechanisms of interpersonal communication; physical possibilities; and means to affect the material world

Encountering these strong interconnections between LARPs (especially educational LARPs) and my approach to immersive theater, I decided to look further into the writing that that falls within the broad oeuvre of LARP literature. What constitutes a "good" LARP? How are these "good" LARPs, then, given a written form?

Analyses about LARP writing/creation suggest four elements that shape "good interaction": "Mirroring, Consequence, Social Context, Freedom" (Simkins, 2015:68–69). Mirroring and consequence are seen as a conceptual pairing, where the former alludes to each individual participant's impact on other participants, and the latter refers to an individual participants' impact on the world of the LARP (Simkins, 2015:68–69). A character is said to be mirrored "when other characters react to them as if their actions, appearance, and [their] presence had import" (Simkins, 2015:68–69). And when a character's action "affects the life of other characters, it has a consequential effect on the game" (Simkins, 2015:68–69). Furthermore, these affects/effects of mirroring and consequence only become possible within a particular social context that is "linguistic, cultural, and physical"; a social context which also effectively constructs the participants' "freedom" and allows them to make "significant decisions [as] characters in game," constrained only "by physics," "by safety," and by social context (Simkins, 2015:68–69).

So, if these concepts of mirroring, consequence, social context, and freedom were taken from LARPs to the immersive theater aesthetic in this book, practically speaking, what are strategies that might warrant consideration? In thinking about this question, and in considering the similarities/difference between LARPs and immersive theater as articulated earlier, the first point of consideration that precedes the construction of each script is the *number of parallel narratives* that each would contain. How would the inclusion of five, versus ten, versus twenty parallel narratives impact the mirroring, consequence, and freedom that might be experienced by spect-actors? In speaking to the importance of parallel narratives in a LARP, David Simkins (2015) suggests that scripting these scenarios might be like the process of "writing a short story that is intentionally left unfinished"; a short story that allows its participants "to imagine and act out the remainder"; a short story each character in a LARP tends to have their own narrative arc, "which establishes their relationships, goals, and dramatic tensions once the LARP begins" (Simkins, 2015:14–15). For example:

> *Under Angmar's Shadow* has 40 characters. Each character's personal history is its own short story, occurring within roughly the same time frame and about overlapping events [...] The character backgrounds vary in length, but include around eight pages of personal narrative, two pages of description of the character's capabilities, and two pages of brief description about the [relationships with] the other characters. Together, this 10 to 15 page document becomes the information unique to the character. [In *Under Angmar's Shadow*, for example]. Each of the 41 characters has their own personal information. The author also writes 54 pages of shared informa-

tion, given to each participant. This packet includes an 11 page information document, with brief information about each faction in the game, and a 43 page Player's Guide [...] Each player is therefore expected to read and absorb 64 to 69 pages of material. In total, the author write 546 pages of unique material for the players and distributed 3200 pages of material, once each player was provided their own complete set of information [Simkins, 2015:14–15].

Now, although none of three scripts in this book is contains quite as many parallel narratives as in the example above, each Prelude does carefully consider the number of narratives that might be included within the world of each piece.

The second point of consideration in the writing of each script is the *level of co-authorship*, i.e., the extent of freedom afforded to the spect-actor in the unfolding of that immersive world. Given the centrality of the playwright (myself) in this process, the scripts in this book resonate most closely with a single-event (rather than a multiple event) LARP—since it has been said that "[b]ackground for single-event LARPs are almost always written by one or more writers who write all of the characters [and the] world information" while multiple-event LARPs "are generally written between the organizers, the person or team who will orchestrate and manage the players and events in-game, and the players themselves" (Simkins, 2015:70). Consequently, a difference (inevitably) emerges in "the level of ownership of the characters expected in the two genres" (Simkins, 2015:70). In single-event LARPs "the writer owns all of the initial characters, and writes them to bring the characters into interesting interaction with each other quickly" and the participants (spectators) generally have limited access and preparation (Simkins, 2015:70). Questions about co-authorship, therefore, and the freedom that is afforded spect-actors in the scripts in this book, are points of consideration in each Prelude. What degree of co-authorship (and subsequently, freedom) would best suit the objectives of the script in question?

The third point of consideration that precedes each of the three scripts is the kind of *pre-performance preparation and spect-actor recruitment* that would best suit the piece in question—exploring and analyzing the ripple effects of these choices on the mirroring, consequence, and freedom that each text seeks to inspire. While this approach might be counter to that adopted by more conventional theatrical scenarios where anyone/everyone is welcome to attend, LARP scholarship suggests that "[o]ne of the more straightforward ways of achieving harmony is by recruiting players to the LARP who have a narrow band of desires" i.e., where there is some cohesion about what is expected from that experience (Simkins, 2015:122). And given the higher levels similarity between LARPs and immersive theater environments vis-à-vis expectations placed on the participants, I would agree that (contrary to more conventional, staged scenarios), "no player is well suited to all LARPs" or immersive theater environments, and no LARP [or immersive theater experience] is well suited to all players" (Simkins, 2015:122).

The careful pinpointing of spect-actors and actors also becomes important in my approach to immersion, because of the applied theater ideologies underpinning these scripts. If the theatrical event is somehow expected to go beyond its own borders; to "do" something; to be applied toward a larger purpose, I have come to think that a careful selection of spect-actors and actors is of incredible importance. For instance, is it important for performers to have lived experiences of the issue that lies at the heart of each script, so as to navigate the ethical minefields of representing voices from a contentious social or political issue? Or, is it integral that performers and spect-actors do *not* have any experience with the issue being dealt with in the piece, so as to heighten the potential for learning about that issue to occur? Who performs in an applied theater immersive experience, and whom that immersive theater piece is targeted toward, have significant parts to play in how a performance approaches/distances itself from its goals. As a result, I propose particular conditions for the target performer and spect-actor group in the Prelude to each immersive theater script, and based on these conditions, the preparatory work that might be used is designed, refined, and developed.

Finally, the last point of consideration that precedes the construction of each script is with regards to the social context that is being showcased in each of the three immersive theater environments in his book, and the *extent of realism and/or allegory* that might be useful toward communicating the complexities of that world. Drawing from the spectrum of political LARPs that either "present an interpretation of a real-life political issue or situation" as directly "modelled according to real-life situation (via the interpretation of the modeller, of course)," or those political LARPs that use allegory to present "some central themes of the political issue in a setting differing from its real-life model" (Kangas, Loponen, & Särkijärvi, 2016:112), the Preludes to each script in this book consider how effective realism and/or allegory might be in impacting the spect-actors' reception of the social context contained within the immersive theater piece in question.

Drawing from strategies therefore, each script in this book is framed by the following qualities (see Figure 1).

Moving from this conceptual framing to the practical, formal construction of a LARP and its subsequent application in this book's scripts, the next stage of investigation involved looking at the structure of LARP texts, which are said to generally include three phases: a preparation phase of workshops/discussions to help the participants "rehearse" for the LARP; the LARP itself; a debrief after the LARP. A "generic" LARP script might therefore be said to be constructed around the following structure[7]:

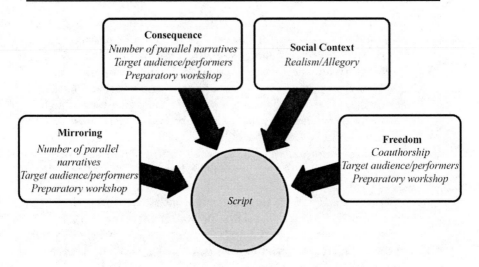

Figure 1: Concepts framing each script.

- **Pre-LARP Preparation:** Eleanor Saitta, Marie Holm-Andersen, and Jon Back (2014:258–259) offer the following examples for what pre-LARP preparation session(s) might include: presentations from/about the organizers/players vis-à-vis the structure of the LARP and their respective motivations for participation; workshops that assist players' characterization vis-à-vis their roles and in building the world of the game; acting out scenes from the LARP manuscript as a form of rehearsal
- **Introduction—Communicates the Vision of the Game:** Describes what the game is about: the setting, the playing style (should the participants be playing to win or lose?), the Game Mastering[8] style, and background on the game and its rationale
- **How to Run the Game:**
  - *Preparations:* What do organizers need to think about before the game, both logistically and in terms of communicating with players? What are the physical logistics (location, food, transport) and how will communication be conducted with the players (questionnaires, casting, communicating about the theme)? Which tasks need to be undertaken right before the beginning the LARP: tasks like taking money at the site, setting up the space, and/or preparatory workshop sessions?
  - *Game Structure:* A short description of the structure, including information about the way in which the individual components, and the overall LARP itself, begin and end

⊚ *Game Walk-through:* Detailed description of the game that says not only what to do, but why it must be done. This walk-through also includes more detailed information for the Game Master (workshop, casting, advice, character creation)

⊚ *Tips, Tricks, and Hacks:* A troubleshooting guide that informs organizers about what can go wrong in the LARP, how it might be fixed, and how to scale the game up/down based on spect-actor numbers/location/funding

⊚ *Closing:* Information about game writers/designers and contact information for players to ask lingering questions and provide feedback about the LARP

• **Game Materials:** Such materials might include character sheets, scene/act/story description, a Game Master cheat sheet that re-states information from the walk-through but very briefly (that can be easily carried by them during the LARP), and other material, depending on the game

With this suggested LARP structure in mind, I revisited the structures put forth by the earlier examples—from tabletop games, different educational contexts, and Red Cross simulations. Then, in conjunction with insights from each of these exemplars, the four conceptual framing factors, and the suggested LARP structure above, I designed the following structure to begin the process of scripting each immersive theater script in this book (see Figure 2).

That said, it is important to clarify that I did not see the format above as being prescriptive or formulaic. Rather, I used the abovementioned structure in conversation with meditations around mirroring, consequence, freedom, and social context—in each individual script—to make final structural choices.

The Gray Zones

Now that I have introduced the starting point for the structure of the scripts in this book, it is necessary for me to speak to the content of each of these texts; content that is framed by the notion of the "gray zones." The concept of gray zones has inspired my work for a long time now, ever since I realized the proclivity of theater about conflicted contexts to reflect a binary opposition between "victim" and "perpetrator." In such efforts—and again, generally speaking—the "victim" is represented as a "recipient of undeserved harm" and thus amenable to/deserving of theatrical/dramatic voice; while "perpetrators" are often seen as being the individuals/groups that are "evaluated as deliberately inflicting harm or hurt on another or assisting in that

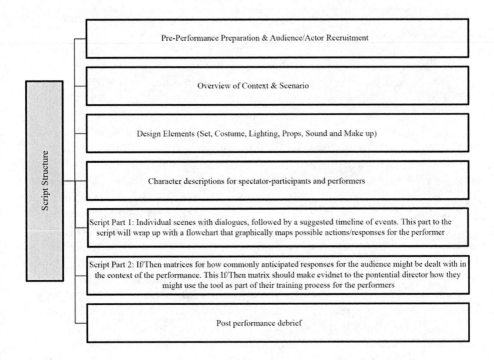

Figure 2: Potential script structure.

harmful deed" (Foster, Haupt & De Beer, 2005:63) and thus, as often falling outside the scope of theatrical efforts. However as anyone who has spent time in settings of conflict will realize quite quickly, a clear distinction between "victim" and "perpetrator" is often hard to sustain over time, especially as an outsider looking in. To an outsider who has no personal stake in/affiliation to a particular conflict, victimhood and perpetration are often two points on a spectrum; a spectrum on which individuals might align themselves, or find themselves aligned, at different points at different times.

While it would be simplistic to say that everyone in a context of war is both "victim" and "perpetrator"—and I am certainly not saying that—what might be said is that the binary between the two notions that have come to define conflict (of victim and perpetrator) is insufficient to capture the many identity-based affiliations that comprise one's positioning. This zone between "victims" and "perpetrators" is what I have come to think extensively about, through the lens of what Primo Levi (in Agamben, 1999:21) puts forward as the "gray zone," a space in which "the long chain of conjunction between victim and executioner comes loose, where the oppressed becomes oppressor and the executioner in turn appears as victim." While I do not seek to apply "gray zones" in this book strictly in Levi's terms, his proposition does function as a point of departure from which I script spaces that are nebulous, unclear, and not black or white. Where "gray zones" refers specifically to Levi's use of the term, it is so acknowledged; however, in a majority of the instances of its usage in this book, the term indicates my interpretation of/approach to this zone as an in-between space; a space that is defined by uncertainty (Dinesh, 2015b:9).

Given my own work thus far, therefore, and my desire to explore gray zones in the texts in this book, each of the three scripts works around a particular conflicted setting in which I have worked. First, *Detention* draws on my work in juvenile detention centers in New Mexico, where—in an unspecified part of the world—spect-actors are immersed within a prison setting. Rather than them taking on the traditionally expected roles in prison simulations though, i.e., the roles of the prisoner or the guard, the spect-actor is asked step into the shoes of an educator who works within prison walls. Then, *War* draws from my experiences working in conflict zones, particularly Kashmir, and places the spect-actor in the role of an "outsider" who is tasked with listening to voices of victims and perpetrators within an area of violent conflict. Set in an unspecified war zone that is framed using documentary material from current/past global conflicts, *War* asks its spect-actors to reflect upon the complex role of being an outsider in a time and place of violent conflict. Inspired by the concept of the gray zone, this piece's pedagogical impetus lies in catalyzing the spect-actors' thinking around the role of an outsider within a setting of war. And finally, *Immigration* is based on my personal encounters with immigration systems in different parts of the world, most recently the United States. This piece asks its spect-actors to take on the role of a low-level bureaucrat and is framed by reflecting on Hannah Arendt's (1963) proposals around the "banality of evil."

The book is divided into three thematic sections: *Detention, War,* and *Immigration*. Each section consists of:

- A Prelude, which frames my particular experience with the issues being dealt with in the following script and the particular pedagogical objectives that I have for that text. The Prelude also includes a meditation on social context, consequence, mirroring, freedom vis-à-vis the number of parallel narratives, the degree of realism/allegory, the target spect-actor/performer group, and the type of preparatory work that might be necessary in the following script
- Each Prelude is followed by the script itself
- Finally, each section concludes with an Interlude—a section that is written with autoethnography in mind; an autoethnographic approach that I have used in all my writing to date. In so doing,

the Interludes in this book put forth two different, yet intersecting points of consideration: one for the immersive theater "director"; the other for the immersive theater "playwright" (realising, of course, that the terms "director" and "playwright" apply differently in this context). Each Interlude discusses one particular element of "traditional" playwriting that had to shift to accommodate the immersive form, as revealed by the preceding script. Each Interlude also proposes a "global" strategy, which might be used by immersive theater practitioners that are interested in staging original interpretations of the immersive texts in this book. The autoethnography, then, comes into play in two ways: in the self-reflexive observations that emerge through the script writing process, and that are then fuelled into creating strategies for other playwrights and directors through an exemplar-based approach.

On we go, then, to the first section: *Detention*.

Detention

My work in New Mexico's youth detention centers began in 2015; first as an independent theater project with a group of incarcerated young men that culminated in a performance entitled *Lives Behind the Walls* (Dinesh, 2017). This introductory and exploratory project was then followed up by my becoming the faculty mentor for a peer-to-peer interaction program that takes students from the international high school at which I teach (referred to, from this point forward, as the College), to get to know and interact with peers at a juvenile facility in the state. This interaction program takes two forms: the first is a weeklong intensive initiative, where students from the College work on a creative project with their peers in a detention center. In 2016 and 2017, these weeklong initiatives resulted in the creation of a short publication that incorporates writing and artwork from both groups of youth. The second form of the interaction program is through a twice-a-month, experiential education program that takes College students for shorter, three hour long sessions that are partly led by the young people and partly by adult mentors, including myself. These sessions include a range of activities, some of which are extremely informal and intended as a way for the groups to "hang out." Other activities are more structured and involve the young people preparing sessions that have specific goals or themes that are explored. In the last academic year, for instance, one group used "Utopia" as the theme for all their visits to the detention center—engaging, during each visit, with different dimensions to that thematic focus. As I write this, my students and I are in the midst of serious considerations about how to make our interaction programs stronger, in their delivery and their objectives. Are we simply looking to get two groups of youth people to interact with each other as form of cultural and/or learning exchange? Or are we working toward larger goals of education and/or the reduction of recidivism rates? And in either case, how can we design activities with more intentionality?

The program is evolving; I daresay it always will be in a state of evolution, because of the ethical questions that surround the College's interventions in the detention center.

Mentoring these different detention center-based programs has been an entirely new experience for me, and consequently, has come to be one of the most poignant components to my life in New Mexico. Even as a (self-proclaimed) socially and politically conscious adult, and one who has participated in the facilitation of theater projects in different contexts of conflict, there was very little that I knew/know about the criminal justice system in the United States (in general), and in New Mexico (in specific). Becoming involved in the world of juvenile justice has not only made me aware of my own ignorance in these matters; rather, the forums that have opened up as a result of my work in these spaces, have made me realize that the complexities of these settings are unconsidered by/unknown to many, many people. And when speaking about spaces of incarceration, I am not referring solely to the issues surrounding the criminal justice system in the U.S., which have gained more mainstream attention in recent years. Rather, I refer to the topic of juvenile justice as being part of a wider, global conversation surrounding the ways in which we (in the largest sense) deal with crimes and transgressions within our societies and communities. Do we seek to punish or rehabilitate? Do we seek re-educate and reintegrate, or discipline and isolate? One could argue that such considerations will always remain timely in a world such as ours—where people will always transgress the bounds of the law; where we will always have to carefully consider how those transgressions are engaged. For all these reasons; for all the ways in which criminal justice occupies my thinking; it seemed only appropriate to make the broad theme of detention form the crux of one of the scripts in this book.

I knew from the outset of conceptualizing *Detention* that I did not want to make the spect-actor in the script become either the prisoner or the guard; not least of all because initiatives like the Stanford Prison Experiment (SPE; Zimbardo, 1971) stand testament to the consequences of giving individuals—even within a simulated context—power over each other. As the reader might recall, the SPE had to be cut short from its originally intended duration because of the extremes to which both prisoners and guards were taking the characters assigned to them; because of the ethical and behavioral lines that were being crossed despite the simulated nature of that environment. And it is not only the SPE that has shown us this darker side of human nature that can emerge, given the "right" circumstances. Stanley Milgram's obedience experiments and the various permutations of simulations that teach about oppression in the classroom (the infamous blue eye/green eye experiment [Peters, 1987], for example, where students with particular eye colors were given power over each other for a day) have all contentiously demonstrated the extreme capabilities of human nature. When approaching the *Detention* script in this book, therefore, I wanted to ensure that the work would steer away from the better-known complicities surrounding how individuals bow down to larger oppressive systems; better-known complicities, for example, like the prison guard in the SPE being far more abusive to the prisoners than they needed to be; better-known complicities, for instance, like those exhibited by the teacher in the Milgram experiment who was often willing to harshly discipline the pupil, when asked to do so by someone in a position of power.

In the spirit of accessing less well-known narratives, therefore, in wanting to access the gray zones of incarcerated juveniles' experience, one of the immediate decisions I made was *not* to ask spect-actors to become an Other who is a prisoner or a guard. Rather, I wanted to ask spect-actors to step into the shoes of a less considered Other within the juvenile justice system; an Other who embodies more "murkiness"—not only because of that Other's positioning within the detention center's systematic hierarchies, but also because of the silence surrounding their narratives in mainstream realms. That said, in addition to my desire for spect-actors to embody a more "murky" Other, this choice—of intentionally *not* characterizing spect-actors as prisoners or guards—was influenced by an ethical dilemma that stems from my never having been a prisoner or a guard myself. How can I give respectful voice to experiences that I do not have any lived experience of? How can I frame voices from juvenile detention centers, without falling prey to some type of stereotyping? It is also because of such questions, then, that the Other chosen for *Detention's* spect-actor is one whose positioning I identify with, and have lived experience of: that of a short-term, volunteer educator who works in a youth detention center.

As I have noted in *Scripting Detention* (2017), the positioning of the educator within a justice system that is designed to regulate, control, and discipline its inhabitants, presents a multitude of contradictions.

> For example, when there are guards who are always present to control inmate-students behavior and actions, how much freedom do educators really have in the delivery of their pedagogy?
>
> When educators do not get to see the fruits of their labor, as it were, because their inmate-students are constantly being released or paroled out of that educator's classroom by the rules that comprise the justice system, how do teachers continue to find motivation in their profession?
>
> When inmate-students from various backgrounds, ages, and learning capabilities are put within the same learning space—based on sorting criteria that has more to do with the nature of their crime

rather than anything else—how can an educator be expected to ensure that all the youth in their classrooms are being served effectively?

How might these educators overcome their own implicit/unconscious biases that stem from a knowledge/perception of the crime/transgression that the inmate-student has committed, so as to have been brought to that facility in the first place?

How do these educators keep the faith in the young people they work with, when they see the same youth return to prison time after time?

In my limited interactions with educators at the New Mexican detention center in which I mentor programs, I have not come away with the best of perceptions. When conducting a rehearsal for a performance that used some of their school teachers' classrooms, for example, I found myself and the inmate-students being met with a territorialism and belligerence that was extremely concerning. However, while such interactions left me worried and frustrated about the functioning of the education machinery within that particular detention center, I must admit to the young people speaking very positively, in future encounters, of some of the very same teachers that I had less that constructive interactions with. Having said this, I must clarify my intentionality here and state that it is not my intention with *Detention* either to glorify or demonize the role of the educator within a juvenile detention center. Rather, what I seek to do is structure the script in a way that effectively and affectively puts forth some of the specific challenges that emerge, when working within a context of incarceration—whether or not those conditions lead to "positive" or "negative" experiences depend, entirely, on the quality of participation that is brought in by the spect-actor in question.

With *Detention*'s intentionality clarified, the script's conceptualization process began with the following questions

- How would I approach realism and allegory vis-à-vis the social context of *Detention*?
- What would the script's target actor and spect-actor demographic be?
- What would be an appropriate duration for the experience, given the above-mentioned intentions?
- How many parallel narratives would *Detention* contain?
- What would it take to ensure an ethical approach to characterization, which did not resort to stereotyping any of the characters involved?

Conceptualizing Detention

Let's return now, to the concepts with which I have chosen to frame the writing and structure of the scripts in this book (as presented in the Introduction); concepts borrowed from Live Action Role Plays' (LARPs) frameworks for "good" interaction: mirroring, consequence, freedom, and social context. The reader will note that, as I move through each of these concepts, I write both in the past *and* present tense about choices framing each script. I make this writing choice consciously, so that the reader gets a more personalized insight into constant evolutions behind the choices that shape each script.

Social Context

The first point I considered when beginning *Detention* is the extent of realism/allegory in the social context that is encompassed in its immersive world. On the one hand, I knew it would make sense for me to create the entire piece as a documentary account from one of New Mexico's juvenile detention centers, since that is the setting that I have most lived experience in. In this vein, I also considered the option of crafting the social context of *Detention* as being the U.S.—in general—drawing from the specific New Mexican context to excavate present day socio-political conversations surrounding the criminal justice system in this country. All this to say, couldn't the immersive world in *Detention* be entirely realistic?

While I immediately saw benefits to invoking this kind of realism within the scripting process, in that creating detailed frameworks for spect-actors' experiences would be facilitated more easily through widely available archival information, this choice also seemed to pose particular problems that I did not want *Detention* to contend with: the primary drawback with a realism-based choice being the consequent prioritization (within the script) of issues surrounding education and juvenile justice as being specific to a particular place. And, consequently, as being less relevant to other parts of the world. In going back to my objectives with the piece, therefore, and revisiting my larger vision for *Detention* to inspire dialogue about the functioning of education within "rehabilitation" programs for young people in various contexts, I began to lean further away from realism.

That said, I was also fairly certain from the outset that I did not want *Detention* to be entirely allegorical; I did not want to transpose commentaries about juvenile incarceration and education to an entirely different world that only contained parallels with the context of a youth detention center. I was certain of this because—unlike the issue of immigration, for instance, about which there is far more visible cognizance in the current global political climate—

juvenile justice still remains a fairly niche subject area. As a result, since questions surrounding juvenile incarceration, as it stands, form part of a lesser-known realm (at least in the circles that I inhabit), I thought it important to frame *Detention* as being identifiably specific to that issue. While, as mentioned earlier, wanting this framing to be broad enough to be applicable to any geographical context of juvenile incarceration/justice/rehabilitation/reintegration/education that a production team might want to create the experience in.

It is for these reasons that the script that follows is set, specifically, within a youth detention center while also *not* being framed as occurring in one particular country/place/locale. The spect-actor in *Detention* will be aware that the context that they are stepping into is one that has to do with juvenile incarceration, but my hope is that they will not (intentionally, anyway) associate the piece as being limited to the U.S., or to India, or to any other location—unless the production team decides to add this specificity; an issue that I will address in the Interlude following the script. As such, although I draw primarily from my experience in New Mexico, my aesthetic decisions in *Detention* are both drawn from archival research into juvenile incarceration systems in different parts of the world; from my informal education initiatives in the New Mexican detention center context; from my own imagination, of what it must be like to teach in a more formal capacity within that setting (more formal than my own, more informal, initiatives). On this note, I must underscore the fact that I have not yet taught a formal class in a detention center with state-mandated curricula over an extended period of time. And as a result, there are limitations to my imagination in *Detention*—limitations that I will readily admit to. What I will suggest, however, is that that any individual or group interested in staging *Detention* also brings on board a consultant from the local context, who has lived experience as being a detention center educator in that specific setting.

Freedom

Having reached this decision about creating an anonymized, but realistic, context in *Detention*, the next concept that warranted consideration in my script writing process was the notion of freedom. How much co-authorship and/or freedom could spect-actors really have in a setting that is founded on rules; rules, which seek to control the behavior of everyone within it—inmates and staff alike? How much freedom could spect-actors be given, essentially, to maintain the reality of the world within *Detention*, while also allowing for mirroring and consequence to occur (i.e., for an individual spect-actor's characters to impact other actor and spect-actors; for all participants to be able to "mark" the world of the experience)?

In thinking about these questions, it became apparent to me that spect-actors in *Detention* could *not* have extensive freedom; they could not impact the world of the experience or their fellow actors/spect-actors beyond a certain degree. And in order to clarify this, I realized that a careful calibration would need to occur: because even within the strict environment of a detention center, even within all the rules that suffocate an environment of incarceration (in most contexts), there are scales of relative freedom. Guards and educators always have more freedom than inmates; educators and guards have more or less freedom than each other, based on the particular space within the prison walls that is being used. For instance, the educator might have more freedom within the classroom, while the guard would have more freedom in the residential area. However, sometimes, even space doesn't make the manifestation of power dynamics straightforward. Sometimes, detention center educators might have more freedom in the delivery of their lesson, but the guards might have more power if/when disciplinary issues arise within that space. So, if an inmate says or does something inappropriate to the educator, it could go either way as to whether the educator or the guard would have more freedom to intervene. One of the struggles in crafting *Detention*, therefore, was to find a way in which I could write in such degrees of freedom; degrees that would implicitly/explicitly demonstrate the complexities of prison power dynamics.

With these considerations about degrees of freedom, I had to ask: what are aesthetic choices that would allow for relative freedom to occur for spect-actors who are asked to embody detention center educators? Could I create a "teacher training" of sorts, at the beginning of the experience, in which spect-actors would have the freedom to design the lessons they would teach in their classrooms—but still have to get their lesson plans "vetted" by someone who has more power than them in the immersive world? Could I choose *not* to incorporate dialogues for actors playing the inmate-students, instead creating character frameworks within which each performer might respond differently to different spect-actors? Could such choices allow for the notion of relative freedom to become central within the written text of *Detention?*

Target Actor and Spect-Actor Group

In thinking about such options for writing in degrees of freedom, the immediate follow-up consideration became to ask myself who the target spect-actor/performer group for a script of this nature would be. Would *Detention* be an immersive, theatrical experience that would be open to anyone who walks off the street, as Jamie MacDonald (2012) says in her demarcation between staged/immersive aesthetics in the Introduction? Or, given the educational objectives of this particular experience, and the issues that it seeks to raise vis-à-vis learning, pedagogy, and juvenile justice, should *Detention* be targeted toward a particular subset of a larger population? In this vein, even when discussing the performers who might partake in *Detention,* should the actors be drawn from a wide demography that invites all who might be interested? Or should the composition of the performing ensemble be carefully considered in terms of the ethical questions raised by the script: where performers with/without particular lived experiences might be preferred based on, for instance, the potential trauma that might be sparked for them in recreating an immersive world about their life experiences? While there is one part of me that values the potential for the scripts in this book to target the widest range of performer and spect-actor demographics, and I shall certainly never advocate that a piece should *not* be shared with those who fall outside a suggested target group, what I will say is that my considerations about the target group of performers and spect-actors is predicated on maximizing the potential of the educational objectives in each script. And therefore, there are suggestions that are always made about who the "right" spect-actors might be; about whom the "right" group of actors might be composed of.

It is not uncommon for applied theater initiatives—as issue-centered theatrical experiences—to include performers and spect-actors who somehow have a "stake" in the scenario in question. It is not uncommon, for instance, for prisoners to perform stories about incarceration to peers from inside/outside prison walls; there are a number of projects, mostly involving the use of Shakespeare in prisons (a simple Google search for this phrase will give the reader a large number of results), which have entered the limelight in recent years. And yet, I would argue that the purpose of such kinds of applied theater initiatives that involve performers with lived experiences of the narrative being showcased, have a larger objective that targets the tangible/intangible development and/or well-being of that population. This is to say that in many prison theater projects, where inmates themselves perform for different audiences—like the first project that I undertook with young men in detention (Dinesh, 2017)—the objectives of the effort are articulated as being more about creating a sense of empowerment for the performer-participants. The effect or affect for the spect-actors in such projects is an important consequence; but is not as integral as the potential consequences for the performers in these works.

Conversely, there are other kinds of applied theater initiatives—Augusto Boal's (1985) Forum Theater being a well-known example—which are far more about the spect-actors' ideas and empowerment than they are about the performers. In such instances, it is important for the spect-actor in question to have the lived experience being showcased in the theatrical performance, so that these individuals are able consider an application of what is being proposed or questioned in the performance, to their daily lives. And between these choices, of course—between focusing on the lived experience of actors and the lived experience of spect-actors—there exist multiple combinations and permutations in which actors and spect-actors' identity markers become important in different ways. In scripting *Detention,* therefore, I had to carefully refine the pedagogical objectives of the script: would it be an experience that catalyzes awareness about education and juvenile justice within a general population? Or would *Detention* be better served by targeting policy makers who might take their encounters in the theatre forward by, ideally, informing their own future policy-making? Should the piece be composed of performers that have been through the detention center education system themselves, either as inmates or educators or guards? Or, in order to maximize the learning potential from the piece, should *Detention* target performers who have had nothing to do with the juvenile justice system?

In clarifying my objectives further, toward making an informed decision about the performer and spect-actor demographic for *Detention,* I decided that it was more important for me to heighten the potential for learning amongst spect-actors and not necessarily focus on the consequences for performers involved in the process. While the process of creating and performing a piece such as *Detention* will always be a learning experience for performers as well, by making a choice to focus on the spect-actors' learning, it became my decision that the actors' lived experience need *not* be a limiting condition. I decided, therefore, that *Detention* could be performed by anyone, with any lived experience—with a prison education consultant from the particular context in which the piece is being experienced, so as to help contextualize and develop more details about/from that environment.

However, in contrast with such an open framing of who the performers in *Detention* might be, in terms of the target spect-actor group—while it could be said that anyone would benefit from thinking about the criminal justice systems vis-à-vis juveniles within the context in which they live—I consider *Detention* to be particularly relevant for two different spect-actor populations. The first potential target spect-actor would be a group of educators-in-training; individuals who are thinking of becoming educators in contexts of incarceration in the "real world," and who want to expose themselves to some of what they might expect in taking on those roles. In the tradition of some of the immersive environments and simulations that were put forward in the Introduction—from the realm of nursing education, for example—this target group of educators-in-training would be able to take away lessons gained from the immersive experience and to consider a direct application of those insights to their upcoming professions.

The second target group that I consider as being most appropriate for *Detention,* is one that is comprised of existing educators who do *not* work in contexts of incarceration but are still teachers. These educators, it is suggested, are those who work in extremely privileged institutions within the context in which the experience is being staged; whose approaches, privileges, and perspectives might be entirely different than their counterparts who work within prison systems. I see such this second target group as being particularly relevant for *Detention* because of the potential long-term affect that might emerge in such a spect-actor group stepping into the shoes of a prison educator Other; I choose this particular spect-actor group for two reasons. One, because educator-spect-actors from more privileged contexts occupy an insider/outsider positioning in relation to the characters being explored in *Detention*: insider in their also being educators; outsiders, however, to the detention center environment. The second reason I find this target group of spect-actors being significant is because of the potential that might occur for *Detention* to then spark relationships between the non-carceral institution at which the spect-actor works, and prison settings that are within their (real world) geographical radius. Since educators within contexts of incarceration can be alienated from their better-resourced counterparts, it is hoped that the resonances from *Detention* might manifest in a real world, potential, avenue for spect-actors' responses to be channeled. That said, I must clarify it is *not* my intention to ensure a "tangible" real-world outcome with this script. However, in recognizing the pedagogical underpinnings of the script, wouldn't it be nice if there could be intersections between the spect-actors' "real-world" lives and their experiences in the world of *Detention*?

Duration

With these target spect-actor groups in mind—of detention-center-teachers-in-training and/or existing educators—I returned to thinking about the preparation process that might be needed for spect-actors in *Detention*. And in so doing, I realized that I would have to make decisions about the duration of the experience, alongside making choices about the structure for the before/during/after that would be part of the detention center world. With regard to duration, I immediately found myself considering two options: a twenty-nine-hour experience, or an eight-hour one; both of which have different benefits and challenges.

Let's consider the first option, i.e., the notion of executing the performance over two consecutive days, where spect-actors will live in the world of *Detention* for around twenty-nine hours. While the immediate concern with this duration is that it might be far more difficult to recruit spect-actors, I continued entertaining this durational choice for a couple of reasons. The first reason is the potential for the experience to be composed of two working days; for educator-spect-actors to teach in a detention center classroom for an eight-hour chunk on Day 1—including a preparation at the beginning of the day and a debrief at the end of the day. Similarly, the participants would have another eight-hour chunk on Day 2, and in having to work over the course of two days, over multiple "lesson" scenarios, could spect-actors experience the student attrition rate that is said to be a primary challenge in detention centers? This is to say that a particularly sincere actor-inmate-student on Day 1, someone who befriends the educator-spect-actors and becomes their "star" pupil, for example—could disappear from the educator's class on Day 2—recreating the student attrition rate that has been often cited as a significant hindrance to prison educators' motivation. The twenty-nine-hour format, thus, would also give spect-actors time to get to know their performer-students, to become invested in the actor-students' development, so that these learners' subsequent "disappearance" from the classroom would be noticed; so that their absences would matter.

Furthermore, in addition to giving the spect-actors an embodied experience of the students who "go away," the two-day format would also allow spect-actors to decompress from the happenings of Day 1 and to adapt themselves to the institutionalization of the prison setting during Day 2; an adaptation that could also bring up problematic connotations of educators in a prison setting being imprisoned in their own right. It is here that the target audience of existing educators once again becomes significant: since experienced educators, one might argue, would be able to adapt their pedagogies to the new conditions that they experience in *Detention*, when given the time to do so. Finally, an additional reason that underpins my desire for using a two working day duration is for the spect-actors to spend some time in the "home lives" of their characters, and to experience what it might be like to go home after a day of working with students who are considered "delinquents." So, for example, after an eight-hour day of teaching in a prison institution, how are prison educators able to communicate their challenges to spouses and children? When they have twelve hours between when they leave work on Day 1 and when they have to go back into the detention center for Day 2—to sleep, to decompress, to connect with family, and to plan for the next day—how can the detention center educator wrap their minds around the contrast between their lives within and outside prison walls? A two-working-day format, therefore, might create the conditions for spect-actors to empathize with personal dimensions to prison educator lives.

While there are these multiple benefits that I see from using a two-day format for *Detention*, however, there are challenges with this durational choice too. Apart from the logistical challenges of finding spect-actors who might be willing to commit so much of their time to a theatrical experience, there is always a risk in such durational works of spect-actors being affected in unanticipated and unpredictable ways; ways that might not be controllable within the immersive world of *Detention*. So, what does one do in such instances of unexpected consequences; of unexpected responses; of interactions that go beyond the participants' control? At what point can spect-actors step out of the world of *Detention* because of their own needs? Can they return to the experience if they leave? Should there be a counselor on stand by, just in case someone is triggered by the experience in the immersive world? Are these questions, surrounding the care that needs to be taken of spect-actors, ones that need to be dealt with by the immersive theater playwright, or by the director/production team?

With these potentials and challenges in mind, I began to consider the second durational option: of creating an eight-hour piece, where the spect-actor is immersed in *Detention* for one regular working day (instead of two). This option is immediately, seemed far more logistically feasible: especially with regards to recruiting spect-actors who might be willing to commit to participation in the event. The eight-hour format also allows for many of the same avenues for exploration as its twenty-nine-hour counterpart. Spect-actors can adapt the lessons before and after a lunch break, and students can "leave" the class during the second part of the day. Although this type of attrition might not have the same kind of impact as the one that might be experienced if student-performers were to "disappear" from the classroom after establishing more of a relationship (over more time) with the spect-actor, won't the point still be made?

While there are possibilities for the eight and twenty-nine-hour scenarios to address similar objectives, what the shorter duration does *not* allow, is a way for spect-actors to access a glimpse into the personal lives of detention center educators in conjunction with their own self-institutionalization within the prison system. Won't the notion of self-institutionalization better achieve its potential if spect-actors have more time to experience the claustrophobia of the detention center setting? It was in thinking through the potential and limitations of these two durational options that I began to wonder if it would be useful to craft *Detention* in "sections": chunks that could be used, or not, by the producers of the script. For instance, could Section 1 be scripted as an eight-hour unit? And consequently, could Section 2 be scripted as a twelve-hour unit where the spect-actor explores their character's home life; resulting in Section 3 being scripted as another eight-hour unit? If this is done, would production teams of *Detention* have the choice to implement one or more sections, based both on the number of performers they are able to recruit and the commitment that a spect-actor pool is able to put forward?

Parallel Narratives

The next element I gave some attention to was the number of parallel narratives that *Detention* would be comprised of. And in addressing this particular element, it was apparent from the outset that the each spect-actors would best benefit from experiencing their own individual path through the immersive world; a path that would be crafted based on each spect-actor becoming a sole teacher in a detention center classroom. Could spect-actors go through a process of defining an individual character for themselves—a character for which they would need to consider and articulate *why* they (as their characters) might want to become detention center educators? Defining individual characters, I thought, might also allow the spect-actor to articulate *what* they want to/are able to teach within the confines of *Detention's* structure. In this way, I began to wonder if spect-actors might also benefit from the comfort of teaching content that they are comfortable with, to counter balance the discomfort these spect-actors might experience within the context of the detention center environment. By allowing spect-actors to explicitly bring in their "real-world" expertise into the sphere of the theatrical experience, I began to wonder if an individual-focused narrative might better allow a production team of *Detention* to decide how many parallel narratives to pursue. A decision that would be based both on the number of performers available for the performance vis-à-vis the number of characters that need to be present for each individual narrative, and of course, a decision that would be influenced by the number of spect-actors that are able to participate in the experience.

Characterization

However, if *Detention* were to be created with this degree of flexibility, where the experience could be executed just as much for one spect-actors as for ten, how would "complexity control" be achieved? This is to say, how could I ensure characters' multidimensionality—regardless of spect-actor group size—so as to not fall into the trap of characterizing all guards as being authoritarian; all juvenile offenders as being bad students; all administrators as being bureaucratic? While I began the writing process with the desire to avoid the creation of stereotypes, I was aware that I would want some character "types" to remain consistent; where, regardless of the number of spect-actors who are able to experience *Detention*, each individual narrative would have certain challenges that are always present, regardless of the unique characterization that is brought in by each spect-actor. Within the creation of the characters in *Detention,* then, I wanted to give the actors and spect-actors plenty of opportunities to have consequences both on each other, and on the trajectory of the performance.

In summary, therefore, before beginning the script writing of *Detention*, there were specific decisions that guided my creative process:

- Not relying solely on realism or allegory but rather, creating a fairly realistic detention center setting, while leaving room for the context to be unrestricted in its geographical specificity
- Not limiting the performer demographic to involving actors that have particular lived experiences
- Focusing on a target group of spect-actors that are either about to enter the detention center setting as educators (in the "real-world"); or spect-actors who are already educators in privileged, non-detention center schools (in the "real-world")
- Crafting the piece in three sections, allowing for the experience to last anywhere between eight and twenty-nine hours, based on the duration (and the sections) that the production team decides to work with
- Creating individual narratives for each spect-actors through the generation of individualized educator profiles
- Ensuring that characterization frameworks are put in place, to frame the unique dimensions that might be brought by each spect-actor i.e., that there is some consistency in that which is experienced

With these ideas in mind, I went into the process of scripting *Detention*.

SCRIPTING DETENTION

The Setting

This experience takes place in an unnamed youth detention center, asking its performers to embody guards and inmate-students, and inviting spect-actors to take on roles as educators within that space. The suggested number of actors required for this experience, the suggested number of spect-actors that the experience can accommodate, and the specific time frames that are mentioned in the section outline are as suggestions and are flexible based on the vision of the artistic team that is taking on this endeavor. Furthermore, the production team of *Detention* can choose to stage only Section 1, if the time commitment that an execution of all three sections demands will not be feasible in the context in which the piece is being produced.

The Characters

Spect-actors

It is suggested that there be a maximum of five spect-actors in each individual iteration of *Detention*: referred to, from this point forward, as TEACHER 1, TEACHER 2, TEACHER 3, TEACHER 4, TEACHER 5. Each spect-actor steps into the shoes of an educator within a youth detention center and in so doing, teaches classes to performers who take on the roles of INMATE STUDENTs. Given that spect-actors need to, literally, teach classes while in the world of *Detention* it is suggested that spect-actors are existing educators from more privileged, non-detention-center institutions in the context in which the experience is being executed. Or that spect-actors be drawn from a pool of detention-center-educators-in-training.

Actors

TRAINER: A performer whose primary role lies in conducting pre-performance workshops and debriefs for the TEACHERs. This is an actor who is always looking out for the best interests of the TEACHERs, advising them—in character—about how they might better engage with the experience of *Detention.*

HEADMISTRESS: One performer plays the role of the HEADMISTRESS of the school, i.e., this is the authority figure that monitors the new TEACHERs and their classes. While the TRAINER seeks to create a supportive environment for the TEACHERs, the HEADMISTRESS is the person who the spect-actors are most wary of. This is to say that she, the HEADMISTRESS, has the liberty to: observe teachers during their classes; to interrupt the classes if things seem to be going awry; to schedule feedback meetings with these educators during their free periods. The HEADMISTRESS is the only character in this experience that has the power to "fire" an spect-actor-educator from their role as an educator in the world of the performance. This action though, is reserved for the especially difficult or distraught TEACHER, whose continued presence in the experience might be detrimental either to themselves or to the world of *Detention.*

INMATE STUDENTS: The actors playing the INMATE STUDENTs represent young people between 12 and 18 years of age. These young people are divided into 4 groups, with maximum of 8 actors per group: GROUP 1, GROUP 2, GROUP 3, and GROUP 4. The INMATE STUDENTS attend classes in groups, and as part of the rules of the world, must move with their groups at all times. Each of the four groups should contain characters that embody each of archetypes articulated below. While performers of all genders are welcome, each group should be composed of individuals who have the same gender identity. If there are insufficient numbers of performers, care should be taken to ensure that the archetypes are balanced out across the different groups.

GROUPs 1, 2, 3, 4 each contain individual STUDENTS, each of whom are characterized according to the eight archetypes listed below:

- STUDENT 1: This archetype is that of a young person who has a stable[1] background, has committed a violent crime, is motivated to learn during the classes, and is determined to turn their life around upon release
- STUDENT 2: This archetype is that of a young person who has a stable background, has committed a violent crime, is completely unmotivated to learn during the classes, and seems indifferent about what might happen to them upon their release
- STUDENT 3: This archetype is that of a young person who has a stable background, has committed a non-violent crime, is motivated to learn during the classes, and is determined to change their life around upon release
- STUDENT 4: This archetype is that of a young person who has a stable background, has committed a non-violent crime, and seems indifferent about what might happen to them upon their release
- STUDENT 5: This archetype is that of a young person who has an unstable background, has committed a violent crime, is motivated to learn during the classes, and is determined to change their life around upon release
- STUDENT 6: This archetype is that of a young person has an unstable background, has committed a violent crime, and seems indifferent about what might happen to them upon their release
- STUDENT 7: This archetype is that of a young person who has an unstable background, has committed a non-violent crime, is motivated to learn during the classes, and is determined to change their life around upon release
- STUDENT 8: This archetype is that of a young person who has an unstable background, has committed a non-violent crime and seems indifferent about what might happen to them upon their release

While GROUPs 1, 2, 3, and 4 all consist of the same eight archetypal INMATE STUDENT characters that are framed based on the stability of the young person's background, the violence of their crime, and that young person's motivation vis-à-vis their future, actors and directors should ensure that there is a complexity that is produced in the overall calibration of how the same eight archetypes manifest as thirty-two different personalities. This is to say that, based on the context in which *Detention* is being produced, the archetypes might need to be sculpted and honed based on the racial, religious, and/or socio-economic dynamics of juvenile incarceration rates in that place; not to mention a consideration of the kinds of crimes that most often lead to juvenile incarceration in that setting.

In addition to these contextual details, complexity within/between the archetypes of the INMATE STUDENTS will be achieved by ensuring that the characterization process—for which more information is provided later— results in individualized responses from each performer. If this is accomplished, each of the four different actors from across the four different groups—all of whom are playing characters that are shaped by the archetype of STUDENT 7, for example—will create unique characters that only share the same points of departure in their profiles. This approach to ensuring complexity applies to every instance in this text, where particular archetypes have been used to delineate between/within a group of characters who are taking on a similar role in the experience of *Detention*.

GUARDS: Each group of INMATE STUDENTS has one actor-GUARD who always accompanies them: GUARD 1, GUARD 2, GUARD 3, and GUARD 4. Like the INMATE STUDENTs' profiles, the GUARDs should also be characterized based on the following archetypes:

- GUARD 1: Optimistic and idealistic, this GUARD really believes in the job that they have taken on. They are extremely fond of the INMATE-STUDENTs that are in their group and do their best to be supportive mentors, rather than authoritarian and disciplinary figures.
- GUARD 2: This GUARD is indifferent to the job that they now occupy. All they care about is being able to take care of their family. This GUARD is often bored while at work, doing the minimum needed to keep their position.
- GUARD 3: This GUARD hates their job; they strongly dislike the youth they work with. They do not understand why the INMATE-STUDENTs, who are "criminals," get to access special classes and resources. This GUARD is disillusioned with the criminal justice system and the number of people they have seen cycle through the same cells over and over again. However, despite this frustration, this official has no idea how to get out of their current place of employment. Their father was a GUARD; their grandfather was a GUARD: it is a family profession.
- GUARD 4: This GUARD wants the job because it allows them to exercise their control and power over a group of people who, in their opinion, are a menace to society. What matters to this

GUARD is not the gravity of the crime or aspects of the criminal justice system. They just like being in charge.

HEAD GUARD: This character is a chameleon and can change their approach based on the situation that is being dealt with. This is to say that the actor-HEAD GUARD can be authoritarian if anything untoward happens within the context of the scenario; they would also be the one to escort teachers to and from their lunch breaks and to/from appointments with the HEADMISTRESS; they would also be the person who assists the HEADMISTRESS if a spect-actors needs to be escorted out of *Detention* for any reason.

FAMILIES: 10 actors play the family members of the TEACHERs and are referred to as FAMILY 1, FAMILY 2, FAMILY 3, and FAMILY 4. They appear in Section 2 of the outline, and are an integral part in providing a semi-holistic insight into the TEACHERs' lives.

- FAMILY 1: TEACHER 1 has a partner who is extremely supportive of their job. They ask the right questions and gauge the mood of the spect-actor when they return "home," to create the kind of atmosphere that would be helpful and healthy: cooking for them; watching a movie with them; leaving them alone; whatever is deemed as being appropriate in the moment.
- FAMILY 2: TEACHER 2 has a partner and two children. Unlike TEACHER 1's partner, TEACHER 2's spouse hates their partner's work; because they think the schedule is too demanding and the pay is insufficient. Once TEACHER 2 comes home, therefore, they also have to deal with passive aggressive behavior—this is not a happy home. TEACHER 2 is given chores to do by their partner, regardless of how tired they might be after having taught in a detention center all day.
- FAMILY 3: TEACHER 3 lives with their parents/grandparents— older, dependent individuals who physically need that TEACHER's assistance and attention when they are back home from work.
- FAMILY 4: TEACHER 4 is a single parent and has a second job, as an after-school tutor. When they go home after a day of teaching therefore, there are two or three students who show up for after-school help in whatever subject area is that spect-actor's expertise.
- There is no FAMILY 5 since the fifth teacher lives alone.

The Character Questionnaires

The questionnaires below have been crafted differently for each role in the experience are integral in how actors craft dialogues and actions for themselves. [The way in which such questionnaires are used in the rehearsal process will be addressed in the Interlude that follows *War*].

Character Questionnaire for the TRAINER

- Name:
- Age:
- Gender:
- Why did you decide to become a trainer for detention center teachers?
- What do you love about your job?
- What do you find most challenging about your job?
- What would be your ideal career? If this is not it, why aren't you pursuing what you wish to be doing?
- What kind of personal life do you have, outside of work?

Character Questionnaire for the HEADMISTRESS

- Name:
- Age:
- Gender:
- Why did you decide to become a headmistress at a detention center school?
- What do you love about your job?
- What do you find most challenging about your job?
- What would be your ideal career? If this is not it, why aren't you pursuing the career you want?
- What kind of personal life do you have, outside of work?
- What kind of teachers do you think tend to be successful in this particular context?
- What qualities do you find most unsuitable for a detention center educator?
- If you could run the school as you desired—instead of being controlled by forces outside your purview—what would you do?

Character Questionnaire for the GUARDs

- Name:
- Age:

- Gender:
- Why did you decide to become a detention center guard?
- What do you love about your job?
- What do you find most challenging about your job?
- What would be your ideal career? If this is not it, why aren't you pursuing your "dream"?
- What kind of personal life do you have, outside of work?
- What do you think of the young people in the detention center? What qualities does a young person have to demonstrate for you to respect them and treat them kindly?
- What is your opinion about the teachers in the detention center (generally speaking)—what kinds of classes do you think are actually useful for youth in these contexts?

Character Questionnaire for the HEAD GUARD

- Name:
- Age:
- Gender:
- Why did you decide to become a detention center guard?
- What do you love about your job?
- What do you find most challenging about your job?
- What would be your ideal career? If this is not it, why aren't you pursuing it?
- What kind of personal life do you have, outside of work?
- How do you assert your authority over the other GUARDs?
- What do you think, personally, about the role for education within a detention center context?
- Generally speaking, how would you describe your attitude toward the youth in the detention center?

Character Questionnaire for STUDENTs

- Name:
- Age:
- Gender:
- How did you end up in the detention center?

- What do you find most challenging about being incarcerated?
- How do you keep yourself going, when you feel depressed/alone?
- What is your relationship with your family like?
- Who are your friends in the center and how did you come to form relationships with each other?
- What academic classes most interest you? Why?
- What do you think you want to do when you are released?
- Do you have any friends in the detention center? What do you talk about with them?
- Where do you think you will be ten years from now?

Character Questionnaire for FAMILIES

- Name:
- Age:
- Gender:
- What do you do during the day?
- How do you feel about your family member's job in the detention center?
- How do you spend time together, when the TEACHER—in their character as someone you have a relationship with—is not at work? What kind of relationship do you have with them?
- If you could, what is one thing you would change about your relationship with the TEACHER, in their character, as someone you have a relationship with)?
- What is your favorite movie?
- What is one thing you have never told the TEACHER, in their character, as someone you have a relationship with)?

The Framework

Section 1

Time	Event
8 a.m. to 11 a.m.	Pre-performance workshop for spect-actors, with the TRAINER. Each spect-actor-TEACHER has a follow up meeting with the HEADMISTRESS of the detention

Time	Event
	enter school, immediately after their pre-performance workshop. After this meeting, TEACHERs are shown to their respective classrooms, where each of them will run *four* lesson periods and have one free period. Each group of INMATE STUDENTS has the same classes, in different orders, over the course of the school day. Like the timetable in most formal school environments, students take multiple classes, switching between classroom areas that have been assigned to particular educators.
11 a.m. to 11:45 a.m.	*Lesson Period #1* GROUP 1 → TEACHER 1 GROUP 2 → TEACHER 2 GROUP 3 → TEACHER 3 GROUP 4 → TEACHER 4 *TEACHER 5: FREE PERIOD*
12 p.m. to 12:45 p.m.	*Lesson Period #2* GROUP 1 → TEACHER 2 GROUP 2 → TEACHER 3 GROUP 3 → TEACHER 4 GROUP 4 → TEACHER 5 *TEACHER 1: FREE PERIOD*
1 p.m. to 2 p.m.	Lunch Break with the TRAINER
2 p.m. to 2:45 p.m.	*Lesson Period #3* GROUP 1 → TEACHER 3 GROUP 2 → TEACHER 4 GROUP 3 → TEACHER 5 GROUP 4 → TEACHER 1 *TEACHER 2: FREE PERIOD*
3 p.m. to 3:45 p.m.	*Lesson Period #4* GROUP 1 → TEACHER 4 GROUP 2 → TEACHER 5 GROUP 3 → TEACHER 1 GROUP 4 → TEACHER 2 *TEACHER 3: FREE PERIOD*
4 p.m. to 4:45 p.m.	*Lesson Period #5* GROUP 1 → TEACHER 5 GROUP 2 → TEACHER 1 GROUP 3 → TEACHER 2 GROUP 4 → TEACHER 3 *TEACHER 4: FREE PERIOD*
5 p.m. to 7 p.m.	Dinner & debrief with the TRAINER. Following a discussion about their day with the

Time	Event
	TRAINER, spect-actor-TEACHERs have to plan their classes for the next day. With relevant guidance from the TRAINER, based on points that might have been raised during the debrief with their peers, and based on their own experience with STUDENTs on Day 1 of classes, it is hoped that the spect-actor-TEACHERs' lessons for the following day will be better crafted.

Section 2

Time	Event
7 p.m. to 7 a.m.	The spect-actors go "home," where they encounter other performers who are playing their respective. TEACHER's family members. FAMILY 1, FAMILY 2, FAMILY 3, and FAMILY 4 place different demands on the spect-actor-TEACHER. All except TEACHER 5, who lives alone.

Section 3

Time	Event
8 a.m. to 8:45 a.m.	The second day of classes commences, with a similar timetable as the previous day, except that events begin and end earlier. The HEADMISTRESS, HEAD GUARD, and the TRAINER will need to be specially vigilant to ensure that spect-actors know where they are supposed to be (the same spaces as the previous day). *Lesson Period #1* GROUP 1 → TEACHER 1 GROUP 2 → TEACHER 2 GROUP 3 → TEACHER 3 GROUP 4 → TEACHER 4 *TEACHER 5: FREE PERIOD*
9 a.m. to 9:45 a.m.	Lesson *Period #2* GROUP 1 → TEACHER 2 GROUP 2 → TEACHER 3 GROUP 3 → TEACHER 4 GROUP 4 → TEACHER 5 *TEACHER 1: FREE PERIOD*
9:45 a.m. to 10 a.m.	Coffee break with the TRAINER
10 a.m. to 10:45 a.m.	*Lesson Period #3* GROUP 1 → TEACHER 3 GROUP 2 → TEACHER 4

Time	Event
	GROUP 3 → TEACHER 5 GROUP 4 → TEACHER 1 *TEACHER 2: FREE PERIOD*
11 a.m. to 11:45 a.m.	*Lesson Period #4* GROUP 1 → TEACHER 4 GROUP 2 → TEACHER 5 GROUP 3 → TEACHER 1 GROUP 4 → TEACHER 2 *TEACHER 3: FREE PERIOD*
12 p.m. to 12:45 p.m.	*Lesson Period #5* GROUP 1 → TEACHER 5 GROUP 2 → TEACHER 1 GROUP 3 → TEACHER 2 GROUP 4 → TEACHER 3 *TEACHER 4: FREE PERIOD*
1 p.m. to 2 p.m.	Lunch and debrief with the TRAINER. Spect-actors depart from the experience.

The following sections of the script will go into each part of the preceding table in more detail.

The Design

The experience takes place across multiple rooms in one building, which serves as the detention center school; smaller spaces that would function as the "homes" of the TEACHERs (these could be apartments within a building, cottages, independent houses, a large area that has been designed to have compartmentalized spaces; whatever is available to the production team). It is possible, based on what resources available to the production team, that spect-actors will need to be transported to another part of the town/city where the experience is being produced, in order to reach their "homes." In this instance, the transport also needs to be considered as part of the immersive world of the performance and thought should be given to how spect-actors might remain within the *Detention* context. For instance, having a detention center bus—which is austere and silent—that drives each TEACHER from the school, to the doorstep of their "home," where an actor in their FAMILY will be waiting to take them into that domestic world. Spect-actor-TEACHERs could be taken back to Section 3 the next day either by the same bus, or by members from their FAMILY driving them back to the primary location.

The building that represents the detention center school should be a larger area that has at least seven smaller spaces within it: one room that is used for the training, coffee breaks, meals, and debrief sessions; one room that functions as the HEADMISTRESS' office; five classroom spaces. Ideally, this would be a building that has minimal windows and wire fences. All the lighting inside the space should be fluorescent and if there is an occasional window, the designers should consider putting bars outside of it. There should be a metal detector at the entrance and heavy, self-locking doors. So, while TEACHERs can have keys to their classrooms, should any other space be accidentally locked, they would have to call the HEAD GUARD to open the door for them.

The building smells sterile. Like it has been thoroughly, and clinically, cleaned.

There is an intercom system that can only be used by the HEAD-MISTRESS and HEAD GUARD. When used, it can be heard throughout the school building and there is a particular sound that is played to mark the beginning and end of an announcement; the same sound is also used to mark the beginning and end of lesson periods and breaks.

The walls of the space are lined with motivational posters—posters that talk about how a change in attitude will help the young people move on to great things. Posters that talk about not being addicted to substances. Posters that talk about role models to look up to. Posters that simultaneously, delineate rules for the ways in which students should *not* behave on the school environment and enumerate the consequences for anyone who crosses the stated boundaries.

The INMATE STUDENTS are dressed in monochromatic colors; different colors for different units. So if GROUP 1 is in all green; GROUP 2 is in maroon; GROUP 3 is in blue; GROUP 4 is in yellow. The STUDENTs wear carefully chosen shoes that, somehow, reflect the individuality of the young person who is wearing them. INMATE STUDENTs cannot wear any jewelry; they cannot wear hats or scarves; some of them can have tattoos, if the general prison cultures in the context in which *Detention* is being executed would make tattoos a relevant choice.

GUARDS are dressed in all black and carry sticks, walkie-talkies, and handcuffs. They wear hats and comfortable shoes; only the HEAD GUARD is allowed to carry a cellphone.

The HEADMISTRESS and TRAINER wear formal clothing, as do the teachers—whatever passes as formal clothing in the context in which the piece is being produced. That said, the HEADMISTRESS could critique the dress code of particular spect-actor-TEACHERs and direct them to a wardrobe closet from which the spect-actors can be asked to re-dress themselves into more formal, detention center appropriate attire.

The Breakdown

Each of the sections in the previously articulated table is divided into specific parts. A detailed explanation of each part, and what needs to happen in that part, can be found below. In each part, there is a sequence of events, actions, and possibilities that has been described—with enough room for actors and directors to bring in their own voices to the piece.

Section 1: Part 1

Before spect-actors arrive at the performance location, they are informed that it is going to be a participatory/interactive/simulation-based/immersive theater piece—I suggest using the terminology that might be best understood in the context in which *Detention* is being executed. Spect-actors are informed that they have to take on particular roles during the experience and that they will have to stay in that character at all times. How this information is communicated will, of course, depend on the context in which the piece is being performed: emails; brochures; telephone calls; in person conversations; whatever.

Below is a brief for what such a pre-experience framing for the spect-actors might involve. This is in addition to, of course, the logistical information that must be provided to spect-actors: the time commitment required of them, the date, the place, the time, and what they might need to bring for their overnight stay in the world of *Detention*. I would suggest that there are two rounds of information provision for spect-actors: in the first, it is the logistical information that is provided a few weeks leading up to the event; in the second, it is the information below that should be sent out, a few days before the experience itself.

When you arrive at our Youth Detention Center [*insert date, time, location*], you will be asked to step into a character that you must remain in for the duration of your experience. You will be guided through every step of the process, but in order to get the most out of your time with us, we encourage you to participate as fully as you can. In order to preserve the integrity of the experience, we are unable to provide you more details at this time but please know that your safety will never be compromised and you are welcome to step out of the experience at any point, should you feel the need to.
Please dress formally. Please be prepared to teach. Please be prepared to learn.
If you are a certified teacher, please bring a copy of your teaching certificate with you.

Section 1: Part 2

When spect-actors arrive at the performance/experience space, they enter a room that has been designed to look like a teacher-training class: a projector; forms; tables and chairs arranged in a semi-circle. There is coffee being served, and snacks. As soon as they are seated, each spect-actor receives a registration form (as below) on which they are asked to craft their own personality. There is one actor in this space, the TRAINER.

NEW TEACHER REGISTRATION FORM

Please use this form to tell us more about who you will become for this experience. You can draw from your autobiographical information or from fictional ideas—we welcome you to be as creative as you want. As long as you stay in the character that your create for yourself for the entirety of our time with you.

- Name:
- Age:
- Gender:
- Educational background:
- What subjects are you qualified to teach:
- Do you have teaching certification (Y/N)? If yes, please attach a copy of your certificate. If no, please explain why you do not have the certification:
- Why do you want to teach in a youth detention center:
- If you have a criminal record, please describe the circumstances of the crime and your subsequent release:
- The names and contact information for three references who can support your application:
- Address & family information: *This section is already filled out with information about the FAMILY that the spect-actor will encounter at the end of Section 1. This is important since it will function as a primer for the spect-actors, when it is time for them to go to their "homes."*

Once spect-actors have had the time to fill out their forms, the TRAINER conducts a warm up workshop that seeks to enable each spect-actors to get into their TEACHER characters in a more embodied fashion.

In this workshop, the spect-actors are first asked to introduce themselves to everyone else in the group, as their character. They are asked to do this introduction in first person, i.e., "I am [*name*] and I want to teach youth in detention centers because [*insert response to question six on the registration form*]" and so on.

Once they have done this introduction, the TRAINER takes them through the well-known Hot Seating exercise. In this, each spect-actor takes turns sitting in the "hot seat," where they are asked to field questions about their character that goes beyond what has been asked of them in the form. The TRAINER starts by asking the questions, but other spect-actors are also welcome to question each other, in the spirit of helping their peers. Potential questions could include:

- What is your biggest fear as an educator in a youth detention center?
- How did you meet your spouse, if you have one?
- What hopes do you have for the young people that you teach in this context?
- What is the best class you have ever taught (as your character)?
- Who was your first love?

Some of the questions are related to the specific role that the spect-actors will take on as an educator in the detention center classroom; others speak to their personal life. The TRAINER must ensure that questions are asked targeting different realms of the character's life, just to ensure that the spect-actors get more time and practice about the person they are about to become. This exercise continues as long as the TRAINER deems fit.

Once all spect-actors have had a chance to be in the hot seat:

> TRAINER: Now, I will set each of you up with an appointment to meet the Head-mistress of our school. Before you meet her, however, there is one more training step to complete. Please take the time to make five lesson plans for your classes today, since the Headmistress will ask to see them.

A copy of the lesson plan template is handed to each spect-actor and they are asked to complete it in as much detail as possible. The entire process of the character work and filling out the lesson plan should take between 1.5 and 2 hours for a group of 5 participants.

LESSON PLANNING TEMPLATE

Notes for all teachers

- Each lesson period is forty-five minutes long. Students have a fifteen-minute transition time to go between classes
- There will be between 10 and 15 youth in your classroom, between the ages of 12 and 18
- We are only able to offer basic stationary: you will have a whiteboard and whiteboard markers. There are also tables and chairs: you are allowed to move them around, if needed.
- Some classrooms might have projectors with computers connected to the internet; some do not have this capacity and if you need this equipment you will need to make arrangements with teachers who do have these materials in their room
- Students will have notebooks and pens/pencils with them. If you need any additional materials for this class, please ask the Headmistress when you meet with her.

- You will receive your personalized timetable from the Headmistress
- You will repeat the same class four times, to four different groups of students

Lesson topic: What is the primary theme and subject that you will teach in your class?

Expected learning outcomes: What do you hope that students will take away from this lesson and how do you plan to assess their learning?

Breakdown of lesson plan: Please explain every single activity that you will conduct with an estimate of how long each of these activities will take

As spect-actors finish their lesson planning, the TRAINER gives the material a quick look and points out any glaring errors. While spect-actors are filling out their lesson plans, the TRAINER is allowed to consult with them and answer any questions that they might have.

Once a spect-actor is ready with their lesson planning template, the TRAINER takes them—with all the forms that they have filled out—to meet the HEADMISTRESS. Once a particular spect-actor has finished their chat with the HEADMISTRESS, the next spect-actor is taken in for their appointment. And so on and so forth. After all five spect-actors have been taken to meet the HEADMISTRESS, the TRAINER's sequence of events is as follows:

Section 1

Time	Event
11 a.m. to 11:45 a.m.	*Lesson Period #1* TRAINER visits TEACHER 4's classroom and takes extensive notes about the teacher's performance. At the end of the class, while INMATE STUDENTs are moving between classes, the TRAINER provides quick feedback to the TEACHER and heads to the next classroom. The feedback is always constructive, i.e., the TRAINER tells the spect-actor what they are doing well; they also tell them what they need to work on with this particular student group. This is also a chance for the spect-actor to ask more questions of the TRAINER.
12 p.m. to 12:45 p.m.	*Lesson Period #2* TRAINER visits TEACHER 5's classroom [same post-class feedback as above].
1 p.m. to 2 p.m.	Lunch Break. The TRAINER has lunch with the TEACHERs in the lunchroom and listens to their discussion. No effort is made on the TRAINER's part to control the conversation, but it is suggested that the TRAINER check in with the TEACHERs whose classrooms they have not had the chance to visit yet.

Time	Event
2 p.m. to 2:45 p.m.	*Lesson Period #3* TRAINER visits TEACHER 1's classroom [same post-class feedback as above].
3 p.m. to 3:45 p.m.	*Lesson Period #4* TRAINER visits TEACHER 2's classroom [same post-class feedback as above].
4 p.m. to 4:45 p.m.	*Lesson Period #5* TRAINER visits TEACHER 3's classroom [same post-class feedback as above].
6 p.m. to 7 p.m.	The initial training space has now been transformed to serve dinner and hold a debriefing session. When the TEACHERs walk in, the TRAINER asks them to grab their food and take a seat in a circle. The TRAINER leads them through a facilitated discussion, with questions such as these: 1. What was your most successful moment today? 2. What was your biggest challenge today? 3. What will you do differently tomorrow? TEACHERs are given the opportunity to ask questions and once the discussion comes to a natural close, the TRAINER asks teachers to take some time to fill out lesson planning templates for the next day. The TRAINER then tells the spect-actors are going to go to their "homes," reminding them—in character—of their home lives. For example: • "So, TEACHER 1, I understand that you have a partner. What do they do?" • "So, TEACHER 3, I understand that you take care of your parents. What are they ailing from?" In so doing, the spect-actor-TEACHERs will be reminded to look back at their teacher registration forms and to get ready for their "home" experiences.

Section 3

Time	Event
Before 8 a.m.	The TRAINER, along with the HEADMISTRESS and the HEAD GUARD, are present at the entrance to the detention center school before spect-actors are scheduled to arrive. As individuals come in, the TRAINER checks in with them about their evening and walks them to the same classroom that they were using the day before.

Time	Event
8 a.m. to 8:45 a.m.	*Lesson Period #1* The TRAINER is present at each of the TEACHER's performance review meeting with the HEADMISTRESS and is an advocate on behalf of the TEACHER, even when the HEADMISTRESS might be extremely critical of them. They always need to defer to the HEADMISTRESS's position of authority within the detention center school, but are also adept at being diplomatic and constructive. For example: • "So, ma'am. I understand that you are concerned about TEACHER 1's use of language with the students. Could you give us some examples of the kinds of words and phrases that you found problematic?" • "I see, so you are concerned about the content's relevance to the students. I just wanted to remind you, ma'am, that TEACHER 2 is working in this context for the first time and I'm confident that they will only improve going forward."
9 a.m. to 9:45 a.m.	*Lesson Period #2* The TRAINER is present at the next TEACHER's performance review meeting with the HEADMISTRESS.
9:45 a.m. to 10 a.m.	Coffee Break. The TRAINER joins the TEACHERs for the coffee break and checks in with those who have not been to their performance review meetings yet.
10 a.m. to 10:45 a.m.	*Lesson Period #3* The TRAINER is present at the next TEACHER's performance review meeting with the HEADMISTRESS.
11 a.m. to 11:45 a.m.	*Lesson Period #4* The TRAINER is present at the next TEACHER's performance review meeting with the HEADMISTRESS.
12 p.m. to 12:45 p.m.	*Lesson Period #5* The TRAINER is present at the final TEACHER's performance review meeting with the HEADMISTRESS.
1 p.m. to 2 p.m.	The TRAINER facilitates the debrief session in very much the same way as that which was conducted at the end of Section 1. Questions such as: • "What were some of the highlights in your classes today?"

Time	Event
	• "Any different challenges than yesterday?"
	Spect-actors are allowed to ask questions but only within the realm of the world of *Detention*. If they break character and try to ask the TRAINER a question that alludes to the experience as a theater piece, they are met with a response like:
	"I'm afraid I cannot answer that question at the moment. I would suggest that you contact <*the person who sent the introductory emails*> for more clarification about that issue"
	The TRAINER thanks the spect-actors for coming to the experience, congratulates them, and gives them a "certificate" for successfully completing their training. On that certificate, there is something along the lines of: "If you would like to continue your training, please connect with <*they are given a list of detention center facilities that are close to the educational institution at which they teach*>.
	Nothing needs to be said about the certificate, or the information on it; the spect-actors are just given that material to do with as they wish.

Section 1: Part 3

The HEADMISTRESS has color-coded versions of each teacher's timetable, with information about the classroom that they will be using, the times of their classes, their breaks, and free periods. These personalized timetables could be pre-prepared (five different schedule sheets for TEACH-ERs 1, 2, 3, 4, and 5) with the HEADMISTRESS only needing to add the name of a particular spect-actor. The timetables could also be created in the moment, with the HEADMISTRESS allocating classroom space based on what the TEACHER needs (in terms of materials) and which classroom spaces contain that equipment.

When TEACHERs enter, the HEADMISTRESS asks them to introduce themselves and to briefly present their lesson plan. As the spect-actor speaks, the HEADMISTRESS takes notes, asks the spect-actor for the forms that they filled out during the pre-performance session, and writes/types her thoughts on a book/computer at her desk. Wherever the spect-actor's plan seems to be lacking in any way, the HEADMISTRESS is allowed to help them, in character.

If the spect-actor needs specific stationary supplies for their lesson, the HEADMISTRESS takes them to a stationary closet that is in her office, and allows them to take what they need. If the materials needed are unavailable, the HEADMISTRESS informs the teacher will have to find a way to improvise around the lack of materials.

If a spect-actor asks for materials that might be used as weapons—like scissors or any other sharp implements—the HEADMISTRESS mentions the potential danger of using these materials with the INMATE STUDENTS. In line with this, the spect-actor-TEACHER is advised to be on guard at all times and not to get close, physically or emotionally, with any student that they might interact with during the day.

Finally, before the TEACHER heads to their room, the HEADMISTRESS asks them particular questions like "what will you do if one of the students becomes violent in the classroom?" It is made clear to each spect-actor that they are to call on the GUARD who is with the group of students for any disciplinary help; that TEACHER is only in charge of delivering the lesson.

Once the spect-actor is seen to understand the rules of the world, the HEADMISTRESS asks the HEAD GUARD to walk the TEACHER over to their classroom and to wait for their first class to begin. Then, the next TEACHER is called in and the same process is followed.

If there is no unforeseen event that arises, that requires an adjustment of plans, it is suggested that the HEADMISTRESS follows the following arc of actions for the duration of Sections 1 and 2.

Section 1

Time	Event
9:30 a.m. to 10:45 a.m.	Individual spect-actor meetings with the HEADMISTRESS.
11 a.m. to 11:45 a.m.	*Lesson Period #1* The HEADMISTRESS visits TEACHER 1's classroom and takes extensive notes about the teacher's performance. Occasionally, she speaks silently to particular students who might be seen as misbehaving or not paying enough attention to the TEACHER. The HEADMISTRESS is generally unaffected by how her presence might impact the TEACHER's instruction—she cares about maintaining the discipline of the environment. As soon as the class is over, the HEADMISTRESS immediately heads to the next classroom without speaking to the TEACHER. The notes that are taken during this observation class will be used as fodder during the performance review meetings in Section 3.
12 p.m. to 12:45 p.m.	*Lesson Period #2* HEADMISTRESS visits TEACHER 2's classroom.

Time	Event
1 p.m. to 2 p.m.	Lunch Break. The HEADMISTRESS stops in on the TEACHERs' lunch break but does not join them—the only person she speaks with is the TRAINER. It is important that a strictly hierarchical relationship is maintained and that she only remains around the TEACHERs as long as she absolutely has to.
2 p.m. to 2:45 p.m.	*Lesson Period #3* HEADMISTRESS visits TEACHER 3's classroom.
3 p.m. to 3:45 p.m.	*Lesson Period #4* HEADMISTRESS visits TEACHER 4's classroom.
4 p.m. to 4:45 p.m.	*Lesson Period #5* HEADMISTRESS visits TEACHER 5's classroom.

Section 3

Before 8 a.m.	The HEADMISTRESS, along with the TRAINER and the HEAD GUARD, are present at the entrance to the detention center school before spect-actors are scheduled to arrive. As individuals come in, if the TRAINER is occupied with another spect-actor, the HEADMISTRESS asks the TEACHER to go to the classroom space that they were using the day before.
8 a.m. to 8:45 a.m.	*Lesson Period #1* The HEADMISTRESS has a performance review with TEACHER 5. The TRAINER is also present. While the HEADMISTRESS does not have to be cruel in their criticism, she is more likely (than the TRAINER) to provide straightforward criticism about observations that were made during the previous day of class observations. There is no part of the TEACHERs' being/behavior that the HEADMISTRESS cannot comment on: she can comment on a TEACHER's use of language; their choice of lesson content; the class design; their approach to discipline; their attitude toward the INMATE STUDENTS; anything that has, or that could potentially have, an effect on the education being delivered in that context.
9 a.m. to 9:45 a.m.	*Lesson Period #2* HEADMISTRESS has a performance review meeting with TEACHER 1 [following the same process as above].
9:45 a.m. to 10 a.m.	Coffee Break. Again, the HEADMISTRESS can stop in but not join the TEACHERs.

Time	Event
10 a.m. to 10:45 a.m.	*Lesson Period #3* The HEADMISTRESS has a performance review meeting with TEACHER 2 [following the same process as above].
11 a.m. to 11:45 a.m.	*Lesson Period #4* The HEADMISTRESS has a performance review meeting with TEACHER 1 [following the same process as above].
12 p.m. to 12:45 p.m.	*Lesson Period #5* The HEADMISTRESS has a performance review meeting with TEACHER 1 [following the same process as above].
1 p.m. to 2 p.m.	Lunch, debrief, departure. The HEADMISTRESS is conspicuously absent from this final session and from bidding the TEACHERs farewell. She continues to work in her office till the last of the spect-actors has left the space.

Section 1: Part 4

GUARDs 1, 2, 3, 4 stick with the GROUP of INMATE STUDENTs that has been assigned to them at all times. The GUARD must walk with their GROUP to and between classes; accompany an INMATE STUDENT if they need a restroom break [in this case, the HEAD GUARD will need to be called so that the GUARD can take that student to the restroom while the HEAD GUARD stays in the room with the INMATE STUDENTs]. The INMATE STUDENTs can never be left alone with the TEACHER.

The GUARDs are encouraged to behave naturally in response to the class that is being conducted. This is to say that they respond to the content being explored in the class in light of their character's interests, goals, and attitudes toward the inmate students.

For example:

- GUARD 1, who loves their job, is always interested in what is going on in the classroom. They participate in the lessons by asking questions of the teachers. They also engage with students during the class, helping them understand concepts if they have trouble, and generally being amenable to students' requests. Even when students misbehave, GUARD 1 always approaches them kindly and gently at first; using force only when there seems to be no other option available to them.
- GUARD 2, the indifferent character, sits back during all the classes

and only intervenes when particular student responses force them to have a response. They don't pay much attention to what the teacher is doing, and instead, looks through any/all materials that they find in that classroom.

- GUARD 3 strongly dislikes the youth and this attitude is visible in how they speak to students as they enter each classroom. During the classes, this GUARD stands behind the students—interrupting their work with snide comments and smirks, as if they are reinforcing all the negative ideas that this GUARD has about them.

- GUARD 4 enjoys the power and is not averse to interrupting the class at the smallest instance to showcase their authority. If the young people are talking while the teacher is trying to present an idea, this GUARD hits the back of the student's chair with their baton. They also call the spect-actor-TEACHER aside, and give them unsolicited advice, if they feel like this TEACHER is unable to handle the class and/or is delivering inappropriate content. They are threatening and authoritarian; the "stereotype" that many have of GUARDs in prison contexts.

Section 1: Part 5

Once all the TEACHERs have been stationed in their classrooms, the HEAD GUARD lets the other GUARDs know that they can now begin taking STUDENT GROUPs to their respective classes.

During the rest of Section 1, the HEAD GUARD does rounds and pops into/out of classrooms, keeping an eye on the goings on. Sometimes, this person is called by the GUARDs to relieve them of their position, if a STUDENT needs to use the restroom. Otherwise, the HEAD GUARD is free to shape their character as best they desire. A participative HEAD GUARD would probably go to classrooms and observe lessons often. A less participative HEAD GUARD would probably walk through the hallways from time to time, but otherwise just stay at their desk near the entrance to the school.

During Section 3, the HEAD GUARD is at the entrance of the school—with the HEADMISTRESS and TRAINER—and watches as each TEACHER makes it to their respective classrooms. Then, the HEAD GUARD walks each individual TEACHER to and from their performance review: they call the TEACHER in question from their classroom and after the meeting, walk them back before getting the next TEACHER for their performance review.

When the HEADMISTRESS and TRAINER are doing the performance review meetings, the HEAD GUARD interrupts the HEADMISTRESS at regular intervals. The HEAD GUARD does not need to say why they are interrupting the meeting, just that the HEADMISTRESS is needed for something else. The

HEADMISTRESS will step outside for a few moments, when she and the HEAD GUARD will step out of the line of sight of the TRAINER and the TEACHER.

Section 1: Part 6

INMATE STUDENTs in each GROUP, as in the character descriptions, have been characterized according to three variables: the stability of their background; the violence of their crime; their motivation (or lack thereof) to extend their education in the detention center. While each GROUP should be of a similar gender identity, there are a few of considerations to keep in mind:

- that STUDENTs represent different ethnicities/backgrounds that are most relevant to the context in which the experience is being staged
- that individuals in each GROUP (the director ensures) encompass a range of ages from 12 to 18 when they flesh out their characters
- that each youth thinks about whether or not they have particular learning/psychological differences that manifest in particular ways in their work in the classroom. It is suggested here that the director and the students undertake research into the ways in which mental health and learning differences play into the juvenile justice system in that particular context

STUDENTS attend classes; that is all they do. But it is incredibly important that, while they are attending the classes, they stay true to the characters that have been crafted for themselves, while also responding (in the moment) to the different lesson plans that teachers might have in store. Preparing actors for this type of improvisation is of crucial importance because each STUDENT's interest in a particular discipline, and that character's likely responses to a particular TEACHER's pedagogy, need to be unique. Potential actions might include:

- One STUDENT who always asks questions and is equally committed to all their classes
- One STUDENT who is incredibly engaged when passionate about a subject but completely disengaged when they do not have an interest in the subject matter
- One STUDENT who interrupts the class with occasional jokes—unless the TEACHER manages to harness their attention in a constructive way
- One STUDENT who is always in their own world—who is hard to get through to unless the TEACHER manages to get them engaged

- One STUDENT who is incredibly shy and even when poked fun at by others in the group, chooses to remain silent
- One STUDENT who always insults other people in the class, at any chance he gets
- One STUDENT who is bright and energetic; interested in learning but unable to retain any information

In all these cases, it is imperative that the STUDENTs respond within the frame of the world being showcased in *Detention*: if the characters step too much out of line and are too disruptive, for instance, they are hauled up by the GUARDs. So, while the actors being STUDENTS are trying to be realistic in their painting a picture of multiple, unique individuals in that classroom, they should simultaneously be careful to ensure that the disruption they cause is "realistic." Detention center environments always involve consequences for any actions that fall outside the rules of the institution, and no one is more aware of the various punishments that can be inflicted on rule-breakers than the young people themselves.

After following the above mentioned directions for all of the classes in Section 1, when STUDENT's return for the next day of classes (in Section 3), it is suggested that:

- One STUDENT from GROUPs 1 and 2 "disappear"—ideally the STU-DENT(s) who were most participatory and were helpful to the TEACHERs. If TEACHERs ask about their absence, it is recommended that the other STUDENTs and GUARDs are vague about the location of the missing student. Perhaps they have been released? Or perhaps they are at a parole hearing?
- One STUDENT from GROUP 3 is "transferred" to GROUP 2. This transfer should be of a character whose presence/absence alters the dynamics in both groups, and thus has an impact on the spect-actor-TEACHER's lesson plan
- One STUDENT from GROUP 4 is in chains over the course of the second day i.e., he had a disciplinary issue the day before and has to walk around with his arms and legs in chains for the duration of Section 3. GROUP 4's dynamic is clearly affected by this and some of the students can—when not watched by the GUARD—try to tell the TEACHER about the event that happened to catalyze the disciplinary action

The rest of Section 3 carries on as Section 1: STUDENTs remain true to their characters, but with the new shift in dynamic caused by the compositional change of their particular GROUP.

If the creators of this piece decide to stage only Section 1, it is recommended that provisions are made to enable the abovementioned "disappear-ances" and shifts in GROUP composition over the course of the first day. Per-haps spect-actors could be paired to teach lessons—with only two groups of student actors rather than four—leading to fewer lesson periods; such that each spect-actor-educator pair teaches two lessons to each group and in the second lesson, has to encounter the changed demographic within that par-ticular group of students? This is up to the director of *Detention* but it is integral to the pedagogical objectives of the experience that TEACHERs under-stand what it might be like to have an inconsistent, yet, highly controlled stu-dent population.

Section 2

The production team finds the most effective way to take the five spect-actors to the spaces that will represent their "homes" between the spect-actors' first and second days of teaching. As mentioned in the character descriptions, each FAMILY attempts to create a realistic setting based on the kind of personal conditions that are meant to frame the personal life of that particular experience. What this looks like will differ for each FAMILY and specific ideas have been included for each of these individuals/groups:

FAMILY 1—When TEACHER 1 reaches their home, they find a warm and supportive space. Their partner is having dinner with their children and when TEACHER 1 walks in, makes them a plate of food. The children are well behaved and all three members of FAMILY 1 ask the spect-actor about their day and provide apprecia-tive feedback when the spect-actor responds to their questions. After dinner, the children go off to bed while TEACHER 1's partner suggests that they watch a movie together. A range of video options are provided to TEACHER 1 and when it's time to sleep, TEACHER 1's partner receives a phone call. On this phone call, the partner is called away to help a friend who is having a personal problem. The spect-actor is asked to go to bed and the partner returns in time to make breakfast for TEACHER 1 and the children-actors—telling TEACHER 1 that they had only just came back home after helping their friend and that's why they were absent over the course of the night.

FAMILY 2—When TEACHER 2 walks home, their partner is cold towards them. They ask questions about the spect-actor's day but when TEACHER 2 gives answers, these responses are met with stinging replies, a rolling of eyes, and smirks. It should become clear through this conversation that TEACHER 2's partner does not like their profession and after an awkward and strained conversation with the actor, the spect-actor-TEACHER is left alone in the living room with a television and some movie options. In the midst of this, the partner storms into the living room, angrily tells TEACHER 2 that they have decided to spend the night at their mother's house, and leaves. The partner does not come back and TEACHER 2 is left to figure out how to handle their morning.

FAMILY 3—When TEACHER 3 enters their home, they hear a voice calling them from one of the rooms inside the house. This voice is found to belong to a very sick family member, who is confined to bed and has a walker by their side. This actor asks TEACHER 3 questions about their day and once conversation has taken place for a few minutes, the sick relative asks TEACHER 3 to make them something for dinner. TEACHER 3 will be expected to go to the kitchen, look at the supplies that are available and make something for them. After the food is served, the family member tells TEACHER 3 to take a break and relax in their living room. But every once in a while they call out to TEACHER 3 and ask them for various favors, the specific nature of which can be decided upon vis-à-vis the characterization of this role.

FAMILY 4—TEACHER 4 goes home to find a young person who contextualizes for the spect-actor that s/he is their child. This actor, after asking TEACHER 4 about their day, asks them about when their first student is coming over for after school tutoring (it is important that the number of students to be expected + the subject to be tutored in are effectively communicated to TEACHER 4 by the TRAINER at the last debrief session). The students who are being tutored by TEACHER 4 arrive at particularly timed intervals and during these sessions, the actor playing TEACHER 4's child also interrupts from time to time, to ask questions of their parent. During the last tutoring session, the child decides to go to bed and does not see TEACHER 4 till they have to be woken up the next morning. The child could wake up their parent, the next morning, under the guise of breakfast needing to be prepared for them.

FAMILY 5—TEACHER 5 lives alone. When they walk in the door, they find a television in their living room and some provisions in their kitchen; it is up to them to decide how they will spend their solitary evening.

In all these cases, it is imperative that there is some way in which TEACH-ERs' concerns about the evening and about making it to work the next day are addressed. It could be that the TRAINER calls each TEACHER at least once in the evening, under the guise of checking in with them after their first day to see how they are doing. If the TRAINER is concerned that any spect-actor might be experiencing extreme discomfort from their home environment, the TRAINER could make a home visit to see how that particular spect-actor is doing. It is also strongly recommended that the TEACHERs get a wake up call either from one of their FAMILY members in character. In the case of TEACHER 5, that the TRAINER call them in the morning to ensure that they are able to get to work on time.

Section 3

All the necessary components to Section 3 have been addressed in their corresponding Section 1 descriptions. The HEADMISTRESS, the TRAINER, and the HEAD GUARD meet the TEACHERs when they reach the detention center on the morning of their second day of the experience. The TEACHERs then go into their respective classrooms and the timetable, as set out, commences.

TEACHERs go through their lessons and have performance review meetings with the HEADMISTRESS and the TRAINER during their free periods.

At the end of the school day, after the final debrief session with the TRAINER, TEACHERs can depart the experience.

INTERLUDE

As mentioned in the Introduction, the Interludes in this book serve to put forth two different, yet intersecting points of consideration. First, this Interlude proposes a strategy that speaks to immersive theater directors who might be interested in staging any one of the three texts in this book. This particular strategy might be of use to directors who are considering the production of *any* applied theater text that needs to be context-specific. The proposal of this directorial strategy is followed by reflections that are aimed more toward immersive theater playwrights; analyses of one element from more "traditional," Realism-inspired playwriting that has to be reconsidered in order to write pieces like *Detention*. Auto-ethnography is particularly important in the Interludes—though its presence can be seen throughout this work—in using the personal to reflect on the bigger picture. As such, the reader will find the tone in these Interludes to be informal … maybe even unexpected.

For an Immersive Theater Director

In the preceding script, the reader will have seen multiple instances where I speak about how particular elements in the script can be adapted so as to make the experience more contextually specific to the precise location in which it is being staged. In the spirit of clarifying what I mean by this, I use the first part of this Interlude as a thought exercise. While *Detention*, as I mentioned earlier, draws from my work in a youth detention center in New Mexico, let's assume in this Interlude's thought exercise, that I want to implement the piece in another context in which I often work—India. How would I, as the director of *Detention*, adapt elements of the script to make the structure and experience more relevant to an Indian context? I present the following discussion as a thought exercise because I don't see myself implementing *Detention* in India any time in the near future. Furthermore, given that it is hard to say that any idea will apply to *all* of India rather than smaller, more self-contained contexts within the subcontinent, I can in no way claim that the modes of adaptation that I suggest in this Interlude will be applicable to all juvenile detention spaces across India. And yet, by putting forth ideas about what I would do to make *Detention* more relevant in India, I hope to present potential directors of the preceding script with approaches and strategies that they might then implement when staging *Detention* in their own contexts. Before going into this thought exercise, however, I should clarify that I have no personal, lived experience of working with detention centers in India, as I do in New Mexico. What I have relied on in this thought exercise, therefore, is information that has been gleaned from diverse sources of archival research—elements from this research have them been utilized to present examples of particular elements of *Detention* that I would adapt. I make this clarification since there might be experiential nuances that are absent in my considerations that follow, for those who might have spent time in India's juvenile homes; to them, I restate that this is, for better or for worse, a thought exercise.

Adapting the Framework

The structure of *Detention*, as it has been scripted, is based on my experience of the formal education system at one youth detention center in New Mexico—a structure that, I have been told, mirrors those that exist across a majority of similar juvenile detention facilities in the United States (U.S.). In this setting, the juvenile offenders are divided into different residential units. This division is based both on the age of the young person in question, and the gravity of their crime; that said, there are mitigating factors that are said to emerge when, for example, two young people who are in rival gangs arrive at the same facility. In such cases, the goal seems to be to separate the two individuals in question, making their age and the nature of their crime a secondary factor of consideration in their living allocations. The residential units are located at a walking distance from a public school that is housed within the larger campus of a detention center facility. The young people in each unit go to school from around 7:30 a.m. in the morning to around 2 p.m. (as I write this, I am aware that the school hours are changing for the following academic year), five days a week. Once they are done with their classes for the day, the youth then head back to their residential facilities where they are engaged in different types of programming: group sessions; individual therapy sessions; homework; time for physical exercise through organized sports groups or informal games; sessions with visiting teachers (like myself), who offer a diverse range of activities. Given the ways in which my understanding of this structure influenced the creation and development of *Detention,* the first element that I needed to understand, when thinking about adapting the piece to an Indian context, was how similarly/differently the notion of a "school" might manifest. And what I immediately encountered is that, the relative autonomy of a public school that is present on a juvenile detention center setting in the U.S.—the autonomy being visible in how staff are hired through the Departments of Education rather than the Department of Corrections; the autonomy also being visible in the absence of the detention center facility's name on the school transcripts that are issued to the youth at the end of their tenure there.

These dynamics seem to function quite differently within the juvenile justice system in India. Juveniles who become enmeshed in the system in India seem to be categorized into two main groups. The first of these groups includes neglected juveniles who are "begging, without homes, destitute, whose parents are unfit or unable to exercise control over them, live in a brothel, lead an immoral, drunken or depraved live, and/or who are likely to be abused or exploited" (Hartjen & Kethineni, 1996:37). The second group is said as encompassing delinquent juveniles who have come into conflict with the law and are adjudicated by the Indian justice system. While both "neglected and delinquent juveniles can be housed together in 'observation' (detention) homes prior to adjudication of the case," youth who are determined as "neglected are subsequently [...] housed in 'juvenile homes' while those judged delinquent may be placed in 'special homes'" (Hartjen & Kethineni, 1996:37). While young people who are remanded to juvenile and special homes seem to receive, largely, informal and vocational education rather than formal education that results in transcripts and diplomas, young offenders between 18 and 21 are sometimes placed in what are called "borstal schools."

In these borstal schools, the primary objective "is to ensure care, welfare and rehabilitation of young offenders in an environment suitable for children and to keep them away from the contaminating atmosphere of prisons" (Krohn & Lane, 2015:61). As such, youth who are in conflict with the law and who are detained in such borstal schools are "provided with various vocational trainings and education with the help of trained teachers" (Krohn & Lane, 2015:61). The "original Borstal School Act required all inmates to engage in drill, study and labour for eight hours every working day" (Krohn & Lane, 2015:61). In this eight-hour time frame, youth are asked to engage in "prayer, parade, physical training, workshops, schools, agricultural training, recreation and games from 5:30 a.m. to 7 p.m." and are staffed (when possible) with "a psychologist, physical education teachers, band masters, secondary grade teachers, carpenters, [and] instructors" (Krohn & Lane, 2015:61). More information than this is hard to come by and it is unclear, in the archives that I consulted, how decisions are made about where young people in conflict with the law are placed—juvenile homes; special homes; or borstal schools. However, even with this limited contextual information, it seems to be that borstal schools are the closest in structure to the school that I have encountered at the New Mexican detention center. One of the first adjustments that I would make to *Detention* in India, therefore, would be the clarification of the setting as being a borstal school. So, for instance, the forms (for spectators) that currently mention "detention center" would be edited to reflect the borstal school terminology. While this adjustment of terminology would be fairly simple, given the already existing ambiguity in *Detention* vis-à-vis context, there are some other shifts that I would make, that would be more significant.

First, given the previously mentioned timetable of borstal schools, rather than following an 8 a.m. start as described in the suggested timeline in *Detention*, I would probably begin the work at 5:30 a.m. Given that the functioning, usage, and passage of time are integral in understanding the experience of incarceration, spect-actors in India should be given an experiential understanding of the way time functions at a borstal school (as below). In so doing, in retaining the target spect-actor group as being existing educators from much better resourced, private Indian schools, I consider the shift in the schedule as being integral to an experiential understanding of the borstal school educators' experience. The existing schedule in *Detention* highlights the struggles that come from being an educator, despite more "regular" working hours in a context of incarceration. When this schedule is made more intense; when educators in India's borstal schools have to work twelve-hour days, what happens to the quality of the instruction that they are able to deliver? How do the borstal school educators deal with their own institutionalization? Consider this adapted timetable that I would use for an India-centric adaptation of *Detention*:

Table 2: Adapted Framework
Section 1

Time	Event—Occurrence
5:30 a.m. to 7:30 a.m.	Pre-performance Workshop with the TRAINER. Individual spect-actor meetings with the HEADMISTRESS. Assuming that a maximum of 5 spect-actors will still apply: TEACHER 1, TEACHER 2, TEACHER 3, TEACHER 4, TEACHER 5.
8 a.m. to 8:45 a.m.	*Lesson Period #1* TEACHERs 1, 2, 3, 4 have classes. *TEACHER 5: FREE PERIOD.*
9 a.m. to 9:45 a.m.	*Lesson Period #2* TEACHERs 2, 3, 4, 5 have classes. *TEACHER 1: FREE PERIOD.*
9:45 a.m. to 10 a.m.	Coffee Break.
10 a.m. to 10:45 a.m.	*Lesson Period #3* TEACHERs 3, 4, 5, 1 have classes. *TEACHER 2: FREE PERIOD.*
11 a.m. to 11:45 a.m.	*Lesson Period #4* TEACHERs 4, 5, 1, 2 have classes. *TEACHER 3: FREE PERIOD.*
12 p.m. to 1 p.m.	LUNCH
1 p.m. to 1:45 p.m.	*Lesson Period #5* TEACHERs 5, 1, 2, 3 have classes. *TEACHER 4: FREE PERIOD.*
2 p.m. to 2:45 p.m.	*Lesson Period #6* TEACHERs 1, 2, 3, 4 have classes. *TEACHER 5: FREE PERIOD.*
3 p.m. to 3:45 p.m.	*Lesson Period #7* TEACHERs 2, 3, 4, 5 have classes. *TEACHER 1: FREE PERIOD.*
3:45 p.m. to 4 p.m.	BREAK
4 p.m. to 4:45 p.m.	*Lesson Period #8* TEACHERs 3, 4, 5, 1 have classes. *TEACHER 2: FREE PERIOD.*
5 p.m. to 5:45 p.m.	*Lesson Period #9* TEACHERs 4, 5, 1, 2 have classes. *TEACHER 3: FREE PERIOD.*
6 p.m. to 6:45 p.m.	*Lesson Period #10* TEACHERs 5, 1, 2, 3 have classes. *TEACHER 4: FREE PERIOD.*

Time	Event—Occurrence
7 p.m. to 8 p.m.	Dinner & Debrief with TRAINER.

Section 2

Time	Event—Occurrence
8:30 p.m. to 10 p.m.	Planning for next day's classes. Teachers go to their homes, where they will have different characters playing family members who place different demands on them. Referred to as FAMILY 1, FAMILY 2, FAMILY 3, FAMILY 4. TEACHER 5 has no family. [Assumption at the moment is that this aspect will not change.]

Section 3

5:30 a.m. to 6:15 a.m.	*Lesson Period #1* TEACHERs 1, 2, 3, 4 have classes. *TEACHER 5: FREE PERIOD.*
6:30 a.m. to 7:15 a.m.	*Lesson Period #2* TEACHERs 2, 3, 4, 5have classes. *TEACHER 1: FREE PERIOD.*
7:15 a.m. to 7:30 a.m.	BREAK
7:30 a.m. to 8:15 a.m.	*Lesson Period #3* TEACHERs 3, 4, 5, 1 have classes. *TEACHER 2: FREE PERIOD.*
8:30 a.m. to 9:15 a.m.	*Lesson Period #4* TEACHERs 4, 5, 1, 2 have classes. *TEACHER 3: FREE PERIOD.*
9:30 a.m. to 10:15 a.m.	*Lesson Period #5* TEACHERs 5, 1, 2, 3 have classes *TEACHER 4: FREE PERIOD*
10:15 a.m. to 12 p.m.	Lunch, debrief, departure.

Immediately, the reader will notice in the adapted schedule that spect-actor-educators in this Indian *Detention* have to work much longer hours: they will have to teach *two* classes during Section 1 (rather than one, as in the current script). The days also start much earlier and end later, and the pace of this Indian adaptation demands a lot more endurance on the part of the spect-actors. The reader will also notice that I make assumptions that the number of spect-actor and performers, not to mention the family dynamics in Section 2, will stay similar to the original script of *Detention*. However, as this Interlude progresses and more information is revealed about the Indian juvenile justice system, those particular choices might very well shift.

Adapting the Characterization

Further investigation into the minimal material that is available about borstal schools suggests that staff members at these institutions often have to create individual lesson plans for their many students; that the "maximum children we receive are ones who have never gone to school and cannot read and write" (Modak, 2015). In terms of strategies then, an immediate consideration becomes whether a young person's literacy becomes part of the matrix of factors that shapes what kind of "student" they are able to become in those borstal schools. So, while *Detention* does not place specific emphasis on literacy, this needs to be reframed within an Indian context. Therefore, while my student character archetypes were based on socio-economic background, violence of the crime, and the youth's motivation to learn in the existing version of *Detention,* it seems like literacy levels will have to be added to the mix when staging *Detention* in India. Additionally, since a challenge particular to the Indian context is that "children in conflict with law and children under care and protection are housed within the same quarters even though the law states otherwise," I would probably refocus the "gravity of crime" from being violent versus non-violent, to being a distinction between a child in conflict with the law and one who is neglected—to make the characteristics of the inmate student population more specific to where it is being staged (Srivastava, 2016).

Studies have revealed that juveniles in such homes/schools in India tend to be from those who are from "economically weaker and vulnerable areas" (Massoodi, 2015)—a trend that is not dissimilar to what is said to happen in the United States. However, whereas in the U.S., the tie between socio-economic circumstances and detention has led to the centrality of race as a mitigating factor in incarceration rates (Alexander, 2012—to name a particularly well-known resource), what would the parallel be in the Indian setting? Rather than race, in the Indian context, might we see a tie between socio-economic vulnerability and individuals who belong to a particular caste or religion? This is a tough question to answer given India's diversity, and the fact that each town/village/state in the country is likely to have slightly different parameters of which group is most vulnerable. In some regions both caste and religion might have a role to play in economic vulnerability and subsequent incarceration; in others, gender might have a role to play in juvenile incarceration rates; in yet others, one's embodiment of gender/sexual orientation (consider the *hijra*[2] population, for example) might become a significant mitigating factor both in socio-economic vulnerability and the subsequent increase in the likelihood of incarceration. Therefore, while the archetypal characters of students in *Detention* are framed by that young person's socio-economic background (with additional meditations on stability and how that term might be best approached), the gravity of their crime, and the student's motivation to learn, if/when adapting *Detention* in India, I would add markers based on the exact village/town/city in which the performance was to be experienced (see the table below).

Table 3: Adapting Character Archetypes

Factors Influencing the Archetypes of Students in the Preceding Version of Detention	Archetypes of Students When Detention is Adapted to an Indian Context
How stable are their backgrounds? Did the young person commit a violent/non-violent crime in order to be incarcerated? Are they motivated to learn?	Is the young person "Neglected" or "Delinquent"? Are they motivated to learn? What is their socio-economic background vis-à-vis caste, religion, and/or other important identity markers in that context? (How does the notion of stability feed into these identity markers?) Is the young person literate?

With these additional factors in play when creating the archetypes of INMATE-STUDENT profiles for an Indian *Detention,* I also spent some time looking at what factors might shape the archetypes of the GUARDs—which, in the preceding script, were primarily centered on individuals' motivations for taking on these particular kinds of positions. And in looking at literature surrounding the challenges faced by detention center staff in the Indian context, it seems to be the case that some of Indian juvenile facilities' staff issues arise from there being a mixed group of juveniles in one facility. This is to say that the inmate population is often composed of both groups: youth who are in the facility because they are victims of neglect; youth who have been detained for having committed a crime. Speaking to the challenges facing borstal school employees as a result of such a mixing of these two groups of juveniles, it has been said, is the way in which "staff-members look at children in conflict with law with a lot of contempt" while taking on "a more sympathetic outlook when addressing children under need of care and protection" (Srivastava, 2016).

Given this information, in the characterization of the GUARDs, I would make sure to include a question in the character questionnaire that asks the GUARD to speak about the difference in their attitude towards particular kinds of juveniles. For example: while the current question is articulated as

"What do you find most challenging about your job?" I would add two sub-sections to this larger question about challenges and ask the actors playing the GUARDs to consider what they find most challenging about working with neglected youth in comparison with delinquent youth. Furthermore, in the process of rehearsing the piece in an Indian setting, I would ensure that these staff biases come through in the verbal and non-verbal interactions between guards and actor-inmates, allowing a perceptive TEACHER to understand that not all the juveniles are in the theatrical detention facility for the same reason; thus making the GUARDs' characterization more specific to the setting of an Indian borstal school.

In addition to this challenge of youth being there for vastly different reasons, when speaking about employees' experience in borstal schools in India, it has been said that "[m]ost special homes in India are characterised by crumbling infrastructure" and "display dilapidated standards of hygiene" where "[b]asic facilities such as bathroom and cleaning facilities are abysmal," and where "food and clothing provided are sub-standard" (Srivastava, 2016). What is worthy of consideration, therefore, is the impact of such conditions on the morale of staff and students—an element to characterization that a director of *Detention* in India would be well positioned to consider during the rehearsal process.

Adding to the challenges of restricted infrastructure, there is one more hurdle that is seems specific to the Indian context: the fact that many unreg-istered juvenile homes exist, making it near impossible to institute quality control and to have a nuanced understanding of the government's positioning vis-à-vis what happens in these homes (Asian Centre for Human Rights, 2013). If a borstal school is actually an institution that is unregistered and thus, illegal, what happens to the youth who leave with transcripts from such a "fake" institution? How do the people who run these institutions deal with their culpability in perpetuating a situation of corrosive injustice? Or, instead of being a situation where resources are being used for nefarious purposes, are some of these "fake" borstal schools actually idealistic spaces for quality education—subverting a problematic system?

There is not much documentation that I was able to encounter about the complexities that arise from the proliferation of unregistered borstal schools and it is most likely the director of an Indian adaptation *Detention* who has more on-the-ground experience than me, who would be able to reflect this layer in Sections 1 and 3. With someone who has no lived expe-rience of Indian juvenile justice though, I would bring in this dimension of registered versus unregistered borstal schools in Section 2—in the home lives of the spect-actors, where particular FAMILY characters bring up the legality of the partner/child/parent's work in the schools in question. This becomes particularly applicable, perhaps, given the stigma that is said to be attached to youth deviance in an Indian context—where it has been said to "stigmatizes the entire family" (CUNY, 2015). Could the stigma pass on to those who work with youth "delinquents" as well? Could the spect-actor-teacher's FAMILY communicate the various biases that surround both the registered status of a borstal school and the problematic of working with these juvenile populations?

In thinking about how to adapt elements of the spect-actor-teacher's FAMILY life, I return to the concept of characterization that has emerged earlier in the discussion above. Given this information above, how would the existing character descriptions in *Detention* need to shift in a generic Indian context?

- **TRAINER:** this character would essentially remain the same, acting as an advocate for the TEACHER while also functioning as their sounding board. In the Indian context though, I would recommend that the TRAINER be overworked and not have the time to visit all the classes and go to all the performance review meetings. Could it be communicated to spect-actors, during the TRAINER's informal conversations with them, that this character has to train multiple groups of teachers and thus does not have the time/resources to focus on one group?

- **HEADMISTRESS:** this character would also function as being similar to the characterization of the role in the preceding script with the added consideration of this character's culpability in the "status" of the school as being registered or unregistered. Is the HEADMISTRESS part of covering up an illegitimate borstal school? This is certainly a direction that might be considered. Also warranting consideration is how much time/attention the HEADMISTRESS is able to provide to teacher performance reviews when the institution is underfunded. Does she have to teach as well? Do the spect-actors see the HEADMISTRESS conduct other chores—through the window in their classroom—communicating the multiplicity of roles that staff members in these contexts have to take on?

- **INMATE STUDENTS:** Four groups with a maximum of forty actors per group. Each group should contain characters with the following archetypes, and while performers of all genders are welcome, each group should be composed of individuals who associate themselves with one particular gender identity. As mentioned earlier, in the Indian context, I would use the markers of socioeconomic class (vis-à-vis religion, caste, and another marker, if there is one), whether the youth in question is considered neglected or delinquent, whether or not the youth in question is a motivated learner, and that individual's literacy levels. Instead of listing out the forty potential combinations that might result from mixing and matching these different characters, I have decided to include a tabular representation of a potential matrix (Table 4), that would also pay tribute to the heterogeneity that is likely to exist in an overcrowded Indian juvenile home:

Table 4: Adapted STUDENT Character Matrix Markers

Socioeconomic Background			Neglected/ Delinquent	Literate/ Illiterate	Motivated/ Unmotivated
Marker 1: Socio-economic Class [below poverty line, middle class, upper middle class, elite]	Marker 2: Religion/ Caste	Marker 3: Gender/ sexuality			

I would, in this adaptation of *Detention* in India, create permutations and combinations for student characters from the abovementioned markers. Practically, this would mean a systematic addition/redaction of particular characteristics from those listed above:

Student 1: Contains Markers 1, 2, 3; is Neglected; Literate; Motivated
Student 2: Contains Markers 1, 2, 3; is Neglected; Literate; Unmotivated
Student 3: Contains Markers 1, 2, 3; is Neglected; Illiterate; Motivated
Student 4: Contains Markers 1, 2, 3; is Neglected; Illiterate; Unmotivated
Student 5: Contains Markers 1, 2, 3; is Delinquent; Literate; Motivated
Student 6: Contains Markers 1, 2, 3; is Delinquent; Literate; Unmotivated
Student 7: Contains Markers 1, 2, 3; is Delinquent; Illiterate; Motivated
Student 8: Contains Markers 1, 2, 3; is Delinquent; Illiterate; Unmotivated

Repeat the process of keeping/removing one/more markers in combination with varia-tions of negligence/delinquency; literacy/illiteracy; motivation/lack thereof—until the target number of characters is reached.

I must note here that *Detention* currently has an equal number of representatives for each particular archetype combination (based on the stability of their background, violence/non-violence of the youth's crime, and the motivation to learn). I made this choice of equal representation because this has been my experience in New Mexico; sufficed to say that the ratios can/should be different based on the particularities of a local context, i.e., if a specific setting has more non-violent than violent offenders, that difference should be reflected in the composition of character archetypes in *Detention*.

When adapting the characteristics based on markers that are particularly relevant to an Indian context, therefore, I would recommend looking at the statistics that might be available from that setting. Using these numbers, if a particular section of a specific population sub-group is more disproportionately represented in borstal schools in that geographical area, I would maintain that imbalance in the creation of the actors' characters.

- **GUARDS and HEAD GUARD:** The general characterization of these characters in *Detention* in India would remain the same, however, with an added question in the character questionnaires about this character's attitude toward neglected versus delinquent youth. Furthermore, given how religious/caste based affiliations still remain significant in many parts of the Indian context, could these characters be further nuanced if their characterization also included potential biases that these GUARD characters' might hold toward the students' religious and caste affiliations? Given the additional factors in this adaptation, in addition to the motivation of the character as in the preceding version of *Detention,* it might be useful to create a matrix (Table 5) for these personalities, just as with the STUDENTs.

Table 5: Adapted GUARD Character Matrix Markers

Motivation to become a guard			*Exhibits biases toward particular markers embodied by the STUDENTs*	*Exhibits biases based on whether the young person is Negligent or Delinquent*
Motivation A *Idealistic: believes in the need for their work*	**Motivation B** *Practical: needs the job to support their family*	**Motivation C** *Cynical: detests the young people and thinks they are incapable of changing their lives, but likes the power*		

With these characteristics in mind, GUARD personalities could be framed as followed:

GUARD 1: Motivation A and exhibits biases based on identity markers *and* on the nature of the youth's negligence/delinquency

GUARD 2: Motivation A and exhibits biases based on identity markers *but* not on the nature of the youth's negligence/delinquency

GUARD 3: Motivation A and exhibits no biases

And so on and so forth.

Once again, I would suggest that based on the contextual factors governing GUARDs' experiences in the place where *Detention* is being staged, that particular combinations of factors are kept or removed.

- **FAMILIES:** While FAMILY 1, 3, 4, 5 from *Detention* can stay the same, given the particular details affecting borstal schools in Indian contexts, I would suggest making a change to FAMILY 2— where one of the reasons for TEACHER 2's family disliking their spouse's profession might be attributed to the stigma that is associated with engaging with juvenile homes. Although the research quoted in this Interlude speaks to stigma toward the family of the incarcerated young person, could extending this prejudice toward those who work with these young people also be a realistic occurrence?

Adapting the Design

In addition to this information surrounding infrastructural challenges helping with the GUARDs characterization, if adapting *Detention* to an Indian context, I would ensure that the spatial design of the immersive environment—either in terms of the "set" or the qualities of a found space—exhibit a dilapidated infrastructure. For instance, while I have recommended fluorescent lighting in the preceding script, given how Indian juvenile homes are characterized have been characterized in the earlier mentioned remarks, I would likely choose to work in a building that, for example, has only one window in each room—and where electricity can only be used after sun down because of the facility's inability to afford the costs. This limited use of electricity would be made obvious through the placement of only one naked bulb in each space; no projectors; no computers; just that one naked bulb that the TEACHERs are allowed to turn on after sun down.

While these restrictions placed on the availability and use of electricity would contribute to one dimension of representing a crumbling infrastructure, there are additional design choices that I would make to further this ambience. For example, the classrooms near the toilet would be enveloped in the stench that emanates from the lack of sanitation. This smell could be one that is created through the combination of particular chemicals, or if being staged in a found space that has already decrepit toilets, I would ensure that these facilities are *not* cleaned for the theatrical immersion. As a result, spect-actor-TEACHERs would have to viscerally experience the "abysmal" conditions that have been recorded. This multi-sensorial experience of a scarcity of resources—especially with spect-actors who are educators from better resourced institutions—would, I think, also extend to the food and drink that is offered to the TEACHERs during the coffee and lunch breaks that have been scripted into the experience.

All this being said, I must emphasize that an incredible amount of care must be taken to maintain some degree of accuracy in these representations of inadequate resources. Given the problematic "slum tourism"-esque representations that often emerge in depictions of the subcontinent in various media, the director of an Indian re-imagining of *Detention* must be careful *not* to over-exaggerate the living conditions in these juvenile homes. There must be an effort to recreate (multisensorially) what these environments feel like—their smell; their tastes; their lighting; the sounds that surround them— as accurately as possible. Hence my caveat in the beginning of this Interlude that these suggested adaptations are contingent upon *where* exactly in India such an adapted version of *Detention* might be staged.

Assuming that these conditions of limited resources and infrastructure were to apply, these (see Table 6 below) would be the shifts that a director could consider when honing *Detention* to an Indian setting:

Table 6: Adapting Design Elements

Design Elements in the Scripted Version of Detention	Design Elements When Adapted to an Indian Context
Two locations: one building with multiple spaces that could comprise the detention center school; multiple cottages/houses or spaces in an apartment building or something else that can simulate the home lives of the people in question. The school building should be a space that has seven spaces in total: one area for the training/break/debrief rooms; the headmistress' office; five classroom spaces. Ideally, this would be a space that has minimal windows and has wire fencing outside. All lighting inside the space should be fluorescent and if there is an	Two buildings: one building with multiple rooms for the detention center and another cluster of spaces that serves as the housing for the educators. While, in a more generic United States' context, small cottages/houses/ apartments seem feasible on a detention center educator's annual salary, the spaces chosen as being the TEACHERs' homes in the Indian context should reflect what is possible vis-à-vis what these educators earn. I recall from my own days of teaching in a private school in India, that my monthly salary of 312 USD was considered as being more than that earned by educators working in government schools. So, what do the borstal school educators earn? And

Design Elements in the Scripted Version of Detention	Design Elements When Adapted to an Indian Context
	based on what they earn, what kinds of spaces can they afford to live in?
occasional window, the designers should consider putting bars outside of it.	The borstal school building should be a space that is cramped, where there is not enough classroom space for all the teachers (while there is certainly space for the headmistress' office). This spatial limitation should be so apparent that the five spect-actor-educators might have to be creative in finding spaces for their lessons. Perhaps they need to double up and share classrooms? Perhaps some of them will need to use an outdoor area as their classroom?
There should be a metal detector at the entrance and heavy, self-locking doors. So, teachers can only have keys to their classrooms and should any other space be accidentally locked, they would have to call the HEAD GUARD to open the door for them.	
There is an intercom system that can be heard throughout the school building and there is a particular sound that is played to mark the end of lessons and breaks. The particular sound that is chosen is up to the discretion of the sound designer.	Each of the limited classrooms room has one window and one bulb that can only be turned on once the sun has set. Maybe there is a fan for the summer.
The walls of the space are lined with motivational posters—posters that talk about how a change in attitude will help the young people move on to great things.	There are no metal detectors or bars; just a fence outside the school that has sharp razor wire and has a tired constable standing at the gate.
INMATE STUDENTs are dressed in monochromatic colors—all green; all maroon. GUARDS are dressed in all black and carry sticks, walkie-talkies, and handcuffs.	There is no intercom system and if word has to go to all the teachers, they either receive messages on their cell phones or a constable at the gate has to be sent to inform each teacher individually.
The HEADMISTRESS and TRAINER wear everyday clothes, as do the teachers. Though, the HEADMISTRESS can critique the dress code of particular teachers and direct them to a costume wardrobe from which they can redress themselves into more formal, detention center appropriate attire.	The walls of this building are bare and have limited posters, maybe just one or two that speak to motivational topics.
	The youth are dressed in clothes that are unkempt; they are barefoot.
	The staff members dress in simple everyday attire.
	The GUARDs wear khaki and do not have anything but a baton.
	The classrooms have some desks and

Design Elements in the Scripted Version of Detention	Design Elements When Adapted to an Indian Context
	chairs but not enough for all the students to sit on. The usage of these materials is also something that the spect-actor-teacher has to deal with. Which students get to use the desks, and when?

Adapting the Actor and Spect-Actor Group

In addition to a limitation of physical infrastructure, it has also been said that—in India—many "special homes face shortage of staff" (Srivastava, 2016). In some cases, "the number of children vary between 120 and 150" with "not enough staff-members to cater to the needs of all the children" (Srivastava, 2016). Furthermore, in many of these homes "12 to 20 children share a room"; a room that is "usually small and feel[s] crammed due to over-crowding" (Srivastava, 2016). This then leads to there being no privacy and "as the spaces are cramped, levels of irritation and annoyance are high, because someone or the other is always around to create a certain level of disturbance. Overcrowding often leads to violent fights over trivial issues" (Srivastava, 2016).

As the reader might remember in the preceding script, I have suggested that each group has 8 students with 1 guard who always accompanies that group: this is a number that I drew from the New Mexico context in which I have worked, where the ratio between staff and students is supposed to be 1:8. If there are any more than eight youth in a particular group, there has to be more that one guard accompanying those individuals. However, in order to represent the overcrowding that happens in Indian juvenile homes, I would probably recommend having four groups of forty student-performers for each guard and spect-actor-educator. While the limit of forty student-performers per group is simply a suggestion, based on the logistics of recruiting performers, I would suggest that the director choose a number that, in conversation with the limited resources, would lead to a very tangible over-crowding of classroom spaces and a fight for stationery. Having a large number of actor-students to deal with, with insufficient classroom space, hardly any electricity, and abysmal sanitary facilities would provide the spect-actor-educator with an experiential understanding of the challenges that staff in borstal schools face.

Clearly, there is a logistical question here, of how 160 actor-students might be recruited—and were I to be directing this piece in an Indian context, there are two options that I would explore to address this logistical hurdle.

The first possibility would be to, in the spirit of applied theater, work with "real world" students who study in a more elite school in that part of India. Just like the pedagogical objective for the target spect-actor group of educators from a privileged Indian school, could the recruitment of student-actors from a similar pool allow these youth an insight into their less privileged counterparts? But how could this be done sensitively and ethically, so that *Detention* does not just become a vicarious insight into the Other for the privileged Indian youth? The second option that I would explore to address the hurdle of recruiting a large number of performers, is using a smaller number of students (fifteen per group, perhaps, rather an forty as suggested above) but to intentionally choose a physically smaller performance location that would feel cramped with this number. I must say that this is where a thought exercise can be liberating; if I had to really take on the logistics of recruiting 160 actors, well, that would be an entirely different story!

The abovementioned adaptations to the framework, characterization, design, and target group retain the "essence" of the preceding script of *Detention*. And yet, in making changes to these different elements, an Indian adaptation of *Detention* will not be the same experience. Culling from the specific thought exercise above to some general steps to follow in adapting *Detention* to a specific context, I would suggest the following (in the order that best suits the nature of the production):

- Step 1: Find the local context's equivalent of the school in *Detention* and situate that institution within the larger conversation surrounding juvenile justice in the setting in question i.e. who is sent to these institutions and why; what are the factors that seem to influence incarceration in that context
- Step 2: Edit (if needed) the framework proposed for *Detention* based on the schedule of detention facilities in setting in which the piece will be performed
- Step 3: Edit (if needed) the number of students and actors that might need to be recruited for an adapted version
- Step 4: Adapt the design elements in the preceding version of *Detention*
- Step 5: Explore factors that would additionally influence the characterisation of STUDENTs, GUARDs, FAMILIEs, and HEADMISTRESS in the context in which *Detention* is being staged

For an Immersive Theater Playwright

Through the process of scripting *Detention* I made the choice to create the framework for a piece that would simultaneously provide structure and promote flexibility. And it was only through the writing process that I realized one major element of "traditional" playwriting that had to be reframed in my desire to script a flexible piece that could transgress contexts: the role of text.

Re-Thinking the Role of Text

In most theatrical scripts, it is the spoken word that is prized above all else—even in the most Postmodern texts, where it is unclear who speaks, and what is staged, there is a centralized assumption that the words on the page are (most often) ones that will be spoken. In crafting *Detention*, then, what became interesting to consider is how the scripting of immersive environments might re-prioritize the focus of the written word. Could it be said the written text, as it applies to immersive theater, might be focused on creating the structure of a world. Whereas, in less immersive texts, the written word is focused on creating structures of spoken text (monologues; dialogues; choral speech)? Might this shift in the role of text be relevant to various approaches to immersive theater, or only to my particular method of creating immersive environments that are parts of applied theater contexts?

In one sense, I believe that the absence of dialogue is incredibly important in the applied theater framing to this book. Given my pedagogical goals, where actors have collaborative input in the staging of a performance, placing the dialogue in the performers'/directors' hands seems to be an effective way of decentralizing the power of the playwright, and of increasing the avenues for co-creation. Furthermore, allowing actors and directors to add their own dialogue seems to be a way to invite linguistic diversity in the experience of *Detention*—where local languages and dialects could easily be utilized to add an additional layer of contextual relevance.

That said, though, despite the absence of dialogue being important to the particular approach that I have chosen in *Detention*, I wonder if this reframed role for text is why we do not see as many "mainstream" texts for interactive forms of drama. Could it be said that scripting for theatrical aesthetics that are multi-sensorial and improvisational—where what is spoken shifts based on who the actors/spect-actors are, and based on where the piece is being performed—contains, at its core, a reconceptualization of the role of the written word? Where words are not about what people say to themselves, or to each other; but rather, about the creation of a structural environment where performers have more liberty in choosing what they say and how they say it?

The table below puts forward a scale of possibilities; with one end of the scale being representative of texts where actors' co-creation is sought, in so far as their collaboration is needed to embody the existing words. On the other end of the scale are the pieces that emerge from the process that is most common to applied theater: devised performances; where creators come together—often as a collective without a "director" per se—and begin to put together a piece through various explorations. Here, a collage of material is woven together and, at least in applied theater contexts, the final texts are rarely scripted; precisely because they are incredibly intimate to the people who have created them. The immersive works in this book, then, fall somewhere in the space between these aforementioned options.

Table 7: Scaling Performers' Co-creation
Levels of Performers' Co-creation

A performance that requires performers to execute a text exactly how the playwright has written it. In this particular approach, the text that is created by the writer pays attention to everything that is said and done by the actor. While the extent of detail on structural/staging information might vary, dialogue is incredibly important in this aesthetic. Performers give voice to what the writers have to say.	A performance that invites actors/directors to become co-creators of the piece. In the scripts of such performances, like the scripts in this book, actors' contributions are integral to every section of the script. As a result, all the focus is on the use of text to craft structure, with there being minimal emphasis on what is spoken.	A performance that is completely devised by the performers, where they are as much writers as they are performers. These "texts" are rarely scripted and in the case that they are, the written word that is prioritized depends on what kind of replication is sought from the piece.

Apart from enabling more co-creation for actors and directors, the absence of dialogue extends co-creative possibilities to the spect-actors as well. Adding more "conventional" dialogue to any part of *Detention* would completely change its essence. Imagine, if you will, what the classroom scenarios might look like if they had to be scripted with the spect-actor still playing the role of the TEACHER. How could the spect-actors be given the freedom to run their sessions as "authentically" as possible, if the actors—STUDENTs and GUARDs—had pre-scripted interchanges that were at odds with the TEACHER's contributions? Wouldn't this be antithetical to encouraging a "genuine" participation from spect-actors? Wouldn't pre-scripting also increase the risks of stereotyping—where the difficult student always remains hard to connect with, rather that this young person also being able to shift how they respond to a TEACHER with whom they are able to establish a rapport? The only way I could see dialogue as being an integral part of an immersive theater script is if there was less co-creation expected from the spect-actors, i.e., where contributions from spect-actors could *not* alter the trajectory of an immersive experience.

It might be useful here, to consider another "scale" (Table 8) that assesses how much co-creation might be invited from the spect-actors. In such a scale, as below, one end would be representative of a more "conventional" production where the spect-actor watches and listens, where dialogue is likely to be an integral part of the dramatic script. The other end of the scale might be representative of the co-creation that is invited in the scripts in this book, where all spoken material is hinged on individual spect-actor responses. In between these two extremes then, there might be the kind of performance in which spect-actors have some agency but not as much as in *Detention*. Consider scripts like *Sleep No More* (2011) by UK-based Punchdrunk, where spect-actors are immersed in the world of Macbeth in a piece that is set in the promenade and asks its spect-actors to wear masks to engage in the experience. In this multisensory experience, actors follow a specific script while also responding to unpredictable spect-actor actions in the moment. So, while there are particular kinds of engagements that spect-actors to *Sleep no more* can put forward, there are specific scenes that must be executed; particular narrative arcs that must be adhered to. It might be useful then, to work with a scale, as follows, to decipher which kind of text is of primary importance— text-as-speech (be it monologue, dialogue, or something else); text-as-structure (descriptions of an environment, sequence of actions, characterization); or text-as-something-else.

Table 8: Scaling Spect-Actor Co-Creation
Levels of Spect-Actor Co-Creation

| A performance that requires audience members to watch and listen, the "creative act," as it were, is primarily in the hands of the performers.

Therefore, in scripting these performances, there is an emphasis on what is "said," verbally, on stage. The text in these dramatic works often/sometimes speaks to setting too, of course [think of stage directions and design ideas that are | A performance that invites spect-actors to engage *but* one that also has particular sections that occur only between the performers themselves.

In scripting these performances there is an emphasis both on what is said/done between the actors themselves, and on text-as-structure in the particular parts in which spect-actor co-creation might occur. | A performance that invites spect-actors to become co-creators at every stage of the piece.

In the scripts of such performances, like the scripts in this book, spect-actors' contributions are integral to every section of the performance. As a result, all the focus is on the use of text to craft structure, with there being minimal emphasis on what is spoken—adhering to a spirit of co-creation. |

often included in these scripts.] However, a bulk of the text focuses on what is shown to the spect-actors.		

Re-Thinking the Role of Context

In addition to this reframed understanding of text vis-à-vis the kind of co-creation desired from performers and spect-actors, another question that arose for me through the process of writing *Detention* is the notion of specificity/ambiguity vis-à-vis the world that is created in an immersive theater script. Going into *Detention*, I had specific reasons for not keeping the context particular to New Mexico—the most important reason being that I wanted the piece to be applicable across multiple geographical contexts and to focus on catalyzing learning for more privileged educators within any locale, about the experience of their colleagues in youth detention centers. Writing the script to prize a contextual ambiguity, therefore, was one of the most significant aspects of *Detention*. And in making this choice, I have had to reflect upon the benefits/drawbacks of specificity versus ambiguity in scripting for an applied theater context. Much of applied theater work is centered on specificity; on creating work with/by/for those who come from the setting to which the performance is being applied. Certainly, in my own work in Kashmir (Dinesh, 2016c), the piece that is being created is hinged on its specificity to the Kashmiri context—where the applied theater principles that have gone into shaping the work make it incredibly important to mention the setting to which the piece is being applied. That said, with *Detention*—and in the other scripts that are included in this book—despite applied theater principles being integral to my experiences in those spaces, it seemed more appropriate to divorce content from context; to separate location from issue.

I have come to think that a significant impact on my decision about contextual specificity/ambiguity in this book comes from thinking about the process of creation and its intersections with the demography and lived experience of the performers. The piece that I work on in Kashmir has been created with Kashmiri colleagues over five years; it is also a piece that is performed by the same artists who played a role in contributing to the performance's vision and content. This is to say that my collaborators in that applied theater context have the lived experience of the content that is being represented in the piece, have consciously agreed to the inclusion of the content in it, and as such, situating the material to the context in which the work was created seems necessary and inevitable. In a work like *Detention* though, where I am creating a script that draws from personal research and from past work, but that does not involve co-writing with stakeholders who have a particular lived experience of the context, ambiguity becomes an ethical, artistic response. Can I, in good conscience, script an immersive theater piece about detention that is super specific to New Mexico, when I have not experienced the ins and outs of that setting? Do I not need to centralize the role of fiction, to visibly acknowledge the role that my own imagination plays in the theatricalization of a range of perspectives, of which I have limited lived experience? Choosing ambiguity in writing *Detention* was, therefore, a pedagogical and ethical choice. Pedagogical in terms of what the piece seeks to achieve in being adaptable to different contexts; ethical in highlighting the fact that I am not talking about one group of young people in one specific place, but rather, about a range of issues that might be shared across contexts of juvenile justice. If there is an important question that I take away from *Detention* then, that I would put forward as a point of consideration to other playwrights who are considering the scripting of immersive theater environments, it would be that of the setting: does it make ethical and pedagogical sense to place the immersive world in one particular geographical location? Or might it be better informed to place the work in a more general context, where there is more room for adaptation; more room for respecting the particularities of lived experience?

It is with these two overarching thoughts in mind—about the reframed importance of text, and the potential of contextual ambiguity—that I went into the writing of the second script, *War*. Based on the questions that emerged through *Detention*, I wondered if the script of *War* would lend itself to being more specific to a particular place; if I might make the script a little more dialogue-centric rather than relying entirely on the directors, creators, and spect-actors of the script to decide how the spoken words would be woven together. That said, it is not the goal of this book to make different choices in each script just for the sake of doing so; rather, the goal is to cull strategies when writing for a specific kind of immersive theater. So, for *War*, while the outcomes from *Detention* influenced the process, they were no more or less than possible points of departure. *War*, like every single script in this book, has its own voice; its own aims; its own manifestation in the world of Immersive and applied theater.

War

PRELUDE

My work making theater in places of war began in 2005: from the experiences of an undergraduate student during a study abroad program in northern Uganda, to working with Theater of the Oppressed techniques in Rwanda, to—as of five/six years ago—finding a "home" for my immersive theater-inspired work in Kashmir. While I have talked about these works in multiple different writing projects, the aspect that I have chosen to focus on in the following script, *War,* is one that I have often considered in the past, but not in the way of giving the topic dramatic shape through immersive techniques. The aspect being the questions that emerge from being an outsider to a conflict zone. This is to say that, while I have always been hyper aware of being an outsider in various contexts of war, rarely have I thought about giving theatrical shape to these experiences as being embodied perspectives from the gray zones of conflict, that might be structured into pedagogically affective/effective theatrical environments.

As I've mentioned earlier, in reference to Primo Levi's (1988) concept of the "gray zones"; I use the term broadly: to apply to the murky areas of a particular setting; the shadowy spaces that are hard to classify; the nebulous phenomena that are difficult to place on the victim/perpetrator spectrum of a specific conflict. Although, generally speaking, such a notion of the gray zone is applied to stakeholders who are indigenous to particular contexts of violence, I would like to use *War* as a means to consider the outsider as part of that spectrum: because the outsider, in lying outside the boundaries of a specific conflict, occupies that does not fit within more obvious manifestations of victimhood and perpetration. While the outsiders' absence on this victim/perpetrator spectrum might seem logical in one sense, I have come to think that the outsider might indeed represent an Other who—somehow—is implicated within the local complexities of a war-riddled context. This is to say that, whether or not one is a complete outsider to a context of war,

91

whether or not one is an insider-outsider to that space, intervening in a highly charged context *does* implicate us (outsiders) on the victim/perpetrator spectrum, whether we want it to or not. Based on whom we choose (not) to engage with in a local context; based on where we choose (not) to go within a conflicted space; based on the kinds of activities we choose (not) to undertake, we make (un) conscious choices about which "side" of the conflict we fall on.

Being an outsider to a particular war zone, therefore, contains various shades of gray. In a context like Rwanda, for example, as an obvious outsider to the genocide that had happened there in 1994, I was never victim to the violence in the region; I was also *not* a direct perpetrator of violence in that or any of the following conflicts that have occurred there. However, there is a nuance here; a layer; that while I am not a "direct" perpetrator of violence vis-à-vis the 1994 genocide, there is a culpability that I must assume as someone who chose to go to Rwanda; as someone who decided to intervene in particular ways apropos the history of that country. A culpability that stems, simply, from my being part of an international community that has, in various ways, been implicated in Rwanda's present: for choosing silence over action; for choosing distanced engagement versus personal involvement; for choosing to leave instead of staying. I realize that culpability is a strong word and that, to some, an outsider's implication in a context of violence is distinctive from the general sentiment that a term like "culpability" invokes. And yet, I have come to think that my personal culpability is indeed a part of the fabric of the international community's response to what happened (in this case) in Rwanda.

This sense of culpability—of being an indirect perpetrator of injustice— is even more heightened when I work in a space like Kashmir, where my being from a part of India that does not question its allegiance to the Indian nation state, is hugely problematic. In paying taxes to the Indian government; in holding an Indian passport; in not being as vocal a critic of the Indian presence in the Valley as I could, if I were not constrained by my own ethical quandaries and fears for personal safety, am I not—in the eyes of the average Kashmiri civilian—someone who represents the "perpetration" of Indian rule in Kashmir? Despite my being a relatively powerless individual, am I not culpable—somehow—for not finding a more tangible way to address the many injustices that are occurring in the region? Isn't there always more that I could be doing, in response to the perspectives that I encounter on the ground? There are no straightforward answers to these questions, of course, and it is precisely because all answers are fraught that—when thinking about a gray zone of war that I could speak to in *War*—it seemed natural to create a work that would speak to the shadowy textures that encompass any outsider's intervention to a conflict that they do not live in; a conflict that they have the choice and resources from which to flee; a conflict that is not "theirs."

Conceptualizing War

Social Context

While the general context was easy to pin down in this sense, to create an immersive environment in *War* that was/is a war zone, I kept going back and forth between the question of realism and allegory; between ambiguity and specificity; a choice that was a primary point of consideration in *Detention* as well. And even though the writer in me wanted to try something different in *War* and set the piece in a "real-world" war zone, I couldn't bring myself to write a piece that would be about Kashmir; or about Rwanda; or about northern Uganda; or about Syria. Like *Detention,* my struggle with using specificity of context is ethical in nature—that, without members from those populations being part of the creative process with me, I have no "right" to be writing about these particular spaces. And while there might be arguments to be made for my past work being sufficient to function as a base for such writing, my personal, artistic, and ethical "code" does not allow for that. Making the choice to set *War* in a specific war zone feels to me like potential appropriation; like a problematic vicariousness that I am wary of condoning, however implicitly. And therefore, although I would have liked to set *War* in Kashmir, for instance, I find myself veering back to ambiguity in my choice of theatrical context—to create an unspecified war zone, in an unspecified part of the world—an ambiguity that intentionally uses the kinds of events and scenarios that might be applicable across diverse geographical war zones.

The subsequent room for fiction, then, is what allows me to write *War* without drowning in concerns about misrepresentation; the space for ambiguity is what permits me to feel less appropriative and less neo-colonial in my approach. That said, the perceptive reader will see some elements of the following script that resonate strongly with elements of Kashmiri realities; other scenarios could very well be read as being based on Rwanda's history; yet, *War* is not only about Kashmir or Rwanda. *War* interweaves narratives from experiences that are intensely personal, to those that are based on more distanced archival research. The point, ultimately, is that the questions addressed in *War* are not specific to a particular place. Rather, the goal is to highlight the contentious positioning of the outsider *across* war zones—that whenever we choose to go to conflicted settings to see, to witness, to learn, whatever; we are somehow implicated within the dynamics of power and violence that operate in those spaces. Separating ourselves from the local conflict is not only impossible; I daresay such a distancing might be naïve. We (outsiders) cannot ignore the ways in which we become part of the webs that exist in the conflict zones that we seek to engage with; this, in essence, is the premise of *War.*

Target Actor and Spect-Actor Group

So, given this particular pedagogical objective—of heightening the spect-actors' critical awareness of the grayness to outsiders' engagements when entering conflict zones—I asked myself who the appropriate target group of performers and spect-actors to a piece like *War* would be. While *Detention* did not limit itself to performers from a particular demographic, there were two specific spect-actor groups to whom the piece was catered: individuals who are in training to become educators in youth detention centers; educators from more privileged institutions who, as a result of *Detention*, might foster future connections with their less resourced counterparts in detention center contexts. Although applied theater is so much more than being about "tangible" impact—and I'm certainly not one to go around measuring what spect-actor members' do/feel as a result of their experiences in my theatrical environments—there are avenues for future impact that I want to create spaces for. Spaces, that, *if* the spect-actor in these experiences wants to "do" something about the issue that they have encountered, might enable a path for them to so engage. From having done pieces in the past that are all about inspiring questions, and about leaving the onus on the spect-actor to figure out what to do with that information, I have come to think about the potential of framing the future possibilities: albeit gently, delicately, and without a particular agenda in mind.

Therefore, when thinking about *War* and what kind of afterlife I wanted the experience to contain potential for, I came to the conclusion that an ideal target group composition for *War* would be—both as actors and spect-actors—young people in organizations such as high schools, colleges, and/or universities that implicitly or explicitly gear students toward international travel; toward social and political engagements that involve these students' embodiment of a global citizenry. I include in this group, for example, students who are part of the College I work at, and its sister institutions—a network of international schools, one of which I work at in New Mexico—that spurs students to think about ways in which they can "change the world" by harnessing their abilities to become "global citizens." I also include in this group, students in social work programs in different parts of the world, who are asked to go into troubled settings as part of practical internships in their field of study. I include in my consideration of an ideal target group for *War*, young people who are likely to join an initiative like the Peace Corps and believe that they want to "volunteer" in places and contexts that are different from their own. I target this piece toward "study abroad" programs as well—a burgeoning array of initiatives the send/receive outsiders into local contexts in the name of "cultural exchange" or "education" or something else. In a way then, I want this piece to target young people who are in relatively more privileged positions, who have chosen—for whatever reason—to engage with contexts that are "less" privileged. And while these "less" privileged settings might not always contain war and violence, I believe the premise of *War* still applies. That any context into which we might enter as outsiders, even if there are some aspects of the locale that make us somehow an insider to that setting, is always full of conflicts that we might not be privy to.

So with young people who are likely to travel and intervene in global contexts being the target spect-actor group for the piece, I also suggest that the same demographic as these spect-actors becomes the performer group. Unlike *Detention*, where I suggest that the lived experience of performers is not important and that prior experience with settings of incarceration is recommended in the form of a consultant rather than being required in performers' backgrounds, I have particular reasons for wanting both spect-actors and performers to be from the same demographic pool in *War*. The primary reason goes back to the pedagogical objectives for the piece; to allow for the creation of spaces in which conversations about *War* might extend even after the theatrical experience has concluded. If young people from the same community also take on the roles of the "locals" who live that conflict, won't there be an increased likelihood of multi-perspectival conversations occurring? An increased likelihood because youth-actors would have time to reflect on what it felt like to be insiders to a community/experience that is then affected by the entrance of outsider-spect-actors? With these questions in mind, I went into *War* thinking more extensively about the post-performance debrief scenarios as compared to the pre-performance, preparatory work that was the subject of focus in *Detention*.

Pre- and Post-Performance Structure

In the Live Action Role Plays (LARPs) and other simulation structures that were presented in the Introduction, it seems to be the case that while pre-performance work can often extend much prior to the performance, post-performance debriefs are quite self-contained and take place immediately after the experience in question, for a short duration of time. Being an educator as much as an artist then, especially for an applied theater piece like *War*, I wonder about how the post-performance debrief component might be potentially extended over a period of time. Could post-performance follow-ups to immersive experiences function as (dramatic and aesthetic) components to the theatrical experience, heightening the potential for affects/effects to manifest and develop? Could there be more than one post-performance session? How might these forums be included in the script of *War*?

I must point out here that until this particular writing project, immersive scenarios I crafted were always with the goal of immediate implementation—where I had the goal to implement a script that I was working on, within a particular context in which I work, in a particular time frame. Perhaps predictably, then, in most (if not all) of these endeavors, my artistic choices for a particular immersive piece would end up being framed by prior logistical knowledge and requirements that would affect the execution of the piece. For example, when wanting to implement a piece at my College campus in New Mexico, armed with the knowledge that the students I teach are unlikely to be able to commit to more than two hours a week for rehearsals, I create the kinds of scripts and structures that are doable within that particular time constraint. Similarly, because I know that I will not be able to recruit more than ten individuals as actors for a project in Kashmir, I—from the conceptualization phase—limit the number of roles in the piece to the number of performers that I am sure I can get. Many of my decisions as an immersive theater practitioner therefore, are seen through the lenses of a playwright, director, *and* producer. And because of these different hats that are always in play, the writer (in me) does not get to "dream" as much as she would want to; because the director and producer voices immediately ask: "Wait a second … how are you going to get this done?" Writing the scripts in this book therefore, has been a much more "liberating" process for the writer in me—I can write the immersive experience with as much imagination as I like, without thinking about the logistics of its implementation. I can write these scripts as a playwright, rather than a director or a producer, and I make this clarification because this freedom from logistical constraints has influenced my thinking around how post-performance sessions might be extended in *War*. The ideas that I have about the post-performance meanderings of the piece are not decisions I might have necessarily made if I were thinking about the piece also in logistical terms. But since I am not constrained by particular schedules/timetables in this regard—and am open to the readers making adaptations as they need for the contexts in which they use the work—I have been able to "dream."

In thinking this through, in considering the potential of a longer debrief process for *War*, one that is segmented over a period of time, I went back to strategies that have worked for me in the past both as an educator and as a theater practitioner/researcher. How much follow up is too much follow up? How much critique about outsider positioning would it take to inspire (potentially) more insightful interventions for spect-actors? And on a related note, how much critique and questioning could result in dampening the young people's enthusiasm and idealism; possibly leading to their paralysis from ever wanting to intervene in contexts outside their own? With these questions in mind, I revisited an event that I was part of organizing in Armenia, while I was working at a College there. In this event, for a month leading up to the

100th anniversary of the Armenian genocide in 2015, a group of faculty members from the College led once-a-week sessions about different topics related to conflict: a series of weekly, one-hour lectures/workshops, over the course of eight weeks, about different theoretical and practical lenses with which that international student population might engage with the Armenian commemoration. Not only were these sessions useful in terms of context and priming, what was also particular effective, I thought, was the overall structure of the eight-week sessions: where the topics moved from being about more abstract concepts, to case studies that were further away from Armenia, to examples that very closely resonated with that context. So, in practical terms, we began with sessions about philosophical concepts surrounding war and commemoration, moving from the abstract to concrete examples from outside Europe/Asia, to particular case students from Armenia and her neighbors, to finally talked about the Armenian genocide itself. These sessions look the shape of lectures, workshops, and film screenings and finally led to a week of different commemorative events specific to Armenia; a week that was officially designated as such by the Armenian government. These events culminated with sessions for feedback; ending, ultimately, with the ritualistic lighting of candles and placing of flowers at a genocide memorial. The way in which the commemoration week was framed therefore, and the way in which it was brought to a close, contained within it an aestheticism that I have come to appreciate in retrospect. It seemed only natural then, when thinking about the potential to extend the post-performance experience of *War*, to borrow somehow from the aesthetic structure of that program in Armenia.

What if, the series of experiences began with the theatrical immersion in *War*, where spect-actors are assigned particular characters with which to engage in the world? What if then, after the first "part" of theatrically engaging with the experience, there were follow up sessions that were geared toward particular/all spect-actors? Could there be once-a-week sessions over the course of a few weeks that might allow for spect-actors and performers to engage more rigorously with the potential problematics of how they engaged with that immersive world? What if, then, at the end of a series of follow up sessions—which would be designed as self-contained events—the spect-actors were given a chance to hear from the "insiders," with feedback that would be useful to their personal development as "outsiders"? And most importantly, if I did decide to design such self-contained follow up sessions, how would I ensure that these events would also be theatrical and aesthetic in nature? How would I make sure that the experience in its entirety and duration, remained "theater"? The structuring of this kind of multi-faceted, theatrically aesthetic post-performance experience is what I went into *War* thinking about.

Freedom

The choices mentioned thus far speak to the social context represented in *War* and subsequently impacted my approach to how much "freedom" spect-actors could have in this world; the ways in which the script might create opportunities for mirroring and consequence in the world of *War*. In *Detention,* I spoke about the need for creating relative levels of freedom for spect-actor-educators—where they would have autonomy over the lessons they taught, but questionable power in other scenarios within the same environment. In a similar vein, there were different manifestations of freedom that I went into *War* thinking about. While I wanted spect-actors to have the autonomy to engage with the environment in as "free" a way as possible—so that they would have the autonomy to act as naturally as they could, thus increasing the likelihood for them to encounter their own biases and prejudices—I was also aware that the spect-actor could not have the freedom to change the context itself.

This is to say that, while I wanted spect-actor-outsiders' actions in the immersive world to have consequences on the performers and on the micro situations in which the two parties were engaging with each other, I also wanted to ensure that the consequences of spect-actors' actions could *not* extend to affecting the world of the conflict zone. I did not want to construct a world where spect-actors could "end the war," or "negotiate a peace deal," or create some type of "fairy tale" resolution to the larger conflict. And while this might not be entirely "fair" within the rules of an immersive world where participants' actions should be able to affect that world's trajectory, I did not want *War* to over-simplify the complexities that surrounding existing conflicts by suggesting tactics for their resolution. Although the immersive environment creates a "game-like" scenario, and games—at least as we have come to experience them—can be "won" under certain circumstances, wars are different beasts. They, mostly, cannot be "won." They, often, cannot be "solved." And this is a complexity that I wanted to maintain in *War*.

In thinking how to frame the spect-actors' "freedom," then—in not wanting to give the spect-actors fake agency, while also encouraging them to pursue the agency that they do have—I began to consider the particulars of the war zone environment that I would create in *War*. While ambiguous, would *War* encompass a context that is currently undergoing conflict, i.e., an active conflict zone? Or would it be a post-conflict zone that is recuperating from violence? Or would it, instead, be a space that lies on the cusp between war and peace? And whichever stage of conflict the space is in, would the larger context be a civil war? Or would it be a war in which international powers are "invading" local communities? Would there a clear victim/perpetrator dynamic? Or would the dynamics of violence and power be far more nebulous? What would be the world of *War*?

There are many possible responses to these questions, but given that much of my current work is focused on thinking about the conflicts in Kashmir, it is that context that I decided to use, to shape *War*. So, in the conflict zone that is created in following script, there is a long-standing conflict that has been occurring vis-à-vis that place's desire for autonomy. Under the rule of a government that seems to have no intention of allowing its self-rule, this region has seen a rise in the number of militant/guerrilla organizations that are all fighting (through different means) for their preferred manifestation of autonomy. There are disagreements, both between different guerrilla groups and between the local civilians, about what "self-rule" might mean. And it is into such a mixed pot of political and ideological ambitions that an outsider-spect-actor steps in.

Framing the conflict zone in *War*—loosely—around what is happening in Kashmir, was a choice that I believed would help me more accurately frame spect-actors' freedom. My own familiarity with the context, I came to see, might allow me to be realistic about actions that might (not) be possible within the script's immersive environment; rather than using contextual factors with which I have no familiarity. That said, although the "kind" of conflict being experienced in the following text shares similarities to Kashmir's histories, this is clearly not the only context in which such a war for self-rule is being experienced. Any region in the world that is battling for its autonomy from the government of another nation-state—Palestine, for example; or Kosovo, before its independence—would contain resonances with *War's* context. Of course, the conditions of the script allow for much context-specific adaptation and the production team is welcome to change elements that might reframe the "kind" of war zone that is being created within the frames of that immersive theatrical environment.

Characterization

Within this active conflict zone then, I also wanted to give the spect-actors different ways of manifesting as outsiders. Each of these archetypal outsiders, I thought, should come in with a different understanding about how they will/are expected to engage with the war. And in bringing these different personalities together, I wanted to simultaneously craft both parallel and paired narratives, where the spect-actors experience their own version of events and yet, experience a commonality of what is witnessed. Furthermore, in thinking about the characterization of these different outsiders, there were various archetypes that came to mind—all of which are based on particular interactions that I've had with specific "types" of outsiders in contexts of war: Who might these outsiders be? Perhaps it could be the tourist, i.e., the person who goes into a conflict zone without any knowledge of the context? Or the volunteer: the idealistic "do gooder" who wants to help? Or the journalist: who wants to document and spread the word about what is happening in the specific site of war? The NGO worker: who is paid much more than local communities might see in a year? The government/institutional representative: who seeks to find a political "end" to the conflict? The artist: who wants to create something out of the destruction they perceive? The businessperson: who believes that capital infrastructure development is the only way to move the context forward? The diaspora member: someone from the conflict zone who grew up elsewhere, who is trying to find a way to reconnect with a tough context, amidst their own ties to that place? All of the above?

Dialogue

With these potential characters in mind, there was one final point of consideration that I took into the writing process of *War*: the place for dialogue. Since the premise of *Detention* was hinged on the lesson plan created by the spect-actor-educator, and that spect-actor's subsequent characterization and execution of their role, there was not much dialogue that could be scripted. Rather, the focus was on the details of the scenario and how the timeline would play out. In *War* though, while I wanted spect-actors to still have the freedom to say what they wanted, I wanted there to be *less* of an emphasis on spect-actors' contributions, i.e., where they could respond within the larger structure of *War* but not change it. Such a choice, it seemed to me, would help showcase the larger structural complexities that govern how war and detention are framed vis-à-vis the specific gray zones that I've chosen to focus on. That an individual educator's approach might have more room to "impact" the world of detention center education in that person's classroom (thought not the world of incarceration); that an individual outsider's interventions in war might affect the ethics and responsibility of small scale interactions with particular situations and people, while unlikely to have an effect on the larger tentacles of the war itself.

In summary, then, I went into the writing process of *War* with the following framing ideas. That I would:

- Create a work that speaks to the shadowy textures that inhabit any outsider's intervention within a conflict that they do not live in; a conflict that they have the choice and resources from which to flee; a conflict that is not "theirs"
- Showcase an unspecified war zone, in an unspecified part of the

world—that would intentionally use events/scenarios that are applicable across diverse geographical contexts

- Target the piece toward actors and spect-actors who are participants in institutions that implicitly or explicitly gear individuals toward travel; toward getting involved in social and political engagements that emphasize the notion of global citizenry
- Design post-performance follow-ups that would function as dramatic and aesthetic extensions of the central theatrical immersion; extensions that might heighten the potential for affects/effects to manifest and develop beyond the events themselves
- Represent an active conflict zone in the midst of a struggle for independence (like Kashmir or Palestine)
- Provide the spect-actors with different ways of manifesting as outsiders, through particular archetypal roles
- Reframe the place for dialogue, in comparison with *Detention*

Onward, then, to *War*.

SCRIPTING WAR

The Setting

War takes place in multiple rooms. I suggest that, where possible, the experience be created in a sprawling location, i.e., instead of taking place in different rooms of one building, that scenarios take place in physical spaces that contain some distance between them. Based on the extent of this distance, spect-actors will either have to walk or take transport between the different spaces and the different scenarios. It is integral that routes between these different spaces are also part of the theatrical environment and that there are installations, multi-sensorial exhibits, actors, or sound effects along these routes—aesthetic choices to help further the immersive world of the conflict zone that the spect-actors are outsiders to.

War is geared toward a maximum of sixteen participants—each of whom will be given a particular "type" of outsider to become over the course of their experience. While more information about each archetypal character is provided a little further on in this script, here is the overview of the different roles that are available to spect-actors:

- 2 Tourists (TOURIST A and TOURIST B)
- 2 Volunteers (VOLUNTEER A and VOLUNTEER B)
- 2 Journalists (JOURNALIST A and JOURNALIST B)

- 2 Non-Governmental Organization Workers (NGO WORKER A and NGO WORKER B)
- 2 Government/Institutional Representations (REPRESENTATIVE A and REPRESENTATIVE B)
- 2 Artists (ARTIST A and ARTIST B)
- 2 Businesspeople (BUSINESSPERSON A and BUSINESSPERSON B)
- 2 Diaspora Members (DIASPORA A and DIASPORA B)

With these particular characters, spect-actors experience *War* in pairs:

- PAIR 1: TOURIST A and JOURNALIST A
- PAIR 2: TOURIST B and BUSINESSPERSON A
- PAIR 3: VOLUNTEER A and NGO WORKER A
- PAIR 4: VOLUNTEER B and REPRESENTATIVE A
- PAIR 5: JOURNALIST B and DIASPORA B
- PAIR 6: NGO WORKER B and BUSINESSPERSON B
- PAIR 7: ARTIST A and DIASPORA A
- PAIR 8: ARTIST B and REPRESENTATIVE B

The eight pairs of spect-actors experience all eight scenarios in *War*—in addition to the welcome and debrief spaces—however, each pair takes a different route through SCENARIOs 1, 2, 3, 4, 5, 6, 7, 8. This is to say that, at any given time, only *one* pair of spect-actors will partake in a scenario, and apart from the welcome/debrief spaces, the pairs should *not* overlap with each other. Each pair follows a particular scenario order:

- SCENARIO order for PAIR 1: 1, 2, 3, 4, 5, 6, 7, 8
- SCENARIO order for PAIR 2: 2, 3, 4, 5, 6, 7, 8, 1
- SCENARIO order for PAIR 3: 3, 4, 5, 6, 7, 8, 1, 2
- SCENARIO order for PAIR 4: 4, 5, 6, 7, 8, 1, 2, 3
- SCENARIO order for PAIR 5: 5, 6, 7, 8, 1, 2, 3, 4
- SCENARIO order for PAIR 6: 6, 7, 8, 1, 2, 3, 4, 5
- SCENARIO order for PAIR 7: 7, 8, 1, 2, 3, 4, 5, 6
- SCENARIO order for PAIR 8: 8, 7, 6, 5, 4, 3, 2, 1

Each spect-actor pair in *War* is assigned an actor playing a GUIDE; this character takes their pair on the particular route of SCENARIOs that has been assigned to them. The GUIDE is largely quiet, and while caring and hospitable in their disposition toward their spect-actors, this character primarily serves to ensure that spect-actors arrive at the right place at the right time. The GUIDEs can occasionally interject during particular SCENARIOs, but the spect-actors should not become overly dependent on them.

Each SCENARIO in *War* has been crafted to highlight a dimension of the conflict that is specifically relevant to one "type" of outsider. While all scenarios contain potential for all spect-actors to intervene, the extra focus in each SCENARIO is so as to make particular parts of *War* hold specific resonance for certain "types" of outsider characters.

Since each SCENARIO has multiple characters for actors, their roles will be described prior to the SCENARIO in question. At this point though, what is provided below is a detailed characterization of the outsider-spect-actors. Please note that the GUIDEs are not characterized in detail because of the "stay in the background" quality to their manifestation in this piece.

The EVOLUTIONs

Each SCENARIO also includes a section named EVOLUTION OF SCENARIO, which showcases how each individual scenario during the follow up experiences that are designed to occur. The exact scheduling of the EVOLUTIONs is entirely up to the production team but imagine something like this:

- Day 1: Spect-actors' experience of *War*
- Day 8, a week after the experience: EVOLUTIONS #1
- Day 15, a week after Day 8: EVOLUTIONS #2
- *There can be as many evolutions as desired by the production team; evolutions for which a trajectory has been provided; evolutions that can be developed with the ensemble*
- Final Day: The Letters

For the EVOLUTIONs, all the actors need to return to their particular SCENARIO worlds. If spect-actors do arrive for these optional follow-up engagements, the GUIDE who worked with them on Day 1 meets them. The GUIDE asks them where they might want to go; if there are specific people they met during their first journey that they would like to see again. The spect-actors are then taken only to those particular SCENARIOs, and once the spect-actors express a desire to leave, they are escorted out and informed about the next time to visit (if there is one).

The "Final Day" will be explained further at the very end of this script.

The Spect-actors' Characters and Their Introduction to War

When spect-actors walk into the first space, eight GUIDES meet them. Around the GUIDEs are eight large banners/cards/some kind of signage; each of which showcases one of the eight "outsider" profiles below. There is an additional board that functions as a counter, informing spect-actors about the number of spots that are remaining in each character profile.

The signs that contain the "outsider" profiles should be easy to read, so that spect-actors have a chance to consider them before choosing one. Perhaps there is a question that accompanies them. Something like: "Which of these profiles best describes the kind of traveler you are?"

While spect-actors are picking a profile, the GUIDEs walk around and answer any questions that they might have. As specific profiles are chosen by spect-actors, the counter numbers change—so that spect-actors know how many of each profile are left for them to choose from. Once spect-actors choose a specific profile, they are paired with their partner by the pair's GUIDE and handed a profile card: each card contains, first, a general contextual overview that is the same for each spect-actor, and that summarizes the conflict that is happening in the region that they are about to enter. Following the contextual overview, the profile card contains detailed information about who that spect-actor is about to become. The other side of the profile card for each spect-actor contains a character questionnaire that they must fill out.

Profile cards will therefore look as follows:

TOURIST A

Profile Card Side 1	Profile Card Side 2
Contextual Overview	**Character Questionnaire**
The war zone you are about to enter is a region that is fighting for self-rule. Under the control/administration/ occupation (depending on who you talk to) of a particular nation-state's government, this region has been at the center of violent conflict for about 50 years. Some of the residents of this region identify with the nation-state that administers it; others do not. Yet others have joined armed militia groups to fight for the region's independence. You, as an outsider with the specific profile below, have come to this conflict zone for various reasons. How will you engage with the different narratives that you are about to encounter here?	*You are welcome to use your imagination to create your characters' background. However, we suggest that you craft information that honors the integrity of the experience that we are trying to create for you: choices that are intentionally disruptive to the environment will result in your being asked to leave.*
	Name:
	Age:
	Gender:
	Profession:
	Personal life:
Profile Information	*[Think about whether or you are married; whether or not you have children; whether you live alone or with others; anything that will help you better craft your personality.]*
You are from the nation-state that governs the region you are about to	Have you travelled before? If so,

enter. You do not know much about the conflicts but you have been told a lot about the natural beauty and historical monuments that are to be seen here. You want to see these sights and get to know this part of your country that has been plagued by violence for decades.	where have you been and why did you go there? What do you most like to do when you travel? Do you tend to take a lot of pictures and what do you do with them? [If you are a taker of photos, you are welcome to take pictures during your time here as well.]

TOURIST B

Profile Card *Side 1*	*Profile Card* *Side 2*
Contextual Overview *Same information as above.* **Profile Information** You are from a place that is far away from the region that you about to enter. You do not know much about the conflicts but you have been told a lot about the natural beauty and historical monuments that are to be seen here. You want to see these sights and get to know this region that has been plagued by violence for decades.	**Character Questionnaire** *Same as TOURIST A.*

VOLUNTEER A

Profile Card *Side 1*	*Profile Card* *Side 2*
Contextual Overview *Same information as above.* **Profile Information** You are from the nation state that governs the region that you are about to enter. You've heard a lot about the violence that is happening in the region and want to help. You are not sure how to help so you have come to this region to understand more about where you might volunteer your efforts.	**Character Questionnaire** *You are welcome to use your imagination to create your characters' background. However, we suggest that you craft information that honors the integrity of the experience that we are trying to create for you: choices that are intentionally disruptive to the environment will result in your being asked to leave.* Name: Age: Gender:

	Profession:
	Personal life:
	[Think about whether or you are married; whether or not you have children; whether you live alone or with others; anything that will help you better craft your personality.]
	Have you been a volunteer before? If so, where have you been and why did you go there?
	What do you think about the impact of volunteerism in the world?
	Are you still in contact with the people you've volunteered with before? If so, what keeps the contact going? If not, why not?
	What kind of career do you see yourself having in your future?
	What made you decide to come volunteer here?

VOLUNTEER B

Profile Card *Side 1*	*Profile Card* *Side 2*
Contextual Overview	*Character Questionnaire*
Same information as above.	Same as VOLUNTEER A.
Profile Information	
You are from a place that is far away from the region that you are about to enter. You've heard a lot about the violence that is happening in the region and want to help. You are not sure how to help so you have come to this region to understand more about where you might volunteer your efforts.	

JOURNALIST A

Profile Card *Side 1*	*Profile Card* *Side 2*
Contextual Overview	*Character Questionnaire*
Same information as above.	You are welcome to use your imagination to create your characters'

Profile Information

You are from the nation state that governs the region that you are about to enter and want to write a news article about the current situation. Your newspaper has asked you to provide an "objective" analysis that clearly states who are the people that are abusing human rights in the region: whether it's the nation state's armed forces, or the armed militia groups. You are on a fact-finding mission to write this article.

background. *However, we suggest that you craft information that honors the integrity of the experience that we are trying to create for you: choices that are intentionally disruptive to the environment will result in your being asked to leave.*

Name:

Age:

Gender:

Profession:

Personal life:
[Think about whether or you are married; whether or not you have children; whether you live alone or with others; anything that will help you better craft your personality.]

What made you become a journalist?

What kinds of issues do you like writing about?

What will, do you hope, come out of the article that you write about this region?

JOURNALIST B

Profile Card *Side 1*	**Profile Card** *Side 2*
Contextual Overview *Same information as above.*	**Character Questionnaire** *Same as JOURNALIST A.*

Profile Information

You are a place that is far away from the region that you are about to enter and want to write a news article about the current situation. The international news agency that you work for, has asked you to provide an "objective" analysis that clearly states who are the people that are abusing human rights in the region: whether it's the nation state's armed forces, or the armed militia groups. You are on a fact-finding mission to write this article.

NGO WORKER A

Profile Card Side 1	Profile Card Side 2
Contextual Overview *Same information as above.* **Profile Information** You work for an NGO that has its headquarters in the nation state that governs the region that you are about to enter—the NGO works with/for young people who have been orphaned by the war. Your employers have tasked you with ascertaining if they can start a branch of your organization in the conflicted region. You are here to do a "needs assessment" about your work.	**Character Questionnaire** *You are welcome to use your imagination to create your characters' background. However, we suggest that you craft information that honors the integrity of the experience that we are trying to create for you: choices that are intentionally disruptive to the environment will result in your being asked to leave.* Name: Age: Gender: Profession: Personal life: *[Think about whether or you are married; whether or not you have children; whether you live alone or with others; anything that will help you better craft your personality.]* What made you become an NGO worker? How do you think your work will benefit this region? What challenges do you anticipate in setting up your NGO work here?

NGO WORKER B

Profile Card Side 1	Profile Card Side 2
Contextual Overview *Same information as above.* **Profile Information** You work for an NGO that has its headquarters in a place (international) that is far away (geographically) from the region that you are about to enter—the NGO works with/for young people who have been orphaned by the	**Character Questionnaire** *Same as NGO WORKER A.*

war. Your employers have tasked you with ascertaining if they can start a branch of your organization in the conflicted region. You are here to do a "needs assessment" about your work.	

REPRESENTATIVE A

Profile Card *Side 1*	*Profile Card* *Side 2*
Contextual Overview *Same information as above.* **Profile Information** You are a member of the nation-state's government and you have been tasked with brokering a peace deal between the armed forces and the militia groups. You have never been to this region before and you are here to understand what different stakeholders want from the conflict, so that a peace deal might be brokered.	**Character Questionnaire** *You are welcome to use your imagination to create your characters' background. However, we suggest that you craft information that honors the integrity of the experience that we are trying to create for you: choices that are intentionally disruptive to the environment will result in your being asked to leave.* Name: Age: Gender: Profession: Personal life: *[Think about whether or you are married; whether or not you have children; whether you live alone or with others; anything that will help you better craft your personality.]* Why did you become a representative for your government/the UN? What is your personal position about the region? Who's at fault: the armed forces, the militia, protesting civilians? Do you have ideas already, about the kind of peace deal that might be brokered?

REPRESENTATIVE B

Profile Card Side 1	Profile Card Side 2
Contextual Overview	**Character Questionnaire**
Same information as above.	*Same as REPRESENTATIVE A.*
Profile Information	
You are a member of the United Nations (UN) and you have been tasked with brokering a peace deal between the armed forces and the militia groups. You have never been to this region before and you are here to understand what different stakeholders want from the conflict, so that a peace deal might be brokered by the UN.	

ARTIST A

Profile Card Side 1	Profile Card Side 2
Contextual Overview	**Character Questionnaire**
Same information as above.	*You are welcome to use your imagination to create your characters' background. However, we suggest that you craft information that honors the integrity of the experience that we are trying to create for you: choices that are intentionally disruptive to the environment will result in your being asked to leave.*
Profile Information	
You are an artist from the nation-state that governs the region you are about to enter and you are here to understand how the arts can help intervene within/respond to the violence in the region. You are an independent artist and fund your own work.	Name:
	Age:
	Gender:
	Profession:
	Personal life: *[Think about whether or you are married; whether or not you have children; whether you live alone or with others; anything that will help you better craft your personality.]*
	What made you become an artist?
	What kind of artist are you (painter, performer, writer, singer, something else)?

	Do you have a vague idea of what kind of artistic venture you will take on as a result of your time in this region?

ARTIST B

Profile Card Side 1	Profile Card Side 2

Contextual Overview
  Same information as above.
 	
Profile Information
  You are an artist from a place that is far away (international) from the region that you are about to enter and you are here to understand how the arts can help intervene within/respond to the violence in the region. You are an independent artist and fund your own work.
	Character Questionnaire
	  Same as ARTIST A.

BUSINESSPERSON A

Profile Card Side 1	Profile Card Side 2

Contextual Overview
  Same information as above.
 	
Profile Information
  You are a businessperson from the nation-state that governs the region you are about to enter and you are here to understand how new business opportunities can be begun in this place. You are of the opinion that new business, and capital, are what is needed to boost the economies of war zones.
	Character Questionnaire
	  You are welcome to use your imagination to create your characters' background. However, we suggest that you craft information that honors the integrity of the experience that we are trying to create for you: choices that are intentionally disruptive to the environment will result in your being asked to leave.
	
	Name:
	
	Age:
	
	Gender:
	
	Profession:
	
	Personal life:
	[Think about whether or you are married; whether or not you have children; whether you live alone or with others; anything that will help you better craft your personality.]

	What made you become a businessperson? Why do you believe that economic investment will help war zones? Is there anything that will stop you from building your business empire here?

BUSINESSPERSON B

Profile Card *Side 1*	*Profile Card* *Side 2*
Contextual Overview *Same information as above.* **Profile Information** You are a businessperson from a place that is far away (international) from the region you are about to enter and you are here to understand how new business opportunities can be begun in this place. You are of the opinion that new business and capital are what is needed to boost the economies of war zones.	**Character Questionnaire** *Same as BUSINESSPERSON A.*

DIASPORA A

Profile Card *Side 1*	*Profile Card* *Side 2*
Contextual Overview *Same information as above.* **Profile Information** Your parents are from this region but decided to move away to start a life in a different country. They have told you some things about the region that you are from and what the conflict is about, but you have never lived here. So, you are back to see the place and to consider whether or not you could live here some day.	**Character Questionnaire** *You are welcome to use your imagination to create your characters' background. However, we suggest that you craft information that honors the integrity of the experience that we are trying to create for you: choices that are intentionally disruptive to the environment will result in your being asked to leave.* Name: Age: Gender: Profession: Personal life: *[Think about whether or you are*

	married; whether or not you have children; whether you live alone or with others; anything that will help you better craft your personality]
	What has your family told you about this region?
	What are you most afraid of, in coming back here as someone from here who has never lived here before?
	Is there anything that might happen, that would stop you rom wanting to move back here?

DIASPORA B

Profile Card *Side 1*	*Profile Card* *Side 2*
Contextual Overview *Same information as above.*	**Character Questionnaire** *Same as DIASPORA A.*
Profile Information Your parents are from this region but migrated to a different country out of fear for their lives—you are from an ethnic minority in this region. Your family has told you some things about the region that you are from and what the conflict is about, but you have never lived here. So, you are back to see the place and to consider whether or not you could live here some day.	

The GUIDEs who are assigned to particular pairs help each spect-actor-outsider with this process. Once all sixteen spect-actor have finished with their characterization process, one of the GUIDEs organizes the entire group into a circle and asks people in the room to introduce themselves. The GUIDEs introduce themselves—as a chorus, perhaps, or as individuals—presenting an example for how spect-actors should introduce themselves:

GUIDES: We are your guides to this place
　　We will take you where you need to go
　　How you respond
　　What you do
　　That, my friends, is entirely up to you.

One of the GUIDEs steps forward.

GUIDE: Take a step into this circle
Tell us who you are
What should we call you?
Why are you here?
Please step into the circle, and tell us who you are
What is your name?
Why you have come to this place?
That's all we need to know ... for now.

As spect-actors step in to the circle and introduce themselves, the GUIDEs are allowed to ask questions that invite the spect-actor-outsiders to say more about themselves. In so doing, spect-actors are given the chance to practice their responses to queries that might be asked of them in the SCE-NARIOs, later in *War*. The aim is *not* to make the space intimidating, where spect-actors are made nervous of what they are about to experience. Instead, this practice is for those spect-actor who might still be struggling with the notion of stepping into a character—that these discomfited spect-actors might be helped through the process, so as to make *War* as affective/effective for them as possible. When spect-actors who are international outsiders step into the middle of the circle—by international, I mean the outsiders who are profiled as being from beyond the borders of the nation-state that governs the region seeking its autonomy—a dot is painted on their right cheek. This is important to distinguish these outsiders from their counterparts who are from the nation state that governs the conflicted region. Once all spect-actors have had the chance to introduce and practice their characters:

ALL GUIDES: Let our journeys commence!

COMMON SCENARIO 1

Characters:
Welcoming committee members. [The number of actors needed is
   flexible.]

Guiding questions for the characters:
What is important to consider during the characterization process,
   though, is *why* particular characters have become members of the
   committee: do they do it out of a belief in the importance of their
   work?
Do they do it for their livelihood?
The intentionality behind each character's participation in the welcoming committee, therefore, should be unique—allowing different kinds
   of interactions to take place between them, and the spect-actors.

All sixteen spect-actor-outsiders are ushered into another space, a COM-MON SCENARIO that is experienced by all of them together. When the spect-actor -outsiders walk into the common space, "locals" from that place meet them. Although there is no specific community or context that is deemed as being the setting for *War,* and although directors/performers are welcome to create their own contextual choices, there is some framing information below that needs to be adhered to. Essentially, the principles below—reflective of the "host" culture; reflective of that conflict zone—should come through in any possible avenue:

- The local culture is one that is extremely welcoming toward international visitors and slightly less welcoming toward people who are from the nation-state that governs the region. Hence the importance of the dots on the cheeks of international visitors
- It is a culture that has a particular kind of drink/snack that is commonly used (chai and biscuits in the Indian context, for instance). This "common" snack is brought out in every scenario where food and drinks are served to the spect-actor-outsiders
- It is a place where the armed forces are referred to as the "Army" and the militia is referred to as "Rebels"
- The clothes that are worn by the locals don't have to come from a specific geographical locations. However, I would recommend that is a concept behind what is worn—that there are enough patterns and commonalities between what people wear to make for a local "flavor"
- Whether the culture is matriarchal or patriarchal is up to the discretion of the director. I would suggest, that in order to heighten the "foreign-ness" of *War*'s setting, that it is women who constitute a majority of both the rebel and army soldier populations. While both men and women work and run domestic chores; the men are not "subservient" by any means. Rather, for whatever reason in this culture's evolution, women are the "warriors" and tend to take on solider and rebel roles. If spect-actors ask why this happens, all that needs to be said is "Well, that's how it always has been." Again, this is a suggestion and the production team is free to decide how gender roles and norms will be structured.

In the first COMMON SCENARIO, there is welcoming committee from the region that is present to welcome the spect-actors as they enter: the committee is carefully calibrated so that there are "locals" of various genders; that there are individuals across the age spectrum. This welcoming committee invites the spect-actor-outsiders in, and does so in a manner that somehow reflects the local customs. If the context for *War* is an imagined one, incredible care needs to be taken to see that the fictionalized host customs do not prob-lematically exoticise any group of peoples who inhabit the world. Rather, in the spirit of full force of fiction, I would recommend crafting creative and unique local customs. It is one such designed custom that is used to welcome the spect-actor-outsiders; these designed customs that then form the avenue through which the local food and drink is given to the visitors.

Members from the welcoming committee walk around this space and make conversation, informally, with spect-actors: these chats happen one-one and in these private interactions that occur in different parts of the space, spect-actor-outsiders are asked various questions that they had to answer in the character questionnaire that they had to answer at the beginning of the experience. Although these conversations are not centralized in any way, each spect-actor gets multiple opportunities to practice their characters and to get an insight into the world into which they have entered. Once a GUIDE notices that the spect-actors in their pair has had the opportunity to converse with a number of people in the welcoming committee, s/he leads their spect-actor-pair to the first stop on their route.

The COMMON SCENARIOs don't evolve in the same way as those that follow. More on this later.

A general note for all routes is that if one SCENARIO is ongoing when another pair arrives, the GUIDE of the incoming group keeps their two spect-actor-outsiders waiting until the previous SCENARIO has ended. It is for this reason that the note on design at the beginning of the script asks for the tran-sitory routes to also be designed in some way to be part of the immersive world—giving spect-actors something to engage with even when they are not inside a particular scenario.

SCENARIO 1

Focus on the TOURIST (and on everyone else)

Characters:
Performers. [The number of actors needed is flexible.]

Guiding questions for the characters:
What is important to consider during the characterization process, though, is *why* particular characters have become performers: do they do it out of a love for the arts?

Or do they perform, so as to educate outsiders about their culture? Or have they become performers to earn an income?

Or, do they struggle with their jobs—wondering if they are putting their culture "on display" to entertain tourist?

The intentionality behind each character's participation in the performance should be unique—allowing different kinds of interactions to take place between the actors and the spect-actors.

As spect-actors walk in, there is a performance that is already in progress
and is created, intentionally by the directors and creators of *War,* as a type
of "fusion." All that performers need to be conscientious about is, again, *not*
Orientalizing and exoticising particular parts of the world.

When the spect-actors enter, there is an allocated amount of time during
which the GUIDE tells them to take available seats and to watch/listen to the
performance that is in progress. There are other actors playing "visitors" who
are seated in some of the chairs, who are taking photographs of the performance and generally, being overenthusiastic about their cultural consumption.
Over the course of the performance, however, the performers reach out to
the two spect-actor-outsiders and invite them to join in the performative
event. It is entirely up to the spect-actors whether or not they join in.

After the performance ends, the actors take photographs with the spect-
actor-outsiders and there is a sense of the spectacle to this scenario—that
they are all part of "selling" this "host" cultures' customs and acts. There is
a deliberate silence about the conflict, and the only way in which any questions about the political issues surrounding the region can emerge, is if spect-
actor-outsiders bring up these issues in conversation with the performers. In
these instances, if spect-actor-outsiders ask questions about the conflict to
an actor who is playing a part in this tourist spectacle, the performer simply
smiles and moves on to speak to someone else.

The only way to really affect the scene's outcomes would be for one of
the spect-actor-outsiders to take charge of the SCENARIO and to ask to converse with the actors, in the presence of the entire group, about the place for
these "performances of culture" in the context of a war. When we know that
what we are seeing, as outsiders, is a "cover"—a beautiful cover—that seeks
to obfuscate more grim realities, how do we intervene? Do we go along with
what is presented to us, because we are "guests" after all; or do we risk being
aggressive (and yet, possibly, more (un) ethical)?

En route between two SCENARIOS in the experience (any two SCENAR-
IOs; not necessarily this one and the one that follows, though that is certainly
an option), there is an installation as follows: along one passageway, one of
the walls is covered with picture of beautiful landscapes; of "local" cultural
forms; of the kinds of things that a stereotypical tourist might choose to
engage with. On the other wall are photos of active conflict: taken through
windows; through cracks in the walls. Both sets of photographs can be staged
or be from specific, real world, conflict zones. It doesn't matter. What does
matter is the image that each kind of image perpetuates. What the spect-

actor interprets through this installation, whether or not they connect the images in one passageway to the SCENARIO above, is entirely up to them.

EVOLUTION OF SCENARIO 1

In the post-performance sessions to which spect-actors are invited, the performance shown in SCENARIO 1 doesn't evolve. The same performance is shown, as many times as there are follow-up sessions; the same kinds of photographs are taken; the same kinds of conversations take place. The only way anything can shift is if the spect-actor-outsiders, somehow, take ownership of that situation...

SCENARIO 2

Focus on the VOLUNTEER (and on everyone else)

Characters:
Volunteers working on various tasks. [The number of actors needed is flexible.]

Guiding questions for the characters:
What is important to consider during the characterization process, though, is *why* particular characters have become volunteers: do they do it out of problematic, naïve good intentions?
Or are they really best positioned to create an "impact" in this role?
Or are they honest about being selfish in their volunteerism; in doing it to build their resumes, for instance?
Or, do they struggle, constantly, between what they do and why they do it?
The intentionality behind each character's volunteer profile should be unique—allowing different kinds of interactions to take place between the actors and the spect-actors.

When the spect-actor-outsider enters this space, they see a lot of activity that is going on. There are people at table who are wading through mountains of paperwork; others who are cleaning windows and floors; one team is painting a wall. There are enough hands on deck and it is clear that there are a substantial number of "locals" who are both sprucing up the space and working on creating "something." The team that is performing *War* can decide the exact nature of that "something": perhaps the group is constructing a new cultural space? Perhaps they are building a new school? Whatever it is, it should be a task that can be broken down into parts that multiple people can work on at the same point.

As the two spect-actors enter, the GUIDE who has accompanied them stays outside the entrance. The spect-actor-outsiders are free to just watch what is happening on around them; or they can go up to an actor and ask them what is being done and how they can help. What is important is that the actors do *not* approach the spect-actor-outsiders. The performers only engage when they are spoken to.

If the spect-actor-outsider asks for something to do, or how they can help, the spect-actor-outsider is given a mundane task to work on: for instance, someone who is already painting the wall is asked to stop and to teach this spect-actor-outsider how to finish that section. At certain points, there are loud noises that come from outside the room; perhaps there is a sound installation of protests right outside the door; the volume for which is controlled by the GUIDE. As the sound increases, some of the actors in the room run out—there is concern in the air—the activity stops. Every time this happens the actors in question return after a minute or so, and tell the others that everything is fine.

When the next group of spect-actor-outsiders arrives at the entrance of SCENARIO 2, the GUIDE with the pair who is already in the space comes in and tells his spect-actors that it is time to leave. So, they would have to leave their task mid-way—unless these spect-actors explicitly choose *not* to leave till they finish whatever little task they are in the midst of. If the outsiders do decide to stay and finish what they were doing, there is a celebratory "toast" that is held in their honor at the end of the completion of their task. If, however, the spect-actor leaves immediately when the GUIDE tells them that it might be time to go, this public recognition is not provided to them.

Whatever the tasks might be, the essential point of this scenario is to communicate the hassles and complexities that come with harnessing an unskilled labor, which is mostly based on "good will" and nothing else. But that despite these limitations, if there is a certain degree of commitment, there are still things that can be accomplished—however small; however intangible.

EVOLUTION OF SCENARIO 2

If/when the spect-actor goes back SCENARIO 2 in the follow up opportunities; all the work that had been done to the space has been destroyed because of the conflict. The walls that were being painted during the first experience are now falling apart; the floor that was being cleaned is now covered in dirt and sludge ... the work has to begin all over again.

SCENARIO 3

Focus on the NGO WORKER (and on everyone else)

Characters:
CARETAKER
GIRL 1 and BOY 1
ACTOR IN AUDIENCE 1
ACTOR IN AUDIENCE 2

Guiding questions for the characters:
Why has the CARETAKER taken on this particular profession?
Is it because a genuine care for orphaned children?
Or is the CARETAKER attempting to take advantage of the situation of
    the vulnerable, for his own benefit?
Or is the CARETAKER the rare strategic idealist, who combines acu-
    men with empathy?
How have GIRL 1 and BOY 1 come to be orphaned?
How do they feel about living in the home?
How do they feel when they are asked to perform for the spect-
    actors?
What are the motivations behind the ACTORs in AUDIENCE desire to
    help the children?
Why these children?
Why now?

As the spect-actor-outsiders walk in, they must understand that they
are in some sort of orphanage—one that is falling apart, physically, and one
to which no cosmetic "changes" have been made to dress it up for the spect-
actor-outsiders. Inside the room is a group of children—orphans; we are
given to understand—that is being looked after by an actor playing their
CARETAKER. The CARETAKER facilitates all the conversations between the
children and the spect-actor-outsiders. When the spect-actors are assembled
and seated,

> CARETAKER: We are so glad to have you all here and to know of your interest in
> providing support to the children of this home. These young people are all
> orphans of this land and have lost everyone they know to the war.... I have
> asked them to prepare a small program for you, to tell you their stories and
> also to present you with a program so that you can tell how talented they are,
> and that bright, young people will use your support.
> GIRL 1: Hello ... [*Silence*]
> CARETAKER: Go on ... tell them your story.
> GIRL 1: I am 15 years old and I am from a small town in the north.... My father, he
> joined the militia about ten years ago and since then, the soldiers.... The sol-

diers started coming to our house every day. The house where I lived with my mother and grandmother. They would not stop coming ... asking us where my father was.... They wouldn't believe us when we said that we have no idea.... You think the rebels are going to be stupid enough to tell their families where they are going? You think they don't know that the army will come knocking at our doors? (*Pause*) We told the army officers this but they would not believe us. Sometimes in the middle of the night, we'd hear knocking on our door.... It finally got too much. My mother and grandmother decided to go across the border and find jobs; they will send for me once they are able to make money.... I ... I was going to be fine living alone but ... now I am here and I am glad to be here.

BOY 1: My mother was part of the police force.... She was really well known and well respected but ... when the rebel groups started again ... she ... we became a target. She was killed in an encounter about five years ago. My father remarried—to someone else ... but she ... she didn't want us. So the two of us (*points to another child sitting next to him*), we are here now....

Based on the number of actors there are to play orphaned children, the stories abound; the contentious culture of testimonial story telling that has come to dominate how conflict zones interact with the outside world ... the stories are always "abject"; always desperate. The testimonies implicate different parties that are involved in the conflict: just as GIRL 1 one implicates the army, and BOY 1 implicates the militia and civil society (in BOY 1 not being accepted by his father's new spouse). At the end of all the testimonials:

CARETAKER: Do any of you have questions for these young people?

Spect-actor-outsiders are given the chance to ask whatever questions they have. In each case though, unless the spect-actors stop the CARETAKER explicitly, this character overtakes the question and interrupts the young person who is going to speak. What it results in ultimately, therefore, is an atmosphere where the CARETAKER is the only one speaking; the dialogue "devolving" into a monologue. It is unclear whether the CARETAKER is doing this with malicious intentions of controlling the children's narratives, or if the CARETAKER is simply looking out for the young people. Ultimately, I would like for this character's intentions to be unclear. Once the question and answer session has had some time to evolve:

CARETAKER: Now our young people have a performance to show you—to show you their talents.

What follows is a series of "kitchy" performances, with the young people trying to "impress" their visitors with pieces that they think will be liked. What is important here is that the young people are performing pieces/styles/genres that are *not* "local" to them—it's as if they've been told to showcase that which is "Other"; that which is seen as being more palatable to "outsiders"; so that the local children seem smarter and more talented. At the end of the last performance:

> CARETAKER: Once again, thank you all for coming to this event and for your interesting in helping our children. With the support that you give us, we hope to recruit more young people like them and to help these youth build our future. We want to move beyond this war. We want these young people to overcome their odds and to move forward with their dreams.... Having heard and seen all these young people's stories and talents, as you leave, please let me know if there is something you would like to pledge as a contribution, to help them.

The CARETAKER goes to the door and as spect-actors exit, asks each spect-actor what they would like to contribute. ACTORS in AUDIENCE start the responses as below:

> ACTOR IN AUDIENCE 1: I would like to offer to cover the costs involved for five youth per year.

If someone has promised monetary contributions, the money is collected and receipts are provided. If spect-actor-outsiders offer something in kind—like a workshop or something else (like ACTOR in AUDIENCE 2, below)—a date and time is fixed for them to return, vis-à-vis the schedule of the "evolution" sessions.

> ACTOR IN AUDIENCE 2: I would like to offer to teach painting workshops to the youth.

The CARETAKER turns to the spect-actor-outsiders and asks them what they would like to offer. Whatever is offered is met with thanks. If nothing is offered, the CARETAKER simply smiles and moves to the next person.

EVOLUTION OF SCENARIO 3

If/when spect-actors return to this scenario, there has been some progress to the young people's/the orphanage's situation, and yet there isn't. Some improvements seem to have been made to the physical infrastructure of the space—it might be cleaner and/or better decorated—but it remains unclear how the young people are moving forward. The children always run to greet the visitors and make the outsiders feel loved and appreciated. There might be some new additions to the group of children and maybe one youth who "disappears."

When the children go to meet their visitors the second (and following) time, the CARETAKER is less present. The young people thus have more of an opportunity to converse with the spect-actors and say things that are somehow ... problematic. Statements like "Can I ask how much money you sent to him?" and when a response is given, "Do you know what he did with that?" What the spect-actor need to take away is a conflict between the young people and the CARETAKER; one that is not explicitly visible, but nevertheless, is alluded to in multiple instances.

If the spect-actor is supposed to lead a workshop or session (as scheduled with the CARETAKER in the original experience) but come in with nothing prepared, the children ask for the visitors to help them with their homework. The actors should decide on the homework topic/s that it would be feasible for the young people to be working on and during this process, statements are made about the CARETAKER's problematic role in that setting.

SCENARIO 4

Focus on the REPRESENTATIVE (and everyone else)

Characters:
MILITARY REPRESENTATIVE (REP)
MIITIA REPRESENTATIVE (REP)
CIVILIAN REPRESENTATIVE (REP)
ACTOR IN AUDIENCE

Guiding questions for the characters:
Why did the MILITARY REP join the armed forces?
How do they feel, personally, about the war—how are their personal sentiments exhibited in their everyday interactions with civilians on the ground?
Why did the MILITIA REP join that particular group (rather than others)?
Are they in it because of a romantic idealism? For practicalities of finances? For fear of repercussions? Can they be bought?
Which particular segment of Civil Society does the CIVILIAN REP represent?
Do they represent the voices of civilians that might not agree with this particular group's positions?
What do they consider to be a "solution" to the conflict?

The spect-actor-outsiders walk into a banquet. It is a fancy evening and it should be clear from the décor that the spect-actor-outsiders are in the presence of "important" people in that context. There is something different in this scenario though, because there are smaller tables set up in different areas of that room. And at each of these tables, there is a representative from a different group/perspective in the conflict.

A gong sounds in three- to five-minute intervals and when this happens, the spect-actors are asked to move from one table to the next. There are is an ACTOR in AUDIENCE, in addition to the two spect-actor-outsiders, to make sure that each REPs table has someone sitting in front of them, listening to the representatives' views. Scripted below are the smaller conversations that happen at each table, with the Prelude presented by the REP in question. The spect-actor/ACTOR in AUDIENCE at a particular table can choose to respond to that Prelude with any questions that they might have for that REP.

What is particularly important in this scenario is the design: there is some sort of physical partition that is in between each of the representative tables (see Figure 3). The partition is translucent; where there are aspects that are visible through the screens, and things that are not. Every time the bell rings and the spect-actors, or the ACTOR in AUDIENCE, seated at that table move to another seat—the REPs have a choreographed move of some sort: where they move to the translucent partition, try to look through it, and just when it seems like they will be able to see the other side, they turn back and go to their seats. This movement should sync with the movement of the spect-actor/ACTORs in AUDIENCE—everyone sits at the same time

The gong sounds. Spect-actor-outsider 1 sits with the ARMY REP; spect-actor-outsider 2 sits with the MILITA REP; ACTOR in AUDIENCE sits with the CIVILIAN REP.

The ARMY REP greets the person seated at their table and asks them about themselves: why have they come to visit their region? After spect-actor-outsider 1 has introduced themselves:

> ARMY REP: You know, I have been here for over 10 years now. And every time I think that we've made some headway; some progress in making people in this region feel like they are part of our nation-state … something happens. A gunshot is heard. A stone is thrown. And everything…. I really worry about the morale of our soldiers here. So many of them ask me "what are we doing here?" … They feel isolated, lonely, disenfranchised. Do you have any ideas about what we can do to make the people here feel like they are one of us?

The ARMY REP carries on a conversation with the spect-actor-outsider, in their specific role. The ARMY REP negates any idea that is put forward by a spect-actor-outsider as being unworkable in that context. On the rare occasion that an idea is seen as being potential worthy in which case all that is said is "We should follow up on that."

Simultaneously, the MILITIA REP greets the person seated at their table and asks them about themselves: why have they come to visit the region? After spect-actor-outsider 2 or ACTOR in AUDIENCE has introduced themselves:

> MILITIA REP: You know how much those army fellows have tortured us? Our families? Even those who do not believe in the militancy will have a point in their

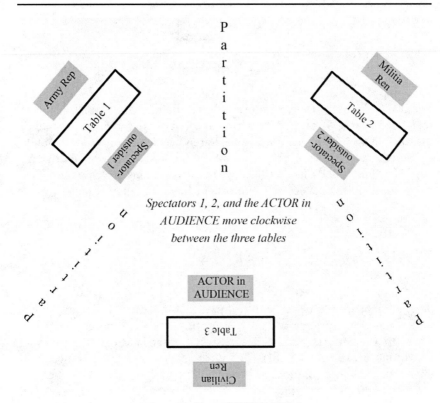

Figure 3: Map of SCENARIO 4.

lives where something is done to their families by the army and then, like us, they will not have a choice. They will have no choice but to fight. But to become one of us. But you know … whenever they want to ignore us they just call us terrorists. They say we are murderers, killers … and somehow, our truth is lost in the chaos. How can we make them listen to us? How can we make them understand that we are using violence because we have no choice? Tell me … what can we do?

The MILITIA REP carries on a conversation with the spect-actor-outsider, in their specific role. Whatever ideas are put forward by spect-actor-outsider 2, are somehow negated by the MILITIA REP as being unworkable. Rarely, an idea is seen as being potential worthy in which case all that is said is "We should follow up on that."

Simultaneously, the CIVILIAN REP greets the person seated at their table and asks them about themselves: why have they come to visit the region? After ACTOR in AUDIENCE has introduced themselves:

CIVILIAN REP: We are stuck. Between guns and more guns. Some of us … we don't even know what is being fought over anymore. Why don't they talk to us? The ordinary man/woman who is not out there fighting the occupation of our land … we are … we are doing our best to move forward. But we don't have many choices, you know? We are desperate…. And we are at a loss…. How do we make the government hear that they need to try something different? How do we get them to listen to us?

The CIVILIAN REP carries on a conversation with the ACTOR in AUDIENCE, in their specific role. Whatever ideas are put forward are somehow negated by the CIVILIAN REP as being unworkable. Rarely, an idea is seen as being potential worthy in which case all that is said is "We should follow up on that."

The gong sounds. The REPs move to the partitions in a choreographed movement while the spect-actor moves clockwise to different tables (under indications from the GUIDEs).

EVOLUTION OF SCENARIO 4

The spect-actors return to find that there are a few more representatives now: perhaps from different political parties, different stakeholders within militia and civilian groups, and differently positioned armed forces personnel. There are more representatives now … which means more partitions; more voices; more "seeing the Other" that does not happen…. It is almost as if these representatives (the ones who were there the last time) do not remember the people they see; that they do not remember the ideas that they seemed to find useful. After all, as the conflict burgeons and more stakeholders begin to emerge, how do these representatives keep track of who is after what?

SCENARIO 5

Focus on the ARTIST (and on everyone else)

Characters:
ARTIST

Guiding questions for the characters:
Why has the ARTIST become an artist?
Was there acceptance in their family?
Are they pressured to support a partner and/or children?
Do they think their art is a legitimate response to the reality of their
    community's conflicts?

The room is covered in blank canvas. Every inch of the floor, the ceiling, the walls—blank canvas that slowly gets filled as more spect-actor-outsiders pass through and contribute to the mass of emptiness. When spect-actors walk in, they see a lone artist in a part of the room. This actor is blindfolded. There is a soundscape playing: sounds of war; of protests; of occasional silence. The artist is painting despite the blindfold; responding to the sounds.

After watching the ARTIST for a bit, the GUIDE approaches individual spect-actors and almost ritualistically, gives them a blindfold to tie around their eyes, and materials to paint with. This process has to be done with the spect-actors' consent, and if for whatever reason, the spect-actor seems dis-comfited at the idea of blindfolding themselves, the GUIDE requests them to simply close their eyes or look down at the floor. The spect-actors remain blindfolded, responding to the soundscape, till the next GUIDE reaches the space with their two spect-actors in tow.

EVOLUTION OF SCENARIO 5

When spect-actors return, the room is no longer blank: the canvases that have been filled by the various artists who have passed through them. This time, when spect-actor-outsiders enter, they see the ARTIST silently whitewashing the space—painstakingly erasing everything that was on there before. It's the same soundscape. This time, the ARTIST is not blindfolded and once s/he becomes aware of the people who are watching her, s/he silently gestures toward the spect-actor-outsiders to join in the whitewashing—in the erasure—of what was created in that space.

SCENARIO 6

Focus on the BUSINESSPERSON (and on everyone else)

Characters:
HOST
ACTOR IN AUDIENCE
Additional ACTORS in AUDIENCE to pitch in evolution of scenario

Guiding questions for the characters:
Why does the HOST think his occupation is important?
How did he come to occupy this particular position?
How does each ACTOR in AUDIENCE negotiate between their entre-
    preneurial quest and the realities of the war?
Do they really believe in the potential for their ideas? Or are they
    simply interested in the money? Or in a means to distract them-
    selves? Or in the fame that might become possible?

HOST: Welcome, everyone, to our annual pitch meeting. Please take a seat at one of the computer terminals that have been set up for you. In the next 10 minutes, we ask that you give us a "pitch"—for a new business that you would like to start in our lovely home. Some of you have been here for a long time; others of you might be new. But remember, it just a pitch. Let us know what you think a business idea could be for our region! Your GUIDEs will help you with your pitches.

As the spect-actor-outsiders sit at the terminal, the GUIDEs sit next to them and talk them through their idea. Essentially, the GUIDE is a sounding board that helps the spect-actor come up with a proposal for a business venture that will be both socially responsible and potentially financially viable. How does the venture help, potentially, end the war or reduce negative outcomes from the violence? How will the venture sustain itself financially? How will the venture contribute to local economic development? These are the three questions that the GUIDE uses to help spect-actors develop their pitches.

Once ready, the space transforms: a stage; a projector; a spotlight. All eyes are on the person who is pitching an idea.

HOST: Ladies and gentlemen, our first pitch for the day, The Dreamers' School!
ACTOR IN AUDIENCE: Thank you, host. Hello everyone and welcome to our pitch of the Dreamer's School—the first high school in this conflict region to offer a diploma that will be recognized across the world. Not only with this school enable the creation of a new generation of leaders for this space; it will also follow a cross-subsidy model where the more well to do members of our community will help pay for the less-well-of families in our midst. Through this cross subsidy model, we aim to increase the sense of social responsibility amongst us. Any questions to this pitcher from our other applicants?

The spect-actors are allowed to ask questions of this project before it is their turn to pitch—hopefully, seeing the person go before them will assuage any nervousness that they might have been feeling.

EVOLUTION OF SCENARIO 6

Designed to be like a talk show/pitch competition, when/if spect-actors walk in this time, they are asked to become judges on a panel. Pitches are put forward by a number of actors: the pitches showcase different kinds of businesses from conflict zones. For example:

- Starting a film studio that would both generate revenue, provide social commentary, and jobs to locals
- Founding a restaurant that uses locally sourced materials and thus gives back to farmers from that conflict zone
- Anything else

After all the pitches are finished, the judges get together and talk about which of the pitches they might prefer to fund. While the actor on the judging panel does not have to be difficult just for the sake of it, what would be nice is for this actor-judge to help the spect-actor-judge nuance some of the decisions that they might make. Are they (the spect-actor judges) making considered decisions about who should "win" the pitch competition? Once the judges decide on a winner the HOST announces the winner with much flourish and the SCENARIO ends with a spirit of hope, of celebration.

SCENARIO 7

Focus on the JOURNALIST (and on everyone else)

Characters:
PROTESTERs, as many as allowed by actor recruitment
ARMY PERSONNEL, as many as allowed by actor recruitment
MILITIA, as many as allowed by actor recruitment

Guiding questions for the characters:
Why is the character protesting? As resistance? As a way to make money? As creativity? How do they define the "success" of their protest?
How does the army officer feel about quashing protests? Do they agree with the means/the end of the PROTESTERs' struggles?
How does the militia person feel about the means/the end of the PROTESTERs' strategies, in comparison with the path that they have chosen?

This SCENARIO takes place in one of the passageways or outdoor areas that are present between other indoor scenario spaces. As spect-actors walk through this passageway, they hear sounds coming their way. Encouraged by their GUIDE, the spect-actor-outsider pairs who have reached that SCENARIO are asked to hide—to not draw attention to themselves. Once the spect-actor-outsiders hide, the actors emerge. From one end of the passageway emerge a whole range of protesting civilians who are carrying balloons filled with colored paint or water. So much so that whenever the well-aimed balloons hit anything, it leaves a large mark. From the other end of the passage way emerge the army personnel to combat the protesting civilians. They are armed with pellet guns—aiming to burst the balloons in the air before they come crashing down on them. Skulking around in the passageway, hidden from everyone but aiming to sabotage the army personnel, are the rebels. Their role in the situation is unclear. Except that they have something to do with what's going down. Perhaps they are the ones supplying the protestors with paint for the balloons?

In hiding from this situation, spect-actor-outsiders are free to engage with the events however they like. They can join the protest, take pictures, and/or interview people, whatever they think would best suit their character as an outsider in the world of *War*. The GUIDE simply keeps an eye on what they are doing and does their best not to interfere in the action. If, however, there is a particularly quiet or reticent spect-actor who does not find a way to get involved, actors playing the protestors, army personnel, or the rebels can approach the spect-actor and ask them questions about why they are there. Based on the nature of the outsider then, and on whether they are from across international borders or are from the nation that "administers"/"occupies" this region, the reactions can be varied in their intensity.

It is possible for an outsider to choose to be a hero. You know, to step in front of the protesting sides and try to broker something. And if that happens, the actors carry on in as realistic a way as possible: perhaps the GUIDE, the outsiders' friend in that context, drags them back? Perhaps the army personnel try to save that person? Perhaps civilians try to save that person? If the outsider does something incredibly surprising and potentially effective, the performers should improvise around the spect-actor's action and develop the situation to the best of their abilities (within realistic bounds, of course). After all, it's not about telling spect-actor-outsiders that there is *no* way to intervene. Simply that finding a way to intervene can be incredibly difficult to do.

EVOLUTION OF SCENARIO 7

If/when spect-actor-outsiders return to *War,* they witness the same kind of protest/battle just in a different passageway. The same parties are involved—using similar forms of resistance and attack—how/when do conflicts actually change? What, if any, is the role of the outsider in changing them?

SCENARIO 8

Focus on the DIASPORA [and on everyone else]

Characters:
Internally Displaced Peoples' camp residents, as many as allowed by
    actor recruitment.

Guiding questions for the characters:
How did each person come to be resident in that camp?
How many people do they live with?
How do they feel about the outsiders who come to "look" at their
   condition?
What hopes do they hold for their futures?

An area—outdoors—that is set up to look like an Internally Displaced
Peoples' (IDP) camp. Rows of tents are set up very close to each other; it
looks like a fire hazard. People are milling around this space engaging in different activities. There is a group of people—a particular subgroup from the
context that is more privileged within the world created for *War* (men, if it
is a patriarchal context, for instance)—who are playing a game. Another
group of people is cooking. Another group is washing clothes. Another is
staring into space. There are myriad different activities happening in this
IDP camp and it should be clear, somehow, that the residents of this camp
are members of a minority community that has had to leave that region
because of some type of discrimination against them—the same community
as is represented by the spect-actor-outsiders playing DIASPORA 1 and DIAS-
PORA 2. Spect-actors are not directed in one particular way and interact
based on the response that is given to them by particular members of that
IDP camp:

- Response 1: At a sudden moment, a person begins to yell at one of
  the outsiders "Why aren't you people doing anything to help us?"
  This person keeps screaming this refrain until other members in
  that IDP camp have to come over and tell this individual to quiet
  down
- Response 2: One or more people who are hospitable and love the
  fact that outsiders are coming to listen to their stories. These individuals give the visitors food and drinks, both of which are some
  slight variation of the national/regional food and drink that is local
  to the region served in the first common scenario/welcoming ceremony. This variability being important so as to highlight the links
  between the majority and minority communities while also highlighting the differences between them
- Response 3: A group of people who don't seem to care about the
  outsiders and remain caught up in whatever they are doing, unless
  directly approached

When another GUIDE arrives at the camp, existing spect-actor-outsiders are
escorted out and the ne pair is brought in.

EVOLUTION OF SCENARIO 8

The IDP camp still remains exactly as it was.... Nothing seems to have changed except that there now seems to be more polarization between the residents. We learn that the government has just announced a policy to resettle members of the community back into their old homes and the IDP camp residents are now split between those who think this is a good idea and those who are opposed to it. While this difference in opinion is less obvious in the beginning, an argument erupts among the group that is playing a game. People come to blows and have to be separated; the calm after the fight being the impetus for the residents to share the recent policy developments with the visitors.

COMMON SCENARIO 2

Characters:
Welcoming committee members as in COMMON SCENARIO 1

Guiding questions for the characters:
The number of actors needed is flexible. What is important to consider during the characterization process, though, is *why* particular characters have become members of the committee: do they do it out of a belief in the importance of their work?
Do they do it for their livelihood?
The intentionality behind each character's participation in the welcoming committee, therefore, should be unique—allowing different kinds of interactions to take place between them, and the spect-actors.

At the end of all the eight different scenarios described earlier, the eight different pairs of spect-actors end up in another common scenario where the welcoming committee (from COMMON SCENARIO 1) is back in action. This time, the event is more formal and everyone is seated around one large table. Food and drink are served and when all GUIDEs and spect-actors arrive:

> HOST: I hope you all have found what you came here for. I would ask that each of you say a few words about your time with us.... What do you think about our little corner of the world?

Spect-actors are given the time and the space to say what they want to reflect on as long as they continue to stay in character. After all spect-actors have had the chance to speak, the GUIDEs step in and usher the spect-actor group back into the first space in which they received their characters at the very beginning. Once in that space:

GUIDE: Will you come back here?
 Or will this be the last we see of you?
 We will be here every _____ [the day(s) for the week],
 from _____ [the specific times],
 for the next _____ [the duration for which these follow up sessions will be possible].
 Will you come back?

It is recommended that the timings chosen are explicitly those that will be accessible to all spect-actors—so that their choice *not* to attend is entirely a choice and not a logistical consequence.

As mentioned earlier, there can be as many EVOLUTIONs as the production team desires. The ideas provided in each evolutionary section can be built and developed as per the particular reality of the war in question—all that is imperative is that there is no "simplistic" solution that is created, where all warring parties live "happily every after."

Wars are complicated. Learning to be an outsider in a war zone, fraught. There is no escaping that.

The EVOLUTIONs

Evolutions occur once-a-week, for however many weeks are desired by the production team. The trajectories mentioned are points of departure, and each ensemble should develop the suggested narrative—in the spirit of being structured improvisation. This is where the rehearsal strategies proposed in the following Interlude will be of particular use.

The Final Day

When spect-actors come to the last and final event of the experience, at the end of all the evolutions, they are again met by their GUIDE.

The GUIDE gives them a letter—a letter than has been written to them by one of the characters in *War*, who the spect-actor most left a mark on. That character speaks to the spect-actor honestly: about what they enjoyed about that spect-actor's interactions; about what they found problematic about that person's responses and interactions. The letters are written in first person; for example:

Dear X,

 Thank you for visiting my home. It was a pleasure getting to know you and I

appreciate the way in which you patiently painted the walls of our office. I was disappointed not to see you again.... I thought you would return and give us ideas on
how to develop the work. Some day, perhaps, you will be able to talk to us *(and so
on)*

The space is set up like a café; like a reading room. Each spect-actor is
given something to eat and drink, while reading the letter. The GUIDE hands
the letter to them and leaves. There can be actors who play servers—who
serve the spect-actor more food and drink, but these actors remain quiet.
Spect-actors can choose to stay for a while and talk with each other about
their experiences, about their letters. Or they can leave immediately. It's up
to them.

INTERLUDE

Like the Interlude that came after *Detention*, this one is also made up
of two sections. The first, speaks to a "global" directorial strategy that might
be applied across the scripts in this book; the second section is centered on
an element of more "traditional" playwriting that might need to be reframed
and reconsidered in the context of creating an immersive theater script that
has social, political, and pedagogical underpinnings. In the Interlude following *Detention*, the global strategy that was attended to, was how to create
context-specific adaptations of the scripts in this book. Through a thought
exercise in which I considered how *Detention* might be specifically adapted
for an Indian context, *Detention*'s Interlude culminated in the proposal of a
series of steps that might be taken in such an endeavor. This possibility of
contextual adaptation remains with *War* as well, and by following the steps
proposed in the previous Interlude, a carefully constructed piece that is particular to say, Syria, could be created and performed:

- *Step 1*: Research the Syrian context vis-à-vis the particular dimensions that have been explored in *War*. How do the perspectives in
  each of *War*'s SCENARIOs, become specific to Syria's conflicts?
- *Step 2*: Edit (if needed) the timeframe and schedule for *War*'s
  events based on the logistical restrictions of the educational community in which the piece is being performed
- *Step 3*: Edit (if needed) the number of spect-actors and actors that
  might need to be recruited for an adapted version
- *Step 4*: Adapt the design elements
- *Step 5*: Explore factors that would additionally influence the characterisation of each of the characters in *War*

For an Immersive Theater Director

Given that dialogue does not have as central a role in the texts in this book as it does in, say, a Realism-inspired text, how does a director go about training performers in an immersive theater piece that is being used in applied theater contexts? How do the more "conventional" procedures that are used for script-centered pieces have to shift so as to train the performer for the requirements that are placed on them by the immersive form?

Designing Auditions

"Conventional" rehearsal procedures usually begin with an audition process, which is then followed by a cold reading of the text. Then, the cold reading is built on through extensive rehearsals of each scene/component of the script, with the blocking (movement) taking up a large chunk of time for the directors and performers. In addition to blocking, there almost immediately commences a process of "line learning" for the actors; the interweaving of technical elements occurring at different stages within the process, and full technical rehearsals taking place closer to the launch of the live performance. Finally, after this process—a process that could take weeks, months, and on the rare occasions, years—the performance takes place.

With an immersive theater text like *War*, however, the rehearsal process needs to be very different—first, because of these scripts' aesthetic of centralizing the role for in-situ improvisation between actors and spect-actors within the framework of the immersive world. In a piece like *War*, therefore, auditions cannot function as competitive processes of selection: this is due to a few reasons. First, the fact that applied theater often involves working with community members who might not have any performance background could lead to a self-defeating process in which amateur performers are dissuaded by the competition that is embedded in a traditional audition process of reading/performing extracts from the piece's script. This then links to a second challenge that immersive scripts (at least the ones in this book) do not have dialogue/text that can be read—rather, the texts that do exist are focused on the performer's skills to react in the moment to responses from spect-actors that might/might not be anticipated. Yet another reason why actor recruitment needs to function differently in pieces like *War* is because of the pedagogical principles that underpin them, where particular target groups are specified as comprising the group of performers (students in a school in the case of *War*); thus restricting the pool to which the audition might be advertised. Finally, again related to the pedagogical underpinnings of applied theater, it seems counterintuitive that there would be a process in place to exclude performers based on the director's perception of some kind of "ability." As a firm believer in the idea that theatrical skills can be taught, based on an interest and commitment, competitive auditions—I think—will most likely be antithetical to what texts like *Detention, War*, and *Immigration* seek to do in a larger sense. All this being said, what might an "audition" look like for a piece like *War?*

I would suggest that "audition-esque" sessions are designed as workshops, for a maximum of fifteen to twenty people at time. In these workshops, the auditioners would be given a character from *War* when they enter the space and are subsequently asked to go through different improvisation exercises in which their ability to respond in the moment might be tested: this could include anything from a hot seating exercise in which the aspiring actors are asked to answer questions in the character assigned to them. Actors could also be asked to go through particular kinds of situational improvisations in which they are asked to create and develop a scenario, with only a summary of the situation's evolution to guide them. Again, the goal with these workshop-based auditions is not to judge the participants and to exclude people from the performance. Rather, the objective is to get a sense of the ease/difficulty with which particular performers might be able to access the form of immersive theater: like a teacher who is trying to assess the skill levels of each student in their classroom, using that information to create focused pedagogical approaches.

Once the performing ensemble has been created, the steps of organizing cold reading sessions of the text, rehearsals for blocking, and the inclusion of tech, work similarly in intention to more "conventional" theatrical pieces— except that each of these steps makes different demands on each stakeholder. Performers are asked to approach characterization as something that is hinged on heightening the potential for individualized responses in the moment of engagement with a spect-actor. Designers have multiple sets to think about— since the promenade quality to the piece, and the scenarios' existence in a diversity of spaces, leads to an array of "stages" that have to be considered. Directors ... well, directors become are far *less* "powerful" when staging pieces like *War*. The relative insignificance of a pre-scripted text, for instance, and the extensive nature to the scripts in their encapsulation of multiple scenarios, necessitates the kind of collaboration and "stepping aside" that is not as essential when directing a script-centered performance in the proscenium. My own process, as a director, of engaging with the staging of immersive theater texts has involved many moments of such powerlessness; it has also involved (and continues to involve) a lot of trial and error. As a result, the suggestions I make below about the rehearsal process for immersive theater scripts, and about the exercises that might need to be used when training actors for such forms, are far from being prescriptive. I do not claim to have found *the* answers, and yet, in having made multiple "discoveries" over the last five years or so, I have some ideas to share. Ideas that, I hope, will function as good points of departure for other practitioners who are interested in immersive forms of theater making; points of departure that will help my colleagues make different mistakes.

Designing the Rehearsal Process

When thinking about how to train actors for pieces like *Detention* and/or *War,* the first step is to understand whether the performers are amateur, less experienced, or professional vis-à-vis immersive theater. Especially given that script-based proscenium theater is what defines most people's understanding of the theatrical form, and the diverse understandings of terms like "immersion," "participation," and "interaction," I have come to find it necessary to begin the rehearsal process with an introduction to the notion of immersive theater. In this vein, I have used different strategies to conduct such an introduction; strategies that are ultimately influenced by the amount of time that is available to me in a particular context. As a result, my immersive theater-introductory strategies include: lecture centered approaches in which I talk to the performers about my approach; a "show and tell" session in which I show a video that exemplifies my immersive, aesthetic framework; readings that function as points of departure from which the group discusses immersive concepts. When time is not a mitigating factor and I do not have to "rush" the introductory process, I find it particularly effective to use experiential pedagogical approaches through which performers can explore my specific application of immersive theater.

Since this experiential pedagogy is also the one that I have found to be most effective in conveying a nuanced introduction, and given that this strategy is more complex than using a lecture or a video or a reading, the section below takes the reader through a sequence of exercises that might be used to frame immersive theater for performers who are participating in *Detention, War,* and/or *Immigration.*

This was a particular workshop design that I adopted when first introducing immersive theater to my colleagues in Kashmir in 2013, at which time none of them had experimented with the form. The ideas below, therefore, draw from exercises and strategies that I have "tested"; they also involve some changes from that initial execution based on my observations of each exercise's outcomes. Sessions 1 through 4 below refer specifically to how immersive theater might be introduced to a group of actor-participants that have not worked with the form before. Sessions 5 and beyond describe techniques that could be used in a rehearsal and staging of *War* and like the earlier ideas, these proposals also draw from work undertaken for the immersive theater experiments that I conduct in my theater "laboratory" in New Mexico

(Dinesh, 2016b; Dinesh, 2018). I would postulate that these techniques could be used for any training process that precedes the performance of an immersive and applied work.

Session 1: Participants (actors) work with the concept of an "emotional polaroid" and are guided through creating static images about different themes; images that its observers then interpret. For example: actors stand in a circle and it is ensured that everyone understands what static images are (a frozen sculpture, as it were). The director then tells the actors that, after someone in the group announces a theme, participants step into the middle of the circle and take a pose in response to that theme. However, only one person can join the image at a given signal—for example, a clap from the director. So, for instance, let's assume that the director chooses the theme, "Wedding." At her signal, a clap, Actor 1 steps into the middle of the circle and takes a pose as the officiator of a wedding ceremony. At the next clap, maybe Actor 2 steps into the circle and chooses a pose that, somehow, adds to the image of Actor 1—maybe they become the mother of the bride, who is whispering to the officiator. Once Actor 2 chooses their position, the director claps again, and Actor 3 steps into the image. This continues until half the actors in the larger group are part of the image.

The other actors in the group, i.e., those who are "watching" the emotional polaroids use nothing but their sense of sight to watch the process of their colleagues. Drawing from some of the work from Augusto Boal's (1985) Image Theater—where corporeal images are used to speak to themes of social injustice and oppression—these montages can be static or dynamic, as long as there are no verbal or audio-based components to what the actors create. This exercise continues as long as the director needs, to sense the actors' comprehension of the aesthetic strategies in question.

Once everyone in the group seems to have garnered an understanding of image-based theater that hinges only on an engagement of spect-actors' sense of sight, the actors are split into two groups. Each group is tasked with devising an image-based performance around a theme that is chosen by the performers themselves, or by the director. There is one requirement that is placed on the performers for their creation: that when the other group of actors comes to their piece as spect-actors, they (the spect-actor group) will be asked to use only their sense of sight i.e., the piece must *not* employ any other sensory stimulus.

After each of the two groups showcases their sight-focused performances, there is a debrief session to reflect on the exercises of the day—what were some responses to the use of one sensory stimulus? What might have changed with the inclusion of more stimuli?

Session 2: All the actors are blindfolded and with their eyes covered, are asked to respond to recorded or live music/sounds. This could be done in multiple ways: with each person responding in an isolated fashion in their own space within the room; as "contact improvisation" with bodies moving in response to the auditory stimulus, with the condition that one person's body is always somehow in physical contact with another's; as image-response-improvisation where participants station themselves next to an object of some sort—a wall, a table, a chair—and when responding blind-folded to the auditory stimuli, create positions in relation to the object that is next to them and hold that position for 10 seconds before moving on to the next image.

Actors are then divided into two groups and asked to create a "radio drama"—where spect-actors will have to close their eyes and will have to only listen in the roles as spect-actors.

With this done, and with the notion of soundscapes considered and established, the actors are divided into small groups again and this time, they are asked to create *two* scenes around a theme chosen by the group (ideally, the same theme as the day before). There are two requirements placed on the work that is created: (1) there should be *at least* two scenes that take place in two different rooms; (2) one of the scenes should take place in one room and ask the spect-actors to use *only* their sense of sight; the second scene should take place in another room and ask the spect-actors to use *only* their sense of sound. If the actors want to add more than two scenes, they are free to decide how those additional components will be structured. Regardless of the number of scenes, the creators will need to consider how they will orches-trate the movement of spect-actors from the first room to the second.

As always, the sharing of the devised performances is followed by a debrief session: what changed when sound was added to the piece? What were the major challenges that were encountered in moving spect-actors from one space to another? Can we discuss sight-based and sound-based montages when the senses work in isolation, versus when the same visual and audio worlds are experienced in interaction with each other?

Session 3: After an exploration of sight and sound, the following session would invoke a consideration of three senses: touch, taste, and smell—all as working together. As a warm up exercise, actors are split into pairs, where they talk to each other about their strongest memory that is associated with a particular food. Then, through acting out that story, they have to find a way to get their spect-actors to smell that food item; perhaps even to touch and taste it. Are there ways to get spect-actors to experience these senses without the physical food item present? Is there something different that happens when we do use "real" food with which spect-actors need to have an interaction? Yes, actors should be encouraged to use food in this exercise.

This introductory exercise and discussion are followed by a devising exercise. The actors are divided into small groups again and there are, yet again, requirements that are placed on the work that is created: this time, they are asked to create at least *three* scenes around a theme chosen by the group (maybe the same theme that was explored during the prior sessions; maybe a new one). One of the scenes should take place in one room and should ask the spect-actors to use *only* their sense of sight; the second scene should take place in another room and ask the spect-actors to use *only* their sense of sound; the third scene should occur in yet another space and ask the spect-actors to use *only* taste, touch, and smell (through the invocation of food). If the creators choose to devise more than three scenes, they are free to structure the remaining scenes as they see fit. Finally, just like the previous day—keeping in mind the challenges that were discussed—the creators in each group need to consider how they will move spect-actors between the different spaces in which the scenes are being shared.

Session 4: Using the framing ideas of the "five senses," and the concept of the "promenade" where spect-actors move around the theatrical spaces—ideas that should be well understood from the previous sessions—I recommend that this fourth session is when a concrete example of immersive theater is given to the participants. Rather than falling into the trap of presenting oversimplified definitions that cannot adequately present the various discussions that surrounding the terminology of "immersion," I would suggest that existing examples are used to frame *War.*

In the past, I have used examples like *Un Voyage Pas Comme Les Autres Sure Le Chemins Del'exil* (Haedicke, 2002) and *This is Camp X-Ray* (UHC Collective, 2003) to talk about how the usage of multisensory aesthetic strategies and a movement-based usage of space might manifest in the theatrical placement of a spect-actor into the shoes of an Other. Once such exemplars are put forward, actors are asked to (in small groups) create a promenade theater piece that is multi-sensorial, and that asks its spect-actors to become a particular type of Other (i.e., the spect-actors should be given a character that they need to become). There are no limits placed on the number of rooms/number of spaces that are used as long as the spect-actor is asked to embody an Other, to use multiple senses, and to traverse through multiple spaces.

Session 5: With an understanding of this approach to immersive theater being established, I would suggest a reading of the script (*War* being used as an example in this case). The reading would primarily involve one individual going over the different scenario structures—with the occasional integration of more voices to read the dialogues that might be present. This, I must note, also reduces the need for literacy being a pre-requisite amongst the performers. As long as there are a couple of people in the ensemble who can read the text and clarify the scenario to their colleagues, the lack of dialogue in *War* would actually make it quite easy to produce with actors who do not read or do not read English. I suggest that such an initial reading of *War* is accompanied by intermittent discussions, to ensure that all the performers understand that structure and objectives of the piece.

Once the piece in its entirety has been understood, decisions are made about who can play whom (based on an intersection between the interests of individual actors and their skills). Conversations will need to occur about how *War* will be adapted: both in relation to a specific geographic location and based on the number of performers that can recruited (given that challenges with recruitment is a perennial, legitimate concern in applied theater environments). While the Interlude following *Detention* speaks to how the scripts in this book can be adapted to specific regional/national contexts, a more extensive discussion and consideration about performance "scaling"— the term I use to refer to the process of adapting immersive scripts for more or less actors—occurs in the Interlude following the next script, *Immigration.*

Session 6: Once all the actors are familiar with the larger premise of the piece and the characters they will be playing in *War*, much like a "traditional" rehearsal, I would suggest that the text is broken down into sections that function as self-contained bits that can be rehearsed in isolation from the rest of the performance (each of the SCENARIOs and their evolutions, for example, in *War*). While the SCENARIO breakdown is fairly clear in *War*, *Detention* will require a different kind of breakdown to facilitate its sectioned off rehearsals. This approach, of course, is up to the director and/or stage manager, based on the logistical aspects framing the rehearsal schedule.

In the first of these SCENARIO rehearsals, I suggest that work is done on the character questionnaire that accompanies each of the scripts in this book. For this part of the process, each performer reads the script for emergences of their character and fills out the questionnaire once they have understood every single entry/exit/presence of that character in the world of the script. While answering their own character's questions is one part of the process, once performers have had the time to do this, everyone in the smaller (SCENARIO) group should get together—with the director inviting each individual actor to share their responses with everyone else who will share that SCENARIO with them. This sharing is necessary and integral so as to ensure that characterization choices made by an individual performer are not in contradiction with choices that are made for another character in the scene. Sharing character profiles, especially in a devised process with less experienced performers, can be integral when thinking about potential— unscripted—interactions that could occur in the world of the immersive world.

Session 7: The more verbal and intellectual process of characterization in Session 6 would benefit from then being followed up by more physical forms of improvisational characterization. For instance, actors could be guided through the well known "character walks" exercise where performers begin by walking around a room and at particular moments, change the way that they walk/sit/stand based on certain directions given by the director. For example the director could give the performers directions like: "Walk the way your character in *War* would … think about the way they hold their shoulders; how they hold their head; how they use their feet." Slowly, incrementally, additional directions could be given: "Think about how your character walks when they are angry"; "How do they carry themselves when they are disappointed"; "How do they tend to use their hands when they are calm?" Chairs, tables, and other kinds of objects can be slowly added to the space and actors can then be asked to consider how their characters would sit, move, stand, and so on, in response to different circumstances.

The character walks could be followed by a "hot seating" exercise, where each character takes the "hot seat"—a chair in front of all the other actors— and is asked a series of questions by the director and by other performers in that SCENARIO. The questions asked can begin with those on the questionnaire, to make sure that the information that was created has been retained. The questions can also extend to issues and themes that are *not* included in the questionnaire but serve to push that performer to consider whether or not they have created a holistic character for themselves. Actors are advised to ask tough questions of each other but not with the intention of making each other fail i.e., the ensemble is specifically requested to refrain from questions that are crafted with the sole purpose of tripping each other up. The exercise is to push each character to be as extensive as possible since, given how much improvisation actors are called upon to use in a piece like *Detention* and *War*, there's no telling what element of a character's background might become useful in responding to a particular spect-actor's response.

Session 8: After the performers have established a better understanding of their characters, they are asked to revisit their SCENARIOs and in so doing, write down specific lines where none have been provided for them. The reader will notice that dialogue is occasionally scripted—more so in *War* than in *Detention*—but is also, more often that not, left open to interpretation by actors and directors within a detailed outline of events that need to take place in that scenario. Given this stylistic choice, and given the pedagogical objectives of pieces like *War* in applied theater contexts, I would suggest that performers be first given the opportunity to come up with the lines as best fit their characters within a particular section of the script. Where two characters are scripted to interact with each other, the actors should decide amongst themselves how they will script their interaction—with the understanding that all dialogue in the piece will be honed and refined during the rehearsal process.

Session 9: It is only after the abovementioned steps around characterization, scenario understanding, and dialogue creation have occurred that I would suggest the actors begin a physical enactment of their particular segments and scenarios. In the first round of these physicalized readings, I would suggest that the actors are given free reign to incorporate movements as they best see fit. The reasons behind actors designing their blocking, instead of the director telling them where to move and what to do, are twofold. First, to ensure that the performers—in their characters—have acquired an understanding of what needs to happen in that scenario. The actors are also encouraged to explore their own blocking at this stage so as to augment the collaborative processes that should, I think, underpin applied theater processes. Extensive notes follow this actor-led blocking, with the director identifying the moments of dialogue, characterization, and physical movement that seem to most need attention. Again, the amount of time that might be devoted to this process entirely depends on the logistics of the project and the schedule in question. More on this in the Interlude that follows *Immigration*.

Session 10: Based on how much time there is in the particular rehearsal process, these sessions that focus on blocking and refining the lines/characterization of the different performers should be followed by a rehearsal of individual SCENARIOs, wherein actors in one segment of the performance become spect-actors for the actors in another scenario. So, for example, actors from Scenario 1 in *War* could come in as spect-actors for a rehearsal with actors in Scenario 2, and vice versa: so that there is an introductory understanding of how the scenarios in an immersive piece might shift based on the presence and interaction of spect-actors.

I suggest that such a trial—with a spect-actor group composed of other actors from the play—is conducted for three or four sessions. In the first few sessions, there should be no intervention on the part of the director; the other actors in the piece decide how they would react as spect-actors. Once there is some comfort that has been reached with having spect-actors, I would also suggest that the director asks the actors coming in as test spect-actors to be of a particular "type" so that the performers in the scene get some practice. For example, intentionally directing some actors to be "shy" spect-actors who do not say a word; asking others to be "overactive" spect-actors who want to overshadow the actors in their contributions; asking some actors to also be whatever they consider as an "ideal" spectator—the last option is so that the director can get a sense of what actors consider ideal spectator participation to be (this will reemerge as being important during the final stages in the rehearsal).

In addition to asking other actors from the team to function as spect-actors for each other—choosing modes of participation that are defined by themselves and/or by the director—I would also recommend that videos are taken of each rehearsal with every different type of test spect-actor so that performers can learn by watching each other react to the different conditions that will no doubt be presented by spect-actor personalities and responses. Additionally, throughout this phase of the rehearsal process, I would recommend that directors provide extensive notes at the end of each rehearsals. Notes to hone performer choices, of course, but also to generate material for an If/Then matrix that will be explained in the next section.

Session 11: Once performers in a particular scenario have had the opportunity to work with other actors as spect-actors, and to run their scenarios a number of times with different spect-actor personalities, I suggest the use of an If/Then matrix for actors to work on. In this exercise, actors are provided with a table (as below) that has specific conditions written on it; conditions that have emerged as warranting consideration from the director's observations of responses generated during the rehearsals with test spect-actors. For example:

Table 9: If/Then Rehearsal Matrix

If *[something the spect-actor says/does]*	*Then* *[how you would respond in character]*
If, for example, a spect-actor asks to use the restroom in the middle of a scenario	I will, for example, escort them to the restroom in character. Or (in the case of an authoritarian character) I will tell the spect-actor to wait.
If the spect-actor feels unwell in the middle of the experience and needs to leave	*The performer is asked to fill in the possible response they will give in such a situation*
If the spect-actor is really difficult and does not stick to the rules of the world	*I would also suggest the inclusion of blank cells under the "If" column, so that actors can add to the list of conditions that might*
If the spect-actor gets so into character that they get emotional	*arise in the presence of a spect-actor.*

Once actors have had the chance to think about and fill in their responses, I would encourage them to share their answers with each other—so that actors within a scenario have an understanding of what to expect from their peers in a particular type of situation.

Session 12: Once performers have been taken through the If/Then process above, the time might be right to invite "test" spect-actors from outside the performers' ensemble. These "test" spect-actors might include spect-actors who are either not part of the right target group for the *War;* or they could be spect-actors that want to experience the piece beforehand, because they are unable to participate in final experience. I would suggest that these rehearsals, for a few test spect-actors, continue to take place in the divided segments (i.e., not the experience in its entirety). And only once actors have tried particular sections with different test spect-actors over the course of a few rehearsals, does it become the right time to have "final rehearsals" of the whole experience for a set of spect-actors that are as close to the target demographic as possible. After having been through the various steps above—of testing scenarios first with actors from other scenarios being their spect-actors; of then rehearsing their scenarios with spect-actors who are from outside the performing ensemble—actors should be now be well positioned to take on the immersive experience in its entirety.

Session 13: After the performers have had a chance to rehearse the entire experience once, it might be the right time to return to a discussion based setting and to talk about each actor's experience in interacting with specific spect-actors through the various stages of rehearsal described above. Beginning with more anecdotal experiences in which actors freely discuss their memories of particularly poignant interactions, I would suggest that the director then leads the discussion into a conversation around what "good" and "bad" participation might mean for the actors: were there particular kinds of responses that all the "good" spect-actors came up with? What made these responses particular appealing to the performers? Did the same response from a different spect-actor—based on their age or gender or race—seem to impact the actors' judgment of that response? Do the actors have some anecdotes of "bad" or "less than ideal" responses that they received during the rehearsal process? How did they consequently deal with responses that were "bad" or "unexpected" or "less than ideal"? What is the "unexpected" and are we more open to surprising responses from people we know rather than people that we do not know? There are four larger concepts that should be targeted through an anecdotal sharing of spect-actor experiences from rehearsals: good participation; bad participation; unexpected actions; expected actions—and the various intersections between them, based on the specific identity markers embodied by the spect-actor in question.

Once some overarching ideas have been identified in relation to good/bad participation and expected/unexpected actions, I would suggest following the discussion up with activities that seek to address the notions of implicit/unconscious bias vis-à-vis the target spect-actor group. In the case of *War,* for example, since the target spect-actor group for the experience includes young people from the same community as the actors—students who are likely to be the kinds of future citizens who will travel to other parts of the world and attempt an engagement as outsiders—it is entirely possible that the actor/spect-actor groups will have preconceived notions about the other; notions that will affect how actors and spect-actors respond to each other in the world of the piece. For such a group then, I would use exercises as the ones below, in my final rehearsal sessions with actors around their potential implicit and unconscious biases.

Exercise #1: Print out pictures from the directory at the institution that the performance is set to take place in and give each actor a copy of all the student photos. Performers are asked to look at the photographs and pick three images: one of the images should be of someone that they consider to be a very good/good friend; the second image should be of someone they consider to be an acquaintance; the third image should be of another student from the school community who is a stranger to them. Then, the actor looks at each of the three pictures in front of them and in knowing what they do about each of these three individuals, write down a brief statement about the kind of spect-actor that they think this person will be. No qualifying words like "good" or "bad" should be used; rather actors should be encouraged to anticipate participation based on what they know/think they know/do not know about particular peers in that school community. Once the performers have had the chance to do this for all the three images that they have chosen, the ensemble comes back together and without mentioning names, individual actors are asked to discuss how they described the participation of very good friends versus acquaintances versus strangers. I would suggest that the director does not interrupt the process of sharing until all the performers have mentioned their particular notes; the director only takes notes during the initial sharing and considers (perceptively) the different ways in which expectations are framed by particular actors toward individuals that they have varying degrees of closeness with. For example, "Actor A, I noticed that you speak about your expectations from your friend in far more detail than you do about your acquaintance. Could this mean that you might actually be more critical of a person whose reactions you think you can anticipate? Especially if this person were to go outside the bounds of what you consider being "good" participation from them?" Questions that follow the sharing of statements are meant to be provocative; to encourage performers to think about the ways in which they might respond to people who participate in the performance; in, no way, to shame performers about biases that they will no doubt hold. While this process is particularly relevant to a situation like *War,* where the target spect-actor and performer group are from a closed community in which many members are likely to know each other, it can't be ruled out in larger communities either.... In the latter case though, instead of using photographs from a school directory, I would suggest asking the performers to bring in photographs of friends, acquaintances, and strangers from the local population, especially those who are likely to come to the performance.

Exercise #2: Another exercise, based on the student composition of the school, would be to create a questionnaire around "markers" that seem to be of specific importance to the social dynamics within that setting. So, for instance, for the demographic in the College I teach at in New Mexico, that is composed of 16 to 19 year olds from over 80 countries, I would start designing questions by considering the main demarcations of inclusion/exclusion within the context of the College environment: the often, problematic, racial groupings that exist i.e., the Caucasian kids from North America and Western Europe generally sticking together; with the Africans/Latin Americans forming groups with individuals from their specific regions. These group formations are not malicious and most often, seem to be based on the quest for a cultural resonance that becomes necessary at an international residential school. And yet, they occur. And these groups' existence becomes a potentially problematic marker of how sameness and difference are experienced at the College.

Like race, another (unconscious) grouping factor at the College seems to be the division of the student body based on their preference for social activities—the "party goers" and those who prefer less party-like social situations—which, causes fault lines (generally) along lines of socio-economic backgrounds (can you afford to pitch in with the costs?), religion (does your religious practice allow you to be comfortable around those who are engaging with stimulants/behaviors that might run contrary to what you believe in?), and personality (do you like being around large groups of people?).

With such markers identified, in a rehearsal session that occurs closer to the date of the final performance, I would split the actors into pairs and ask them to answer the questions/statements in the questionnaire below:

In pairs, and using the scale below, please rate each of the statements that follow (each actor should fill out one of these forms).

There are no wrong answers so please be honest!

1	2	3	4	5
Very Comfortable	*Comfortable*	*Neutral*	*Uncomfortable*	*Very Uncomfortable*

Section A:

(i) _____ *You go to dinner in the Cafeteria and find yourself sitting at a table with all Spanish speakers*

(ii) _____ *You go to dinner in the Cafeteria and find yourself sitting at a table with all Japanese speakers*

(iii) _____ *You go to dinner in the Cafeteria and find yourself sitting at a table with all English speakers*

(iv) _____ *You go to dinner in the Cafeteria and find yourself sitting at a meeting that has already started about Queer Rights on campus*

(v) _____ *You go to dinner in the Cafeteria and find yourself sitting at a table with people talking about a science experiment*

Section B:

(i) _____ *Your friend takes you to a loud party which has lots of people drinking*

(ii) _____ *You friend takes you to a book reading at a local book store*

(iii) _____ *Your friend takes you to a philosophy lecture*

(iv) _____ *Your friend takes you to drink coffee on a Friday night*

(v) _____ *Your friends organize a dinner at home as your weekend party plans*

Section C:

(i) _____ *Your character in the play has to interact with someone who you know to be a practicing Christian, to whom what you say will be offensive*

(ii) _____ *Your character in the play has to interact with someone who you know to be practicing Muslim, to whom what you say will be offensive*

(iii) _____ *Your character in the play has to interact with someone who you know to be an atheist*

(iv) _____ *Your character in the play has to interact with someone who you know to be homophobic in real life*

(v) _____ *Your character in the play has to interact with someone who you know to be occasionally racist in real life*

Add the Points

_____ *Section A*

_____ *Section B*

_____ *Section C*

Total: _____

Student-performers, in their pairs, would discuss their overall scores in each section but without revealing specific ways in which they rated particular statements. In this way, it is hoped that performers will maintain some comfort in their anonymity and thus be honest in presenting ideas to their partners. After each pair has had some time to discuss their responses, the actors come back in a larger group and the director facilitates a discussion where observations are made about any common trends that might be observed across the groups. More importantly, once the common trends/differences are identified, it is important to consider how any potentially implicit biases that might have been expressed in the exercise might be made obvious and deal with during the theatrical experience itself. What if the responses show no trends or patterns?

Remember, the goal with these exercises around bias is not to shame individual performers and/or to talk about prejudice in an abstract context. Rather, the specific aim to speak to the ways in which the actors' (un) conscious and implicit/explicit performances of bias might feed into the performance itself. As a result even if actors are not entirely honest in how they respond within the framework of the abovementioned exercises, the director should not be discouraged! After all, the point is to get the actor—on an individual level—to think about the biases they might hold. Whether or not they are able/willing to articulate those prejudices in the face of other performers/the director.

With this bias training being the final step in the rehearsal process, I would say that the actors are ready to perform for their final spect-actor group and to carry out the piece itself.

The abovementioned exercises and sessions when rehearsing for an immersive piece, as mentioned earlier, are ideas that I have come upon through a trial and error process in different immersive theater experiments. The latest in the series of these experiments (Dinesh, 2018) explored the impact of spaces and relationships on affects derived from immersive theater, ultimately leading to the creation of implicit bias exercises that might need to be part of an immersive theater rehearsal process. It was this experiment that also led to my understanding that actors' pre-existing relationships/lack thereof, with spaces/spect-actors, do intersect with the judgments that are made in situ, during the performance in question (Dinesh, 2018). And drawing from these empirical findings I would strongly suggest that some form of implicit bias contemplation is incorporated within the training process for immersive pieces like *War, Detention,* and *Immigration*—especially with an applied theater framework that seeks to promote learning for all involved in the theatrical process.

That said, like everything else in this book, the proposals that I make for the rehearsal process are *not* to be seen as formulaic. Rather, the various sessions and exercises that have proposed earlier in this Interlude can/should be adapted based on two factors: the logistics that influence the duration of the larger rehearsal schedule and its smaller components; the particular requirements of a group of target spect-actors/actors vis-à-vis their past experience with theater. For instance, the sessions articulated above could just as well be carried out over a six-week period with an hour-long rehearsal per scenario/segment/section each week, as they could over shorter and/or longer periods of time. Maintaining this kind of adaptability and flexibility in the rehearsal process, I have come to see, is integral in most applied theater contexts where schedules have to shift in response to realities on the ground.

For an Immersive Theater Playwright

Re-Thinking the Theatrical Event

Having spent much time discussing global strategies for directors—of rehearsal designs that might be useful even outside the scope of *Detention, War,* and *Immigration*—the remainder of this Interlude speaks more to playwrights. As such, this Interlude now moves onto a discussion about particular element(s) of "traditional" playwriting that need to shift when writing immersive theater scripts for applied theater contexts. As the reader will recall, the process of creating and writing *Detention* got me thinking about the differing roles for text in more realistic versus more immersive theaters—the former (generally) centralizing the role of text in dialogue generation; the latter in scenario creation. In a similar vein of identifying congruencies and divergences, the process of scripting *War* catalyzed me to look at these scripts' proclivity for also including articulations of processes that extend before and after the boundaries of the central theatrical experience itself. By this, I mean the preparatory workshops that have been crafted for spect-actors in *Detention* and *War.* I also mean the post-performance EVOLUTIONs of SCENARIOs, that function as post-facto events that enable spect-actors to further their experience in *War.* Why did it seem "natural" to include pre- and post-performance sessions as part of the scripting process for *Detention, and War* (and, subsequently, *Immigration*)? Just as the presence/absence of dialogue in immersive texts might serve to highlight the decentralization of director and/or playwright's roles, what does the inclusion of events that occur before/after the central theatrical experience in immersive theater texts tell us about the scripting needs for such aesthetics in applied theater contexts?

Generally speaking, the concept of a preparatory session and/or a post-event debrief is not uncommon: the reader will have seen the inclusion of these categories in many of the examples that were presented in the Introduction. However, while these forums might not be uncommon in other disciplines' use of immersive strategies, the approaches used by *Detention, War,* and *Immigration* to define what happens before and after the central theatrical event are elements that I consider to be quite unique in the realm of scripting drama. For instance, when speaking to what does exist vis-à-vis pre- and post-performance events in the theater world, we see how the Theater of the Oppressed and some other forms of socially oriented interactive drama underscore the use of theater games as exercises as a means to both "warm up" spect-actors and to use theater as a process-based methodology that serves particular political and/or psychological aims. In Forum Theater, for example, where spect-actors are asked to become spect-actors who intervene in the scenario being presented on stage, it is not uncommon for the Joker (the facilitator) to do a few simple exercises with the spect-actors to introduce the modus operandi of interaction in that form. Similarly, like Theater of the Oppressed, there are other theatrical movements—initiatives that fall within the broad realm of Theater in Education, for instance—that often include talkback/debrief sessions as a forum between actors, facilitators, and spect-actors, which takes place (usually) right after the central performance event.

However, the kind of preparatory and debrief work that is scripted in both *Detention* and *War* respectively, is different from these existing examples in two ways. First, the games and exercises that are used in efforts like Forum Theater to warm up spect-actors, are the kinds of activities that can be done en masse—with a large number of spect-actors. Theater of the Oppressed events are not particularly known to restrict the number of people who attend an event (except, maybe, in the context of workshops). And as a result, "call and response" exercises and facilitated interaction with the performance are the kinds of preparation strategies that are used. This is to say that the preparatory activities that are chosen need to be ones those that can be facilitated, regardless of the number of people in the spect-actor group. In contrast with this strategy, within the scripts in this book, the preparatory work is far more small-scale; I would go so far as to say that the preparatory work is personal; intimate, even. Intimate because the goal of these "before" processes is not only to enable the spect-actor to understand the rules of the immersive world. Rather, the objective with these spaces is also about inviting the spect-actor to develop their own character within the performance's world. An ideal example being the way in which *Detention* uses the preparatory session for spect-actors to become their own kind of detention center educator and design their lesson plans. In addition to this focus on each unique individual, what I believe to be unique in the pre-performance preparatory work in this book is the way in which they occur "in world." This is to say that the pre/post-performance events in *Detention, War,* and *Immigration* take place within the world of the central theatrical event. And quite unlike the talk back discussions that are common in applied theater environments—where the central performance ends, the fourth wall (if it exists) is shattered, and where the actors engage with spect-actor "out of world"—the debriefs and preparations in my immersive theater scripts intentionally occur within the frames of the imagined world that is created in the central performance event itself.

The existence of these scripted pre/post-performance "in world" forums in *Detention, War,* and *Immigration* is not accidental; I consider their inclusion to be an aesthetic, ethical, and pedagogical choice. That said, it is important to highlight that this particular choice also serves to distinguish this book's approach to immersive theater from other immersive environments that are not particular preoccupied with what is being "learned" as a result of the performance, as they are with what might be experienced by spect-actors "in the moment." The inclusion of these scripted pre/post-sections in *Detention, War,* and *Immigration* makes these texts unlike other immersive aesthetics that thrive in the grayness of artistic ethics, and embody an explicit desire to discomfit spect-actors—intentionally keeping their spect-actors under-prepared and vulnerable, in terms of those individuals' engagement within that theatrical world. The inclusion of events that extend beyond the central theatrical event in the immersive scripts in this book, therefore, embodies the pieces' focus on the creation of learning opportunities, for performers and spect-actors alike, about issues surrounding youth detention, war, and/or immigration. Understanding that people learn best with an intermediate amount of novelty—something that I have discussed extensively in past work (Dinesh, 2016a)—the preparatory sessions seek to balance the intense novelty of form and content with a provision of "tools" to decode that novel environment.

In addition to the pedagogical principles that guide my desire to prioritize the scripting of the pre- and post-components to the central theatrical events in this book, these strategies are also used to foster more opportunities for ethical representation. In this approach spect-actors are not asked to learn by simplistically and vicariously placing themselves in the shoes of an Other; no. Rather, in explicitly scripting pre-performance processes for the spect-actor in *Detention* to design their lesson plans, for example, I hope to stimulate a more careful and reflective process of blurring lines between the spect-actor's Self and their character's Other. Similarly, in the choice to invite spect-actors to return to *War* on multiple occasions following the central theatrical event, and in the decision to create post-performance opportunities in which evolutions might be witnessed, I hope to demonstrate a more layered picture. In this more complex image, being an outsider is not problematized and critiqued in simplistic binaries. Rather, being an outsider is presented as a process; a process that could have short, medium, and/or long-term ripple effects; except, of course, when the presence of the outsider does nothing at all. The "post" component to *War*, therefore, seek to add ethical textures to the pedagogical base of the piece.

Although pedagogical and ethical questions were central to my scripting decisions vis-à-vis the pre/post-performance sessions, the decision to include these processes as part of the script were also made because of the aesthetic enhancement that they provide to the texts. The choice to design those forums as being "in world," and the choice to see them as integral extensions of the theatrical event rather than ornamental add-ons, makes the inclusion of what comes before and after the central performance a part of the script's aesthetic core. In one way, this decision is aesthetic because it immediately changes the visual form that the written, dramatic text takes—a reframing of text that makes an immersive theater script "look" different, on the page, than its more realistic counterparts. The decision is also aesthetic because scripting these forums as part of the dramatic event makes it something that needs to be carefully rehearsed, designed, and performed; rather than being additions that are made to the central event, not requiring the same kind of artistic rigor as the performance itself. The scripting of forums that precede and follow the central theatrical event, therefore, and the inclusion of these components within the dramatic texts themselves, are important ideas for the immersive theater playwright to consider when seeking to script works that have pedagogical and social applications.

I stress the pedagogical and social applications since, if an immersive theater playwright were to be less concerned about the pedagogical/social trace of the piece and were more focused on the aesthetic experience that is constrained during that central event itself, well, this writer might not need to consider the pre/post-forums with as much attention. In summary therefore, the main points from the discussion above might be summarized as follows (see Table 10 below). The reader will notice that I make sure to craft the information in the table below as proposals rather than "facts" because I do not want to create false distinctions between different aesthetics and genres. Rather, I want to present possibilities that are fluid, based on the particular "mixing and matching" of objectives that any unique theater practitioner might undertake.

Table 10: Impacts of Focus on Pre/Post-Performance Events

Focus of the theatrical experience	*Considerations vis-à-vis what comes before/after the central theatrical event*
Focus on the spect-actors' experience as it occurs during the central theatrical event. This central event could either be a script-based performance that occurs in the proscenium; or an interactive performance where audience members speak from their seats in an auditorium; or immersive aesthetics where extreme novelty is desired and thus, where audience discomfort/vulnerability is actually part of the work's intentionality. With such a focus, even though these performances might have social and/or political themes/objectives, the focus is on what is learned *within* the contained theatrical performance.	In such performances, there is less likely to be a need to script pre- or post-performance sessions that bookend the central event. The scripts of such performances then, when they exist, will *not* contain segments/sections that explain what might take place, for spect-actors, before/after the event in question.

Focus of the theatrical experience	Considerations vis-à-vis what comes before/after the central theatrical event
Concerned with outcomes, however intangible, these performances have a focus on creating particular kinds of "impact"—thus necessitating some consideration of what comes before/after the central event. The exact nature of the content/structure of these sessions will, of course, depend on the specific outcomes desired by that piece; the particular aesthetic that the performance will use. Immersive pieces like *War*, which assign characters to spect-actors, have very different needs from other kinds of interactive/non-interactive counterparts.	If the pre/post-performance forums happen "out of world" i.e., where the theatrical environment created in the central event does *not* need to be maintained, the scripting of such instances are likely to be less extensive and more likely to be summaries of what needs to happen. If the pre/post-forums are to be "in world," then these processes will also need to be visibly present during the script writing process.
There are of course those performance events that place much of their focus on what happens outside a central performance event. Consider Augusto Boal's (2002) *Games for Actors and non–Actors*, for example, where the whole point is the process of exploration and creation that takes place in lieu of what might be considered a theatrical performance. Also consider the use of theater as a form of therapy, for instance, where what happens *after* the use of the theatrical form is where the potential of the effort lies.	In such efforts, of course, what is more extensively scripted is what happens in the "before"—where the "process" is the product and in so being, changes the position of text in the process of scriptwriting. Whereas text in proscenium and Realism-inspired works centralize text as dialogue, and text in immersive aesthetics (as in this book) centralize text as scenario creation, text in such theater work might be seen as centralizing the written word as activity description. Activity in this instance being different from scenario in that there is no "out of world" setting, even in the central event. The spect-actors are rooted in their "real world" identities, using theater-based exercises and activities toward particular ends.

The table above, much like the scales that were proposed in the Interlude following *Detention*, is not about being prescriptive vis-à-vis playwriting. Rather, these articulations are strategies that an immersive playwright might want to consider as part of their creative process. Just as the strategies surrounding context-specific adaptation and rehearsal design have been presented to assist the immersive theater director, the *scale of immersion—*

importance of dialogue and the *focus of the theatrical event—importance of pre- and post-performance forums* matrices are to be of particular use to the immersive theater playwright. Going into the process of writing *Immigration* therefore, I was hoping to identify two more overarching realms of practice to offer the reader of this book: a global strategy that would be useful to directors seeking to stage *Detention, War, Immigration* or other works like them; a conceptual framing that would be pertinent for writers seeking to script immersive works. Let's move on, then, to *Immigration*.

Immigration

PRELUDE

Immigration has been a part of my life since I was 16 years old, when I was getting ready to leave India to study in the United States. "Make sure you wear traditional Indian clothes and a *bindi*[1] and braid your hair when you go to the interview," someone said to me; "also, you know, put the *bhasmam*[2] on your forehead like you were just at the temple. That way, when the U.S. immigration official looks at you and sees you in all this traditionally Indian stuff, they won't be worried that you'll become an immigrant. Because you'll look like you won't fit in." Incredibly surprised at this advice, but given that this was my first time applying for a U.S. visa—well, any visa—I followed that person's advice to the letter. I went to my visa interview in a gray *salwar kameez*,[3] with a braid that was heavily dosed with coconut oil, wearing a *bindi* that had a *bhasmam* line above it. I stood in my first visa interview line ever— trying to look "demure"; like I wouldn't "fit in" in the U.S.; I had no idea what I was doing. Balancing heavy folders full of paperwork both from the under- graduate institution sponsoring my admission and from my father's account- ant; paperwork that would hopefully would assure the official that I wasn't out to drain the U.S. economy, I watched as the young woman in front of me—around my age, also looking to go to the U.S. to study—had her visa denied. "But sir, look at this," she said pointing to the mountains of paperwork she had with her. But the immigration official shook his head and she knew her time was up. No visa. No college in the U.S. She walked away from the visa counter crying. She was dressed exactly like me. I think she'd been given the same advice as me.... For me though, my first visa process was anti- climactic. All my efforts at wearing the "right" kind of clothing, and embody- ing the "right" kind of attitude, seemed to be worthless because the U.S. offi- cial barely looked at me. My interview took all of two minutes. I was asked two questions. There were some brief glances at the paperwork. And I had my visa. I was going be a student in the U-S-of A.

Since that first visa interview, I have become incredibly aware of the downsides to having an Indian passport. I have attended countless visa interviews in the intervening years; been questioned by immigration officials at various borders; been nervous—multiple times—about whether or not a moody official at a desk somewhere, would decide (not) to let me into a country: to continue my studies; to attend a conference; to visit family. While I have been quite lucky thus far, in that I have had only one unsuccessful visa application that continues to haunt my subsequent applications to that country, I never seem to get less nervous about applying for that piece of paper. Every single time, I am nervous. Even after I get a visa, I am nervous that the officer at the port of entry might not let me in … what if they misunderstand something I say? What if they don't like the look on my face? I still get nervous every time I apply for a visa because of the complete lack of power that I have in influencing what I get to do with a particular period in my life. In fact, as I write this book, I am still embroiled in an immigration process: a series of additional steps in a process that has already taken a year of my life; a process that will (hopefully) re-validate and re-authenticate my presence in a country from which my legally wedded spouse hails.

So, although I have immense amounts of privilege and luck on my side— in my fluency in English; in my family's and my own socio-economic background; in my access to educational opportunities; in my never having been a refugee, or an asylum seeker, or an immigrant who does not have enough resources to go through a multitude of expensive visa procedures—immigration, in one form or another, has consumed nearly the last two decades of my life. When I see pictures or read the news about the "current" global refugee crises then—I place current in quotation marks since this particular crisis has been current for a while now—when I read about changes being made to U.S. immigration policy, when I hear of travel bans that are being instituted against people from particular parts of the world, when I hear about yet another instance of someone being told to "go back to where you came from," it's all too personal. I am all too aware that under the right/wrong circumstances, with an official/person who is in the right/wrong mood, my papers could be denied. Or accepted. I could be allowed to stay. I could be deported. I could be told to "go back to where I came from." And life, as I know it at this moment, could very well fall apart.

I say all this because *Immigration* is personal to me in a way that *War* and *Detention* can never be. I've never lived through war myself; the few instances in which I've been caught in war-like situations, I have had the choice and the resources to leave that setting. I have taught in detention centers but unlike the educators that I focus on in the script in this book, my work in that context is entirely voluntary and something that I could stop doing should the experience ever become too uncomfortable or "too much" in any way. *Immigration*, though, stems from a personal place, and given both the choices and serendipitous events that have occurred in the last decade, I am, once again, an immigrant. And this time, there is less choice for me to leave that identity behind. Much of what I draw from in the following script therefore, stems from my own lived experience; a lived experience that is nuanced, simultaneously, by what is happening in the world at this point in time.

Conceptualizing Immigration

I have conducted a few different immersive experiments around the theme of immigration before writing this script—particularly immigration vis-à-vis asylum seeking (Dinesh, 2016b; Dinesh, 2018). And in each of these prior attempts, I have structured the immersive experience such that the spect-actor places themselves in the shoes of the asylum-seeker-Other. Spect-actors are given particular profiles as refugees and asylum seekers, having to undergo interviews with actors playing lawyers and officials who ultimately decide the fate of that spect-actor. While there are benefits and challenges that arose because of the choice to place spect-actors in the shoes of an asylum seeking Other in those particular initiatives, in *Immigration* though, given my desire to consider the "gray zones" of the larger thematic direction of each text, I decided that my focus should lie elsewhere. An elsewhere that was influenced by Hannah Arendt's (1963) *Eichmann in Jerusalem*, which speaks to the "banality" that underlies "evil"; the simple-mindedness that often surrounds actions, which when viewed in their totality, could result in a situation of massive destruction and chaos.

In this particular characterization of the "gray zone," the individual who is carrying out ordinary tasks that they are hired to do, fails to see (or chooses not to see) the ways in which their actions might be implicated within an immensely problematic system of oppression, injustice, and violence. In Eichmann's case, what is highlighted is his being a "banal" individual whose only "banal" task was to organize transport—transport that would take people to face certain deaths in Nazi Germany's concentration camps. In organizing the transport, in engaging with the mundane logistical aspects of taking a particular number of people from one specific area to another, Arendt's writing might be said to characterize Eichmann as someone who exists without a recognition of his actions' import; as someone who was not (chose not to be) conscious about the extent of his complicity within the larger narrative of the Holocaust. In this complicity then, people like Eichmann might be said to occupy a gray area where the choice to perform their duties with a larger system of oppression are hard (for some) to place on the scale of victimhood and perpetration. After all, if Eichmann had refused to do his job, how could he have supported himself and those who might have been dependent on him? If Eichmann had refused to do his job, might his life have been in danger? Was he complicit or did he simply not have a choice? It's questions like these that make Eichmann's experiences—and those like his— difficult to classify and place on a range of victim/perpetrator experiences. In *Immigration,* therefore, I knew that I did not want the spect-actor to be an all-powerful officer or the powerless immigrant; I wanted them to become someone "like" Eichmann.

Social Context

So, who might be an Eichmann-equivalent in today's immigration systems? Who are the "banal" individuals that become part of unjust structures—not only in the U.S., though recent changes to this country's policies have certainly led to it epitomizing an immigration system that is perilous? Who are those who are so caught up in the banalities of what they are doing, that they are/choose to be unaware of the larger oppressions and injustices that they have become complicit within? After much consideration, I contemplated the idea that spect-actors to *Immigration* might be asked to become consular officers in an overseas immigration office for an unnamed country—officers who would assess paper-based applications and in-person immigration applicants (played by actors), and decide whether or not those individuals would be accepted into the officer's country. But after this initial idea on how to frame spect-actor participation, I realized that this type of Other would not be "gray" enough ... that it was not shadowy enough to contain parallels with the Eichmann-like experience that I wanted to recreate. After all, if actors got the opportunity to actually see and interact with the people whose applications they rejected and/or accepted, wouldn't the actors' responses be easier to predict? Wouldn't it be more likely for spect-actors as immigration offices to accept applications when they have the actor-immigrant sitting in front of them? So, what if the spect-actors never got to see the applicant? ... What if the spect-actors to *Immigration* did not visibly have the power to accept or deny an application but to only make a "suggestion," thus transferring responsibility for that decision onto the person in the context who has more power? Would these additional choices make the experience murkier? More morally and ethically ambiguous? More "real," somehow?

As a result of these considerations, the initial idea had morphed and instead of crafting roles for spect-actors wherein they would become consular officers that interacted directly with immigration applicants and make decisions about the applications' acceptance or denial, I decided to craft the spect-actor roles slightly differently. The spect-actors, I decided, might better be crafted as officials who do an initial "vetting" of visa applications (never in person, though; they only evaluate paper-based applications) and make recommendations for those particular applications to be accepted or denied to a more powerful character within the world of *Immigration*. This is to say that these particular officers—whether or not such "vetters" actually exist in real immigration scenarios—would assess visa applications in the first instance and after attempting to validate the "authenticity," or lack thereof, of the application in question, make recommendations to a higher authority: a higher authority, played by a performer, who would then make the final decision on the application. I say that I am unsure about whether or not these "vetters" exist in real-world immigration officers because I have not encountered explicitly articulated positions such as these in my research. However, in the context of *Immigration*, I thought it important that the spect-actor *not* have a say in the final decision that is made about the applications themselves, so as to heighten the spect-actors' being one more step removed from a direct complicity within the given scenario.

I consider these kinds of officers to be the Eichmanns in the immigration world because, while they are simply cogs in the wheels of a country's immigration policies and systems, these officers—in their banal actions of suggesting "acceptance" and "denial" have the power to tear a person's life asunder. Yes, these officers are simply implementing what they have been told to do: you know, the officials who started turning people away as soon as the current president's travel ban emerged, only to immediately allow those same people back in again when, a day later, the ban was stayed by a court. These are the Eichmanns of the immigration world, to me, because they do what they are told to do—without (it seems) a consciousness of how their individual decisions become part of a larger system that discriminates and oppresses. And even if there is a consciousness amongst some of these officers, as I'm sure there must be, I would still consider their narratives as being parallel to those of Eichmann because such individuals are unable/unwilling to take individual stands against a system that they know is unjust. The current injustices surrounding immigration might not have reached the severity of the Holocaust—depending on whom you are speaking with, of course—but what if every single border officer at every single U.S. airport had refused to implement the travel ban on the day that it was announced? What if there had been collective dissent that was composed of various individuals' acts of agency against an executive order that, at the very least in its suddenness, was completely unjust? What is it that makes so many people, despite lessons from history, perpetuate complicit behavior? I do not exclude myself from this critique, of course; there are many ways in which I consciously choose (not) to contribute to larger structures of inequality and oppression. I am simply not highlighting my banal ways of perpetuating oppression because of the immigration setting that frames the following script.

Characterization

That said, despite my scathing critique of mid-level immigration officials' (lack of) actions, I cannot simply demonize these officers and make them out to be a spineless mass. Like any other gray zone, I must consider the dimensions to these individuals' experiences precisely because while they might easily be considered as perpetrators in one sense, some of them might very well be victims in their own right—to their own socio-economic circumstances; to their own familial obligations; to their own needs and desires; to blind nationalism; to ignorance. Since, to me, a gray zone is precisely a space in which it becomes harder to place blame and shame; *Immigration* tries to ensure that spect-actors get a glimpse into the multi-dimensional factors that make mid-level immigration officials less likely to dissent when enmeshed in a system that seems unfair and unjust. Yes, some of these officers might be individuals who get off on a power trip, and others may be entirely unconscious of the larger ramifications of their actions. But what about the few/many who might be aware of the contentious nature of the jobs but feel, for whatever reason, that they do not have a choice but to continue to do what they do? At what point does that individual officer's personal context begin to influence our critique of their (in)action—as witnesses and participants—within a corroded system?

In addition to the officials' characterization, I was also keen to include gray zone narratives within the stories of the potential immigrants—whose narratives would be showcased in the paper-based applications that the spect-actors have to evaluate and vet. By this I mean that I did not want all the immigrants in *Immigration* to be defined as characters who are occupying extreme circumstances. I did not want all the immigrant roles to be crafted as refugees or asylum seekers, or immigrants who are seeking to escape a particularly horrific fate in their home country. I wanted to ensure that there would also be the voices of more privileged immigrants, immigrants who have more of a choice in their departure. I consider this choice to add a "gray zone" component because, implicitly, I hoped that an unexpected, non-stereotypical characterization of potential immigrants would force spect-actor-officers to content with the complexities within their own judgment. Are you, the spect-actor, likely to suggest the approval of an immigrant's application based on the extremity of their story? Or are you, the spect-actor-officer, able to judge each individual applicant based on the parameters of their own story, not looking for their narrative to fit your expectations of what an immigrant experience must look like?

Framework

With these characterization choices in mind, I decided that the world of *Immigration* would take place in a context-unspecific consular office, where actor-immigrants (through paper-based applications) would apply for visas to go to an unnamed country. In this setting, spect-actors would step into the roles of low or mid-level officers who vet immigration applications and make suggestions to a more high-powered official (played by an actor) about whether or not particular actor-immigrants should be provided with the necessary visas to enter their country. The spect-actor-officers would not ever meet the applicants in person; they would only see affected applicants leave the office of the higher ranked official: perhaps in tears; in anger; reactions that—if paid attention to—would inform the spect-actors about the impact of their actions.

So, in order to help support the creation of this environment, in addition to the actors playing immigrants/visa applicants, what other performer roles would need to be crafted? Of course, I knew that I would have to design a particular kind of "powerful" figure; a "boss" or "leader" who would effectively embody the consequences that could arise for the spect-actor-visa officers if they were to step outside the bounds of their roles and deliberately try to subvert the experience by simply suggesting acceptance for every single person that they encountered as an immigrant. This would be the leader/boss who also enacted the consequences of the spect-actor-officers' suggestions on the bodies of the actors playing the immigrants. So, to allow this powerful figure to better exert their authority, could there be a limit on the number of visa applications that spect-actor-officials could suggest accepting—a limit that could *not* be exceeded both at collective and individual levels? This is to say, could the spect-actor group—as a whole—be directed to *not* suggest acceptance of more than 20 percent of the total number of applications that are vetted, with individual visa officers not being allowed to suggest acceptance for more than 2 percent of the cases assigned to them? What if, in addition to this limit, spect-actor-visa officers were given monetary motivations—of being paid $50 at the end of the day if they came in at or under their quota; or if their assessments of acceptance/denial fit with the higher ranked official's decision? What if spect-actors could be "fired" (sent out of the experience) if they did not adhere to the rules, and accepted more/less people than they were directed to? What if spect-actor-visa officials were publically held accountable for their actions, being shamed or praised in front of their peers for their perceived successes and failures? Would such strategies allow spect-actors to truly engage in the gray zone where they both recognize the power that they have, within the context of being simultaneously powerless? And finally, how much time would the spect-actors need in order:

- To experience the ways in which their distance from the bodies of the applicants might alleviate them of feelings of responsibility?
- To experience the shirking of their individual accountability, given the "suggestive" rather than decisive qualities to their occupations?
- To experience the effect that an individual's personal circumstances could have on their complicity within oppressive structures?
- To experience some of their own implicit biases in what makes for a "good" immigrant story?

How much time would spect-actors need in the world of *Immigration?*

Duration

The reader will have noticed different approaches to duration in *War* and *Detention.* With the former, time was shaped in response to the kind of debrief events that were created after the central performance event, i.e., what is important in the experience of *War* is not how long the first theatrical immersion lasts. But rather, what is more important to the objectives of the piece is how the different follow up sessions will manifest *after* that first immersion. This is to say that the structure of the piece makes the duration of the project, in its entirety, a point of consideration; rather than the duration of the central immersive theatrical event alone. However, while *War* shapes time based on events that also lay outside the scope of the central theatrical immersion, in *Detention* my decisions around time were approached differently.

In *Detention,* the duration of the piece was decided based on how much time spect-actors might need to get into their particular roles as educators in a detention center context. The twenty-nine-hour suggested time frame was also based on considering how embodied experiences of educators' institutionalization might be best created; on thinking about when how/when spect-actors might begin to form relationships with actor-inmate-students that could then be broken because of a detention center's floating population; on deciding to include a consideration of these educators' personal lives within the frame of the piece. Furthermore, *Detention* was scripted in sections: sections that could function as independent chunks and/or as interwoven segments. Given these different approaches to time, it might be clear to the reader that my decisions surrounding the duration needed for each of the pieces in this book are based solely on the objectives of the particular piece in question; nothing more, nothing less.

With *Immigration* too, then, my initial thinking around the duration of the piece was similar to what preceded *Detention:* if one of the objectives of this script is to get spect-actors to explore the four qualities articulated above, how much time would be needed to increase the chances of such an affective experience occurring for spect-actors? Should it be the duration of a regular workday (9 a.m. to 5 p.m.), for example, where the world of *Immigration* could be run as a day at the office? Or is less time sufficient for *Immigration*, since spect-actors might well "get" the premise just after an hour of the experience? Or, in the spirit of ensuring spect-actors' potential consequence on the world of *Immigration*, would it better to end the experience when the number of visa applicants' quota is reached—leaving the duration in the hands of spect-actors' actions? Or, unlike *War* and *Detention,* could the duration of *Immigration* be entirely flexible; with different options being articulated in the script itself? What would be the impact of this flexibility and is this adaptable duration "authentic" to the experience that is trying to be replicated? Unlike the other two texts, I did not go into *Immigration* with a specific duration in mind—instead, I decided to let the writing process lead me to a decision, when the time presented itself.

Target Actor and Spect-Actor Group

In keeping with this notion of "flexibility," when thinking about the right target demographic of spect-actors and actors for this particular experience of *Immigration,* I did not think that there need to be restrictions placed on the lived experience of the performers. For the target spect-actor group, however, I decided that there might be *two* possible target spect-actor groups most applicable for *Immigration.* The first target group that I considered as being particularly relevant is one that is composed of individuals who have never had an experience of immigration themselves. So, the ideal spect-actor—in the context of the U.S., for instance—would be someone who has never traveled outside the U.S.; better still, someone who has never/is likely to never meet an immigrant in the course of their lives. The second target spect-actor group that I consider as being appropriate for this experience of *Immigration* is one that is composed of individuals who consider themselves "immigration activists," and are active, loud critics of the immigration machinery. In a more and more polarized debate climate about immigration in different parts of the world, I have often found knee-jerk critiques to be problematic in their own right. Do such opponents of policy (like myself in some occasions), when they ask immigration officials to dissent and to protest, understand the real-world implications for those individuals? In demonizing the immigration machinery and those who are a part of it—is the knee-jerk activist problematically dehumanizing the very individuals whose humanity they need to catalyze, to change the system? Placing spect-actors from this target group into the shoes of immigration officers, I hope, will invite them to consider less polarized generalizations about what exactly characterizes the people who are part of various nation states' immigration policies and structures.

That said, although the script of *Immigration* makes particular recommendations for the two different target spect-actor groups mentioned above, more so than *War* or *Detention,* this particular piece might be most applicable to any spect-actor group. *Detention* requires the creation of lesson plans, which an existing educator would be much better positioned to take on; *War* requires multiple debrief situations—leading to a self-contained group of actors and spect-actors (like members from a school community) being more appropriate; *Immigration* does not require the same kind of shared experience or prior knowledge from its target spect-actor group. With any target group, however, what I also want to add to the experience of *Immigration* is something—an avenue—that the spect-actors might choose if indeed they decide, as visa officers, to dissent against the system.

So, if an individual spect-actor is deemed to be violating the quota rules by the actor wielding the power in the situation, and if this spect-actor was thus "fired" from *Immigration,* then what? Wouldn't the message be inherently fatalistic if *Immigration* were to kick people out from the experience for dissenting, without some consideration of what might happen after? Wouldn't such an approach basically tell people *not* to dissent? Did I really want to leave spect-actors with that particular outcome? It was clear to me in considering these questions that I wanted to add something to the experience—for those who did decide to dissent—so that there would be a further reflection about what comes after. What are the implications of protest? What are the consequences of choosing the less complicit path?

What if, when a spect-actor-visa officer gets "fired" from the experience, and steps outside the immigration office building, they encounter a group of activists who are trying to get their government to change that nation's immigration policies? What if, then, the spect-actor was given an option to join a movement to activate against the situation that made them leave the larger, oppressive system in the first place? Would the spect-actor's decision to join that protest, or not, lead to another ethical choice? The spect-actor's decision then, would not just be about joining the protest or not; but about drawing a parallel between that "simple" decision and the "real-world" decisions that immigration officers would have to face if they in fact decided to leave their jobs and oppose what they deem to be unjust policy making.

This kind of script, therefore, where spect-actors are given avenues to "break the rules" and to then make another decision about how they will continue that dissent into subsequent scenarios, might enable the design of creative pre/post-performance sessions that help draw in spect-actors from across diverse groups. For example, pre-performance preparation for *Immigration* could involve prior information about the visa officer's character being sent to spect-actors a few days before the performance. In so doing, when the spect-actor arrives at the world of *Immigration,* they are arriving at the "office" where they will be briefed on their jobs for the day.

Unlike the pre-performance sessions that were designed for *War* and *Detention,* I see this relatively simple approach for *Immigration* as being part of what might make it applicable for a wide target spect-actor group. Unlike this simplification of the pre-performance process, however, the question of a post-performance debrief is a little more complicated in this situation since, unlike *War* and *Detention,* the pedagogical goal with *Immigration* is a little more nebulous. In *War,* as the reader might recall, the longer term objective is to have students who are likely to volunteer in Other contexts to become aware of the ethics of their actions. *War,* I hope, will help these young people think about the kind of outsider that they will become with more care. Similarly, with *Detention's* affective goal of increasing partnerships between better-resourced institutions and detention center schools in the same geographical context, it seemed to make sense that spect-actors would leave with information about a detention center closest to them. With these two scripts then, the particular gray zones that spect-actors step into are ones in which the target spect-actor group and the structure of the piece allow for some kind of post-performance action to be alluded to; an action that an affected spect-actor could reasonably take within the "real-world" lives in responses to the questions raised in *War* and *Detention.* With *Immigration,* though, it is hard to think about what such a parallel might be. If spect-actors experience the perspectives of immigration officers and listen to multiple narratives about immigrant desires and struggles, they might become more conscious about immigration issues, yes. But what are reasonable actions that can be taken in one's day to day life to manifest the affect that might emerge from an experience like *Immigration?* Would it be about joining more protests that activate against oppressive immigration policies? Would it be about connecting spect-actors with the issue of immigrant rights so that they would think about collaborating with like-minded groups and individuals in their immediate vicinities? Would it be to draw parallels with positions of power that the spect-actor does occupy in their "real-world" lives—as board members, or institutional administrators, or as teachers? Or is it just about the experience, allowing spect-actors to decide for themselves what they want to do with the experience, without the *Immigration* explicitly attempting to frame that channeling in any specific way?

After much consideration, I decided that unlike *War* and *Detention,* the pedagogical objectives in *Immigration* would be more intangible. Yes, there is something to be learned; something to be explored; but the definition of that "something" will be left to the spect-actors. And given this difference from *War* and *Detention,* where the absence of dialogue and the extensive articulation of pre/post-performance work were strongly influenced by the specific pedagogical objectives of the scripts in question, what implications would *Immigration's* more open-ended goals have on the writing strategies that I would need to use in the creation of the script?

SCRIPTING IMMIGRATION

The Setting

This experience is set to take place in a building that, ideally, has a large fence around it. The building is tall and imposing; gray and bleak. It looks like it could be the hosting space for a mortuary, just as much as it could be the corporate headquarters for a fancy company, or an apartment complex, or a penitentiary, or a school. The building is clean and well maintained, both inside and outside. There are minimal windows. There is a flag flying close to the entrance.

Inside this building lays an immigration office that represents an unnamed country; the office is presumably located in a location that is *not* the country itself: for example, the setting might be Indian embassy in Kenya; or the United States Embassy in Vietnam. The setting can be as specific or abstract as the director desires. And if going down the "specific context" route, careful adaptations should be made to the design and script elements that follow. This script, however, is set in an abstract immigration office that represents an unnamed country and operates out of another unspecified nation-state.

As abstract or specific as the setting may be, the spect-actors who come to this experience become OFFICIALs who will vet whether or not the actors— playing aspiring visa applicants—should/should not be allowed access to their country. The immigration/visa applications that the spect-actors assess could be "in person" i.e., where a live actor plays the character of a particular kind of immigrant. They could also be "paper based" i.e., where the premise is that the visa application in question has been sent via post.

Before the Experience...

Spect-actors should receive their character profiles a few days before they come to the theatrical experience and below are the profile "types" into which spect-actors might be divided. Before going on to these profiles, though, it is necessary to mention that the structure in this script allows for the experience to be conducted with as few as one spect-actor; or as many spect-actors as the team is able to get together. Whatever the number, however, it is recommended that there be an equal distribution of the following profiles amongst the spect-actors. So, for example, if there are 10 spect-actors, two individuals should get Profile 1, two spect-actors should get Profile 2, two should get Profile 3, and so on. If there are less than five spect-actors, well, the director is free to decide how the profiles might be mixed and matched so as to create diverse and non-stereotypical characterizations. Essentially, the idea is to facilitate the creation of a scenario where there exists a pool of spect-actor-OFFICIALs, each of whom has a different motivation for having taken on that job; each of whom has a different way of executing that job. And yet, like most human environments, there are certain patterns that can be observed both in the nature of those who come to take on a particular profession; in the ways in which they execute that profession. Hence the need for the following profiles needing to be distributed in a well thought out fashion...

The Spect-Actor-OFFICERs

Different versions of the profiles below can be generated; some potential variations are described below each specific profile:

Officer Profile 1: You are an immigration officer for the country in which you were born and raised. You became an immigration officer because it is a stable job and you have to financially support your spouse and three children. You are desperate to keep this job because you feel lucky to have found the position and are unsure if you will be able to come across anything better.

Potential Variation 1: An immigration officer who was born elsewhere i.e., who is an immigrant themselves. All the remaining characteristics could stay the same.

Potential Variation 2: An immigration officer who is either an immigrant or a "native"—who likes the stability of the job but is *not* particularly desperate to keep it. They believe that they will be fine in another professional environment too.

Additional Consideration: An additional characteristic could be the OFFICER's relationship to the local context. Are they comfortable in their country of employment? How do they interact with "locals"? How do they perceive the "locals"? And how do these perceptions affect the characteristics mentioned above?

Officer Profile 2: You are an immigration officer in the country in which you were born and raised. You became an immigration officer because you are deeply nationalistic and love your country fervently. You are not against immigrants crossing over to your land, but you do want to be certain that any newcomer that is let in will contribute to the nation's economy and not be a drain on its citizens' resources.

   Potential Variation 1: An immigration officer who was born elsewhere and is now a citizen of the country that they represent i.e., this person is an immigrant themselves. All the remaining characteristics could stay the same.

   Potential Variation 2: A "native" or an immigrant, this officer hates immigrants and think they are nothing but a drain on the nation's resources. While they might not openly discriminate against immigrants in unofficial encounters, within the office, their attitude toward immigrant communities is made visible through body language, tone, and/or choice of vocabulary.

   Additional Consideration: An additional characteristic could be the OFFICER's relationship to the local context. Are they comfortable in their country of employment? How do they interact with "locals"? How do they perceive the "locals"? And how do these perceptions affect the characteristics mentioned above?

Officer Profile 3: You are an immigration officer for the country in which you were born and raised. You became an immigration officer because you like being in a position of power over others. You initially wanted to join your country's army, but since you were unable to pass the physical test and thus, were unable to get into the armed forces, you decided to become an immigration officer. What is most important to you, in your job and your personal life, is the chance to show people what a natural leader you can be.

   Potential Variation 1: An immigration officer who was born elsewhere i.e., who is an immigrant themselves. All the remaining characteristics could stay the same.

   Potential Variation 2: A native or an immigrant, this officer could be a megalomaniac who does not only like being in power, but enjoys going out of their way to be authoritarian to anyone; in any situation. This is the kind of person who would challenge even the HEAD OFFICER—though they are well aware of boundaries that cannot be crossed so that they can keep their jobs.

   Additional Consideration: An additional characteristic could be the OFFICER's relationship to the local context. Are they comfortable in their country of employment? How do they interact with "locals"? How do they perceive the "locals"? And how do these perceptions affect the characteristics mentioned above?

Officer Profile 4: You are an immigration officer for the country in which you were born and raised. You hate your job and are only doing it because you are waiting for something better to come along—you just don't know what that something better might be. You've been trying to find some direction in your career but have been unable to do so; you do not know what your passion is. Keeping your job as an immigration official pays the bills till you get your life in order and for you, it's a temporary thing.

Potential Variation 1: An immigration officer who was born elsewhere i.e., who is an immigrant themselves. All the remaining characteristics could stay the same.

Potential Variation 2: A native or an immigrant, this officer hates their job and wants to actually be a scientist. However, you've been unable to find a research/teaching position in your field and find yourself "stuck" doing what you are doing now.

Additional Consideration: An additional characteristic could be the OFFICER's relationship to the local context. Are they comfortable in their country of employment? How do they interact with "locals"? How do they perceive the "locals"? And how do these perceptions affect the characteristics mentioned above?

Officer Profile 5: You are an immigration officer for the country in which you were born and raised. You are a painter and you are an immigration officer during the day because the hours of this particular job allow you to pursue your art. The pay is good and it is stable employment; both of these aspects give you the opportunity to paint as much as you would like without being worried about supporting yourself and your family.

Potential Variation 1: An immigration officer who was born elsewhere i.e., who is an immigrant themselves. All the remaining characteristics could stay the same.

Potential Variation 2: A native or an immigrant, this officer is in the job until their painting career takes off and they can make that their full-time occupation.

Additional Consideration: An additional characteristic could be the OFFICER's relationship to the local context. Are they comfortable in their country of employment? How do they interact with "locals"? How do they perceive the "locals"? And how do these perceptions affect the characteristics mentioned above?

The reader will notice that each of the variations changes particular elements that are contained within the primary profile description and directors/actors of this piece are encouraged to "play" with the profiles and variations as they wish. However, what is absolutely necessary is that there is complexity when looking at the larger group of characters given to the spect-actors: there should *not* be simplistic representations where, for example, all the OFFICIALs are authoritarian. Complexity is an absolute must. Everything else is malleable based on the vision of the production team.

Along with their character profile, in the package that spect-actors receive a few days before the performance, they should be sent a letter that says something like this:

DEPARTMENT OF IMMIGRATION

Dear Sir/Madam,

We are delighted that you will be joining our Department of Immigration as an official. We have no doubt that our country will benefit from your efforts and we appreciate your commitment toward empowering our future.

We ask you to report for your first day of work on *[insert date of performance]*, *[insert time of performance]*, *[insert location of performance]*. Please be on time.

Please dress in attire that is formal and that is representative of your station within our Department.

Attached to this letter you will find a badge and other relevant information. Please affix your picture in the demarcated location of the badge, complete the necessary information, and have the badge fixed on your person when you arrive for your first day. **Please note that you will not be allowed in if you are not wearing the badge.**

All the information in this packet must be read and understood before your first day.

Please contact us if you need any clarifications or any more information.

We look forward to working with you.

Head Officer
Immigration and Visas Bureau, Department of Immigration

[insert phone number and/or other contact information for a relevant member of the production team, should the spect-actor desire more information]

Based on the specific nature of a particular spect-actor pool, additional follow-up introductory sessions might become necessary: either as additional documentation that is sent out; or workshops where spect-actor-OFFICIALs fill

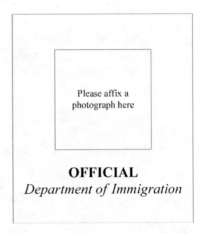

Please affix a photograph here

OFFICIAL
Department of Immigration

Figure 4: Badge for spect-actors.

out character questionnaires and go through characterization exercises; or as more formal question and answer forums where spect-actors can clarify their doubts "out of character," with members of the production team. The way in which these additional preparatory sessions will be carried out, and the extent to which the exact nature of the piece is clarified, is entirely up to the discretion of the production team and their understanding of the local context. Is the spect-actor pool comprised of people who have never attended an immersive theater event before and would need more than the documentation that is sent to them? Is the spect-actor pool comprised of experienced theatergoers who do not need additional sessions? Or, is the context one in which an information session might be needed even before the documentation with the character profile, letter, and badge is sent to spect-actors?

Like the diversity included in the spect-actor-OFFICERs' profiles the character profiles of the actor-IMMIGRANTs who come into the office, the HEAD OFFICER who runs the office, and the GUARDs who perform various tasks, should also showcase different "kinds" of narratives.

The Actor-HEAD OFFICER

The HEAD OFFICER is a character that commands authority; someone who is extremely adept at improvising in response to in the moment contributions from spect-actors and other actors; someone who has a thorough understanding of the rules of the world. The performer playing this role, in consultation with the director, should think about the following dimensions to their personality:

- How did they come to this particular profession?
- Do they, in their personal life, agree with the immigration policies of their country? If they do or do not, how does this personal attitude bleed into their work in the immigration office?
- How do they respond to officers beneath them, who might not respect their authority?
- How do they respond to officers beneath them, who might make a lot of mistakes in the work?

The HEAD OFFICER is the character that uses the spect-actors' suggestions in order to officially accept or deny a spect-actor-IMMIGRANT's application. It is suggested that this character takes as much/as little time as they want to make a decision on an application, based on the character that they have framed for themselves.

The Actor-GUARDs

The GUARDs are the characters that ensure the smooth functioning of the immigration office; they are in charge of maintaining order both within the building and the premises that are contained within its fence. Each of the GUARDs should showcase a range of personalities, where there is not one model of behavior. All the GUARDs—there can be as many guards as needed—wear the same uniform and follow similar protocols of language usage. And yet, each of them is different from each other. Perhaps there is one GUARD who is sympathetic to the immigrants, because he is an immigrant himself—how does this sympathy manifest in small acts of kindness, within a system that does not necessarily create the conditions for kindness to manifest? Perhaps there is one GUARD who has a long-standing grudge against the notion of immigration—how does this character show their antagonism, subtly, to incoming applicants?

The performers playing this role, in consultation with the director, should think about the following dimensions to their personality:

- How did they come to this particular profession?
- Do they, in their personal life, agree with the immigration policies of their country? If they do or do not, how does this personal attitude bleed into their work in the immigration office?
- How do they behave with prospective immigrants coming in for their interviews? Is there a certain "type" of applicant that they are more favorable/unfavorable toward?
- How do they act toward the applicants when they are leaving with a rejected visa and are visibly distressed?
- How do they interact with the OFFICIALs?
- How do they interact with the HEAD OFFICER?

The GUARDs help facilitate the deliverance of the applicant, and communicate with each other through walkie-talkies or phones. So, when the HEAD OFFICER is ready to see a particular applicant, their name is announced through the walkie-talkie; a GUARD goes outside to get that person (actor); they are dropped off at the HEAD OFFICER's space. When the decision has been made, the HEAD OFFICER calls the GUARDs again, to escort the applicant out of the space.

The Actor-ACTIVISTS

There are two kinds of activist groups spect-actors encounter as they leave the location of the experience. One group is fighting for more lenient immigration laws; the other is looking to inspire stricter laws.

What needs particular consideration here is whether or not these two activist groups share a particular common identity trait. For example, is the anti-immigration group more likely to be comprised of Hindus, while the pro-immigrant group is more likely to be made up of Christians? Is the anti-immigration group more likely to be comprised of financially well-resourced individuals, while the other group has people who hail from more humble financial backgrounds? Choices that will depend on the context that is used, or created, for *Immigration's* world.

Within these broader characteristics, like all the characters in this script the ACTIVISTs should embody their behavior in different ways: why did they choose to become activists for this particular cause? Was there a specific incident or law that functioned as a catalyst? How do they behave toward the spect-actor-OFFICERs when they walk out the office, at the end of the day of work?

With this character group of ACTIVISTs, what is important is creating rehearsal techniques where these performers are asked to become "storytellers"—where they create short one or two-minute monologues that communicate something about the character; something personal; something that has to do with *why* they have become ACTIVISTs. For example, where indicated later in the script, one ACTIVIST could speak about the particular moment during which they realized that they wanted to "make a difference." One ACTIVIST could speak about a very specific instance in which they lost their job to an immigrant. One ACTIVIST could speak about a particular success story—their uncle, for example, who was an immigrant to the host country and became a successful businessperson who gave a lot back to their new nation. One ACTIVIST could speak about a particular crime that occurred in their neighborhood, where the immigrant was the criminal. Actors can write their own monologues, or the directors could script them, or the rehearsal process can include creative writing exercises to assist in the process.

The Actor-APPLICANTs

Listed below is a spectrum of profiles for the performers who will be taking on the roles of IMMIGRANTs. Some of the profiles place characters on the more privileged end of the immigrant spectrum; other choices ask APPLICANTs to take on less privileged roles. After all, it is not only narratives of suffering and pain that underscore people's desire to travel ... there are myriad reasons why people choose to leave the place into which they might have been born and the choice to encompass this diversity is an important part of characterizing the actors who play these roles. Showcasing as diverse an array of the narratives below is what is necessary, so as that the experience does not become one more problematic representation of the abject immigrant; while there might well be some who embody that condition too.

When refining the actors' particular APPLICANT personalities—and the application paperwork for each of these applicants—it is up to the director and the production team how to design the details of the characterization process. For example, the actors can create their own application paperwork as part of their character development rehearsals; or there could be a designated person on the production team, whose only job it might be to generate immigration applications; the tech savvy director could find an online paperwork generator. The options are many. Whatever the chosen modus operandi though, since there will be a large volume of paperwork that needs to be generated, there is careful thought that needs to go into showcasing an array if voices and narratives in these applications.

The particular "types" of APPLICANT profiles for the performers, below, have been crafted as a function of three factors: the primary activity that will be undertaken by the immigration applicant (i.e., is the applicant going to the officers' country as a visitor or an asylum seeker?); that person's socioeconomic background (i.e., do the financial conditions of that individual APPLICANT make it more or less likely for them to emigrate/immigrate?); that person's potential contribution to the host country's economy (i.e., does the applicant put forth a skill sets that the host country can benefit from?). Each profile is followed by possible variations of that character and actors/directors can "play" with them, again, as long as complexity is maintained in the overall distribution.

> APPLICANT *Profile 1:* The rich traveler who is going on a holiday in the officials' country, and who has never been denied a visa (to anywhere) before. This person is likely to spend a large amount of money in the host country, and is likely to have submitted all the right documentation in support of their application.
>
> *Potential Variation 1:* The person who is almost always going to be approved but occasionally misses the submission of sufficient documentation. A frequent traveler, they can pay for their papers being expedited and given their extensive travel history/resources, the HEAD OFFICER is aware of who they are. Therefore, even if the spect-actor-OFFICIAL rejects an application, the HEAD OFFICER can decide to pass them through.
>
> *Potential Variation 2:* The rich traveler who has never traveled before. They have plenty of financial information and it seems likely that they will spend a lot of money in the host country. But since they are "new money," can they be trusted? The HEAD OFFICER

can seek to "cultivate" this particular applicant—to see if they can become investors in the near future.

APPLICANT *Profile 2:* The traveler who is going backpacking/camping/volunteering in the host country. This person has been denied a visa before (to the same or another country), because they were unable to prove that they had enough resources to pay for their travel in that particular failed attempt. In their current application, therefore, this traveler hopes that they will have assuaged the fear of the officer by supplying extra paperwork. While there is no particular economic gain from this tourist's entry into the new country, there is likely to be some form of social contribution (however intangible) that stems from the traveler's "good intentions."

Potential Variation 1: This applicant wants to volunteer with an organization that is on the government's watch list for potential terrorist behavior. The traveler is aware of the organization's status (or not) and seeks to convince the officer that they present no risk to the host country. Where the applicant is aware of the organization's status, there can be pre-prepared arguments that seek to counter the officer's questions. Where the character is unaware of the organization's status, there is room for them to be caught off guard. In either case, the spect-actor-OFFICIAL is given annotated paperwork in which the organization's dubious status has been highlighted.

Potential Variation 2: The organization that this traveler is volunteering with is completely unknown to the office. Therefore, the application will need to include extra documentation/proof of status and the OFFICIAL will have to decide whether or not the organization sounds legitimate.

Potential Variation 3: The actor-applicant is on their way to intern or volunteer with an extremely well established international organization (like the United Nations).

In all the instances of this character, based on the resources of the production team, the host organization's website is an "active" link. This is to say that the spect-actor-OFFICIAL can check the website in real time, during the experience, to decide whether or not they want to approve that particular application.

APPLICANT *Profile 3:* This applicant is a businessperson who wants to start a new venture in the officials' country and they are an ideal visitor, in many ways. They have records of good finances and other supporting materials, and are most likely to make a financial contribution to the host country. They are also likely to provide jobs for citizens of the host country and present a potentially sound economic opportunity.

Potential Variation 1: But of course, there could also be the entrepreneur who might bring in a lot of revenue to the official's country but in so doing, will take the market for that business away from locals. The creation of the local jobs could be counterbalanced by the higher-level positions being potentially taken away by "foreigners."

Potential Variation 2: There could also be the businessperson who is unethical and is in the midst of illegitimate deals with individuals and organizations in the host country. The financial paperwork could have multiple loopholes and if, for whatever reason, the spect-actor-OFFICIAL is unable to catch these errors, the mistakes are flagged by the HEAD OFFICER, who either privately or publically calls that spect-actor out on their error.

APPLICANT *Profile 4:* This actor-APPLICANT portrays a skilled laborer who is applying for a work visa at a specific company/organization in the hos country. This person has a great academic and socio-economic background, but is it possible that they are taking jobs away from someone in the host country that might be as skilled? How can this applicant prove that the skill that they have is "special"? How can they prove that they are not "stealing jobs"?

Potential Variation 1: A situation where it is clear that the job in question is being taken away from a citizen of that country. It is clear because the employer's sponsorship letter is unable to explain why/how there is a need for someone from outside the nation-state's borders.

Potential Variation 2: A situation where it is clear that the job is *not* being taken away from a citizen of the host country—the skill set demonstrated by the applicant is phenomenal and there is unlikely to be someone in the host country who can match their qualifications.

Potential Variation 3: An applicant who has an extremely special skill set that is also, somehow, "dangerous." Someone who has a history of working for causes of "radical activism," for example; or demonstrates an identity affiliation (based on race, religion, caste, class, gender, sexuality) that is frowned upon in the host country.

APPLICANT *Profile 5:* This applicant is an unskilled laborer who has no formal degree, does not hail from a strong socio economic background, but wants to work in the host country despite not having a specific place of employment yet. Their visa application to the host country has been denied multiple times but they always keep trying.

Potential Variation 1: This applicant is convinced that they will have a better life, economically, for themselves and their families, if they are able to move to the host country and find work. They claim that they are unable to find jobs in their country of origin and submit different kinds of evidence to try and prove that that is indeed the case: classified advertisements from newspapers; informal anecdotes from a professor at their local university; evidence that is ... well, not from recognized sources.

Potential Variation 2: The applicant could possibly find jobs in their country of origin but wants to go overseas because many members of their extended family live there. However, their family members' legal status in the host country is questionable and the applicant is unable to provide proof of their residency. What should be clear is that they are certain that they can find a job in the host country; that they are passionate about being close to family.

Potential Variation 3: While this applicant has skills that are not particularly special, their family members in the host country are powerful and successful. The applicant does not have a confirmed job yet and their skill-set is not the most impressive, but the portfolio submitted—of their family members—is strong.

APPLICANT *Profile 6:* This applicant is an artist who is being sponsored (or not) for a performance tour. While there is cultural, artistic, and educational value to their visit to the host country, is it enough to get them a visa?

Potential Variation 1: An artist who is widely acclaimed worldwide and who has a recognizable repertoire. This artist is able to provide documented evidence of their reputation in their own country and in different parts of the world. As a result of their status, they have a reputable host in the host country that is willing to sponsor their visit.

Potential Variation 2: This character is an emerging artist who would like to apprentice with a more professional mentor in the host country. They have located an artist in the host country who is willing to host them, but this applicant does not have a strong artistic background and is In the very early stages of their career.

APPLICANT *Profile 7:* This applicant has a higher education degree— like a doctorate degree—and is fleeing from a particular situation of persecution in their home country. This applicant can speak articulately about the reasons that surrounding their seeking refuge or asylum and has a convincing case to present.

Potential Variation 1: There is a strong case made for asylum, however, there are some details that do not add up in this applicant's case. This is to say that, while there might be some truth to their fears, it is unclear whether their life is really at risk in their home country.

APPLICANT *Profile 8:* Like the applicant in Profile 7, this person is also fleeing persecution and is in fear of their lives. However, they do not have formal education and are unable to articulate their case well.

Potential Variation 1: There is a strong case made for asylum (in terms of the paperwork). However, since this person does not have formal education, they are unable to present evidence for how they will be able to find a job/make a living in the host country.

APPLICANT *Profile 9:* A family of applicants wants to visit their relative in the host country. The relative has either had a baby or gotten married (something that is generally considered a positive life event). It is incredibly important to this family that they are able to be present with their relatives. They have average financials and strong ties to their host country, but are they going to return after their visit or just stay and be a "drain" on the host country's economy?

Potential Variation 1: An applicant who wants to visit family in the host country, but because that person has had a life event that is generally negative (a bereavement of some sort).

APPLICANT *Profile 10:* Someone who wants to seek medical treatment for themselves/their family members. This applicant has just enough money for the initial stages of the medical treatment— nothing more, nothing less. Why does the host country need to let them in?

Potential Variation 1: An applicant who is extremely wealthy and can afford extensive medical treatment.

The director can decide the ways in which the characters above are distributed and how the variations will be created/allocated. In addition to the variations above, there are some universal factors that can be added across all the profiles, to help shift circumstances:

- Whether or not the applicant is traveling with family
- Whether or not they speak the language in which the interview is being conducted
- Whether or not they have sufficient paperwork

Based on the resources available to the production team, there could also be an entire technological system that is created, relevant to the world of the experience. Just as there could be real world websites that are created for the profiles of the travelers who are interning/volunteering with specific organizations, spect-actor-OFFICIALs could get email accounts with regular email alerts that tell them about changing policy. For example:

- ALERT: Please make sure that all applicants who declare "Hinduism" as their religion have an extra affidavit that attests to the nature of their participation in religious activities
- ALERT: Please note that policies about asylum seekers have changed and we can no longer accept applicants with more than one child

If this can't be done via email, the ALERTs can be made during the 90-minute feedback sessions that occur—more on this later.

Once actors have been allocated particular profiles, they should be asked to further develop their characters using a template, as below. In addition to the template, actors should be encouraged to create the supporting paperwork that they will need for their application:

CHARACTER SHEET

- Name:
- Gender:
- Age:
- Educational background:
- Occupation:
- Annual income:
- Who comprises your family?
- Why are you applying for a visa?
- What documents will you provide to support the visa application?
- How will you carry yourself, in order to make the most impact on the immigration officer?
- What will you do—in the immigration office, as your reaction—if your visa application is denied?
- What will you do—in the immigration office, as your reaction—if your visa application is accepted?
- What is most challenging, to you, about the visa process?
- If you are allowed into the host country, what is the first thing you will do there?
- Do you have a back up plan if your visa is denied? Somewhere else to go? Something else to do?

With the actors' process, it is recommended that particular attention be paid to how the performers will react in situ, when their visa applications are accepted or denied by the HEAD OFFICER (on the recommendation of the spect-actor-OFFICIAL):

- Do they vocalize their happiness at being granted the visa?
- Do they cry, publically, in front of the officers and the rest of the applicants when their application is refused?
- Do they demand to see the spect-actor-OFFICIAL who suggested the approval/rejection of their application?
- Do they throw a fit of rage—when denied their visa—insult the HEAD OFFICER, and have to be taken out by the GUARDs in full view of the spect-actor-OFFICIAL who might have suggested approval/denial?
- Are they completely submissive, barely speaking until asked a question?

In order to highlight the responsibility of the spect-actor-OFFICIAL— to enable the spect-actor to "test" their complicity within a larger immigration system that is not always just or fair—it is imperative that all actor-APPLICANT characterizations work toward presenting an ethical dilemma for the spect-actor in question. This is to say that there should be some kind of visible response when spect-actors leave the HEAD OFFICER's room, so that the spect-actor-OFFICIAL is aware of their role in a particular applicant's status. Perhaps there is a screen outside the HEAD OFFICER's space, which projects the name of the current applicant being interviewed. So that the entire spect-actor-OFFICIAL population can keep track of how their suggestions are being implemented.

During the Experience...

When spect-actors arrive at the performance location, there is a long line of actor-APPLICANTs who are waiting outside the immigration office. The line is incredibly long, and if it is possible to recruit a large number of actors, the line should snake around the building and extend to the end of the next street. From the demeanor of these actors when spect-actor-OFFICIALs arrive, it should be apparent that these applicants have been waiting outside for a long time. Some are seated on the ground. Others are standing. All of them look incredibly nervous.

When the spect-actors roll up to the building and are allowed to enter it immediately, there is a change in the body language of all the actors who are waiting. They know that these people have some power over them. That these people will probably have some say in what happens to their visa applications.

When spect-actors reach the entryway to the building, they are checked by a GUARD for their badges and are made to pass through a metal detector and/or endure a pat down. If the spect-actor in question has arrived without a badge, they are turned away from the entry. If, for whatever reason, the director decides not to turn spect-actors away (perhaps the mode of pre-performance message transmission is not likely to succeed) the spect-actors with missing cards should be sent to the HEAD OFFICER who will then set them up with a badge before directing them to their work desks. The spect-actors who come in with their badges are directed to their desks by the GUARDs at the front entrance.

The spect-actors enter a larger space that is set up like an office. Rows of tables and chairs inhabit this space. Each table is piled high with individual folders, and has a laptop or desktop computer on it. The walls are gray; there are few windows; fluorescent lights; the smell of disinfectant...

There should be as many cameras as possible in that space, cameras that provide "real time" transmission of the goings on in various parts of the build-ing—parts of the outside area where actor-APPLICANTs are lined up between the door of the office and the fence outside the building, the front entrance, the passage between the front entrance and the office, the entrance to the office, and at angles that enable a view of every single table and chair in the space. The cameras should be connected to the GUARDs' desk at the building's entry way and the HEAD OFFICER's station, where an array of screens are visible—showing real-time surveillance of actors and spect-actors. Essentially, therefore, the spect-actor-OFFICIALs, if they look over to/walk past the HEAD OFFICER's room or the front GUARDs' stations, should be able to witness real-time feeds of themselves and their peers.

There are multiple GUARDs inside the office space as well. One GUARD per row of tables and chairs, perhaps? It should be obvious that even with the relative authority that they have, the spect-actor-OFFICERs are under sur-veillance themselves.

As soon as all the spect-actors are seated at their desks, the HEAD OFFI-CER walks to the front of the room and conducts the training session. There is a projector screen present behind the HEAD OFFICER, for the demonstra-tion that will come a little later—the same projector screen that is used to broadcast the name of the applicant being interviewed at any given time.

> HEAD OFFICER: Congratulations on being the chosen few to be invited to join the Department of Immigration. Today, you will begin your work for our country by assessing whom we should let in within our borders, and who we should keep out. You each have a stack of applications on the desks in front of you.
>
> Part of your job will be to go through each application that lies in front of you, and to decide which ones should move forward to an interview with me and which ones can be rejected immediately. Those that you recommend for

approval will be brought it from outside and will have an interview with me—I will double check the information and decide whether or not they can in fact be issued the necessary permits. Those who you deny, will not make it to the interview stage.

Please do not recommend people for interviews if their applications are sub par. Look at their financial documents—will they have enough resources to live in our country without being a drain on our economy? Look at the reason for which they want to visit our country—does their story seem authentic? Look at their demeanor—do they look like they are telling the truth? ALWAYS LOOK FOR PROOF—if they cannot provide evidence for everything on their application, you should suggest denying them. It's your responsibility to do so. Any questions?

Spect-actors are given the chance to ask questions. HEAD OFFICER answers their questions to the best of their abilities; when necessary, spect-actors are asked to refer to the information sheet that is on their desks (more on this later).

> HEAD OFFICER: Now, please open up the document that has been placed on your computer's desktop.

A file needs to be created such that it can be updated "live" by anyone in the room; the updates can also be seen "live" by anyone in the room: think of something like a Google spreadsheet. Spect-actor-OFFICERs will need to fill out the information below for every single application that they assess on paper. If the spect-actor-OFFICER is unable to fill out any one of these bits of information—except that which is not relevant to the visa type that they are applying for—that visa application *must* be rejected. The recorded information includes:

- Name of the applicant
- Age
- Gender
- Reason they are applying for a visa
- Proof submitted of financial solvency
- Proof submitted of job status (for visitor visa applications)
- Proof of employment (for work visa)
- Proof of danger to self (for asylum/refugee status)
- Whether the visa should be approved/denied
- The official's reason for suggesting approval/denial of the visa.

Spect-actors are taught how to use the spreadsheet by the HEAD OFFICER who projects a sample application form as an example: showing the spect-actors what they are expected to do.

> HEAD OFFICER: You cannot assess an application that is incomplete. I will constantly review the information being uploaded on our real-time database and

> if, at any time, I see that you have entered incorrect or insufficient informa-
> tion—especially when you have also accepted that visa application—you will
> be immediately terminated from your position and be asked to leave *(insert
> name of space)*. Is that understood? Questions?

Spect-actors are given the chance to ask questions. HEAD OFFICER answers
their questions to the best of his/her abilities.

> HEAD OFFICER: Finally as a visa granting institution, we—as an office—cannot
> accept more than 100 applications *(number is flexible based on how many spect-
> actors/actors there are in the experience)* a day. This limit includes both the
> paper-based and in person applications. Is that understood?

Spect-actors are given the chance to ask questions. HEAD OFFICER answers
their questions to the best of his/her abilities.

> HEAD OFFICER: Finally while we, as an office, cannot accept more than 100 appli-
> cations a day, it is also the case that an individual officer cannot accept more
> than 10 applications *(the number is flexible based on how many spect-
> actors/actors there are in the experience)* respectively. So please, be mindful of
> your recommendations. As soon as your suggested approvals reach the per-
> sonal limit, you will have to stop assessing applications for the day. Remember
> that we are all working together for the future of our great country *(Pause)*. It's
> almost time for us to get started. You should have informational sheets in
> front you, which summarize these basic rules and the parameters for the
> acceptance of applications. Please take a moment to locate those sheets.
> *(Pause)*.

At this point, if the production team has been able to set up an internal technological framework with email accounts for alerts and/or locally housed
websites for organizations that are in the applicant paperwork, there needs
to be some training that occurs for spect-actors to use this platform. It is fine
if the spect-actors feel overwhelmed with information. It is ok if they seem
a bit lost at this point.… On each spect-actor's table, there are "cheat sheets"
with the information previously spoken by the HEAD OFFICER.

CHEATSHEET 1

Before suggesting the acceptance of an application, ask yourself:

1. Has this applicant proved that they will not be a financial drain on our
   resources?
2. Has this applicant proved that they have a legitimate reason for entering
   our country?
3. Has this applicant proved that they will not pose a threat to our country's safety?

If you can say YES to **all** these questions—with proof from the application
forms submitted—the application can be suggested for approval.

All other applications must be denied.

No more than 100 applications can be accepted, as an office, per day
No more than 10 applications can be scheduled for interviews, per
OFFICIAL
Keep an eye on our Department's database before making any
decisions.

If there is an internal technological system, there is a third cheat sheet with information on how to engage with it.

As the spect-actor reads the information that they have been given, the HEAD OFFICER walks around and ensures that everyone understands the rules. The GUARDs can also function as providers of information, if there are a large number of spect-actors that might be difficult for the HEAD OFFICER to facilitate all at once. Once all spect-actors are done reading and absorbing the cheat sheets that have been placed on the desk, the HEAD OFFICER resumes their position at the front of the room:

> HEAD OFFICER: Every 90 minutes we will have a recess during which your work and acceptance/denial rates will be publically evaluated. Any official who goes *over* their quota of approved applicants will immediately be dismissed from their position until further re-training can be provided to them.
>
> That said, since you are all new hires, as an incentive for you to stick to the targets that have been set for you, successful employees get bonuses of $100 *(price can be adjusted to the context, of course, but it has to be real money)* at the end of the day.
>
> Any final questions before we start letting applicants in? *(Once all questions are answered)*. Please begin working on the paper applications on your desks.

Each spect-actor's desk has a large number of folders on it—the same number of applications that the office can accept—each of which has an individuals names written on them. So, if 100 people can be accepted by the immigration office, *each* spect-actor-OFFICIAL's desk has 100 folders on it. If 1,000 people can be accepted by the immigration office, *each* spect-actor's desk should have close to 1,000 folders. Ultimately, what these "numbers" are aiming to create is a sense of "overload." With strict limits placed on who can come in—but with an application rate that far exceeds that number—how do OFFICIALs decide whose story is more deserving than another's?

In addition to the quantity of paperwork on the spect-actors' desks, the names on the folders should be, identifiably, from as many different geographic, religious, racial, and socio-economic backgrounds as possible (or they should all be "made up" names that cannot be associated with a particular group of people). This is important—when *Immigration* is set in an abstract context—that attempts are *not* made by spect-actors to associate certain kinds of narratives with certain parts of the world. Unless, of course, the director has decided to go with a context-specific adaptation; in which case it would be appropriate for folders to contain names and applications that are specific to the demography of visa applicants who seek to go to that particular country.

Resources permitting, it is recommended that the "application paper-work" props that are designed be highly consistent across the paper and in person applicants. That said, since the notion of consistent paperwork can be variable—in that some nation-states are likely to have clear paperwork requirements and forms; others are less likely to have clear requirements. This is to say that the paperwork that is ultimately created and designed for iterations of *Immigration* will have to be resonant with the context that is being encompassed within the experience.

Each applicant's folder should contain a completed, generic application form (as below); financial documents; other supporting documents that they might have submitted. Some folders should be complete. Some folders should be incomplete. These differences in quality could be factors that influence the spect-actor-OFFICIAL's decision-making process. Of course, another option would be to ensure that all the applications are of the same quality, putting the onus entirely on the spect-actors to make decisions about who gets accepted and who gets denied—when the visible quality of all the applications is the same. Again, something that is up to the director of this script.

GENERIC APPLICATION FORM

Please enclose supporting documents for every single question on this form: ID cards for yourself/people traveling with you; bank statements; wedding certificates; letters from sponsors; hotel reservations. If you are applying as a refugee/asylum seeker, please include proof as to why and how you are in danger in your country.

Applicant Name:
Date of Birth:
Date of visit:
Reason for visit:

1. Will you be traveling with someone else? YES/NO.
   If YES, please mention names and their relationship to you. Please note that only children under the age of 18 can be included on the same application as the primary applicant. All others must file separate applications.
2. Do you have a criminal record? YES/NO.
   If YES, please describe this in as much detail as possible.
3. Are you/have you ever been involved in terrorism related activities? YES/NO.
   If YES, please describe in as much detail as possible.

4. Have you previously been denied a visa to this country? YES/NO.
   If YES, please explain why your visa was denied and what makes this application different.

Spect-actor-OFFICIALs, after they finish their introductory training with the HEAD OFFICER, begin by working on the application folders that are on their desks. After a few applicants have been approved for an interview by the office, the actor-APPLICANTs playing those characters start to enter, one at a time (escorted by a GUARD). The GUARD takes that applicant to the HEAD OFFICER's room, and their name is projected on the screen. The design aspect is really important here: all spect-actor-OFFICIALs need to be able to see both the name of the applicant being interviewed by the HEAD OFFICER and that actor-APPLICANTs response both during/when leaving the interview.

The actors playing the applicants enter the office at irregular intervals, at the discretion of the GUARDs who are outside the immigration office. For example, if it seems as though the spect-actor-OFFICIALs have understood the scenario well and are going through the paperwork quickly, the actor-APPLICANTs are sent in at a quicker pace. If, however, the spect-actor-OFFICIALs are having difficulty understanding the premise of the "live database" and/or other elements of the work, the actor-APPLICANTs come in at a slower pace.

After ninety minutes have passed, a "break" is announced to all the employees in the office and no more actor-APPLICANTs are allowed into the space until the break has ended. When the break occurs, the HEAD OFFICER closes the doors, turns on a projector, and projects the shared database that all the officers have been entering their information on—everyone in the office should be able to see the information that is being projected. The HEAD OFFICER looks at what is being projected and makes observations/comments based on:

- Whether or not too many interviews have been granted by the group/one individual
- Whether rules of assessment are being broken
- Whether something contentious has emerged in the live surveillance feed that the HEAD OFFICER has been watching. If possible, these contentious behavior recordings are shown to the larger group and the person who has made the error is publically shamed
- Any spect-actor that is not "performing" as they should be in their job is given a stern talking to by the HEAD OFFICER—in the presence of all the other spect-actors. This underperforming spect-actor-officer is informed that they are on "probation" and that if they do not improve that particular aspect to their performance in

the next 90-minute section, they will have to go a re-training session. This rule must be adhered to. Please note that the re-training
session is another room in the building that is manned by one
GUARD. This GUARD functions as a trainer and goes through
every step of the preparatory process again. Once the instructions
have been repeated, the spect-actor-OFFICER must conduct a few
"test" reviews of applications until the GUARD is happy with the
quality of their work. At this point, the spect-actor-OFFICER may
return to the main office and continue vetting applications.

This becomes a constant process: the ninety-minute application review/inter-
view period, followed by public performance reviews, and re-training sessions. If one spect-actor consistently underperforms, they are "fired" on their
third offence. For this, the HEAD OFFICER takes the individual spect-actor-
OFFICER to their office after the relevant public review session and fires
them—after also publically announcing in the preceding review that they are
being let go.

The duration can function in two ways:

Option 1: The experience can end as soon as the office reaches its
approval quota. Then, the shredding begins (described below)
Option 2: The experience continues for the duration of a regular
workday, say 9 a.m. to 5 p.m., with a lunch break and two coffee
breaks. In this option, clearly, there will be more issues that emerge
toward the end of the day, when the application approval quota
gets closer and closer to being reached. If the approval quota and
the shredding (described below) are completed before the end of
the work day, spect-actors are still be asked to sit at their desks till
5 p.m.

An option to further the sense of bureaucracy and dissonance is to have a
live feed of the spect-actors waiting outside available to the OFFICERs, at
their computers or being projected at different places in the room. How do
the spect-actor-OFFICERs react to just sitting around and watching the APPLI-
CANTs, instead of aiming to get more work done? What do they do in the
face of arbitrary rules?

In both options above, when the approval quota is reached, the spect-
actors are asked to shred all remaining folders on their desks—there is a
shredding station in another office. How will the spect-actor reach to this act
of destruction?

When the office maximum has been reached for application acceptance
and the shredding has been done (*as in Option 1*); or when it's close to the
end of the work day (*as in Option 2*), the HEAD OFFICER calls for a "meeting,"

at which time everyone looks at the data again. The HEAD OFFICER highlights a particularly commendable spect-actor-OFFICER of the day and gives them the money that was promised at the beginning of the spect-actors' training session.

At the end of the workday, in both durational frameworks above, the spect-actors leave the office and again, at the exit, have to undergo a security process. When outside, the spect-actors should see that the actor-APPLICANTs who are still waiting outside.... Perhaps, as the spect-actors leave, the GUARDS could come out and announce to the actor-APPLICANTs that the offices have closed for the day? The spect-actor-OFFICIALs will thus have to face a range of responses from those performers: exhaustion; disgust; indifference; deference; anger.

As the spect-actors leave the premises, right outside the gate of the immigration building, there are two groups of performers who play ACTIVISTs with divergent agendas. One group of these activists has an agenda to get the country to adopt more lenient immigration policies—something specific like increasing the number of applications that can be accepted each day. The agenda could be, for example, that the actor-ACTIVISTS in this group are asking to raise the application approval quota from 100 to 200 people per day. As the spect-actor-OFFICIALs walk out, therefore, whether at the end of the day or during the day (if they were "fired" from their jobs for underperforming) the activists speak to these spect-actors as they exit and ask them to join the protest. Similarly, across from this group of spect-actors is another group of activists who are anti-immigration (because of the brain drain it is causing in local communities) and are trying to get their country to adopt stricter policies—they want a reduction in the number of people being accepted each day, from 100 to 50.

When the spect-actors are all outside, the two groups of ACTIVISTs get into a confrontation with each other: the guards accompany the spect-actors and form human barricades to create a passage between the two groups for the spect-actors to walk through. At the end of the passage, when the GUARD human barricade ends and the spect-actors are about to reach their transport, a few actor-ACTIVISTS emerge from the shadows and try to get the spect-actors to join their particular side of the protest.

Different ACTIVISTS try different strategies to and it is entirely up to the spect-actor whether or not they join the protest. The strategies could include: the use of petitions that spect-actor-OFFICIALs can choose to sign, in support of either "cause." Some of the actor-ACTIVISTs could go up to the spect-actors and talk to them, individually, about joining their protest. Perhaps one activist will try to gently cajole the spect-actor into joining their group. Perhaps another activist could try to guilt the spect-actor into joining their group. Some of the activists could be completely indifferent. Others could be openly critical of the immigration officers' role within the implementation of particular policies. The "approaches" could be multiple:

- "How can you live with yourself? They are people too you know."
- "They are taking our jobs. Why do you keep letting them in?"
- "Why don't you use your power to protest the policies you are enforcing?"

Whatever the approach, it is here that the "message" is somehow transmitted to the spect-actor-OFFICIAL in the form of questions and accusations. The message being: at what point within a bureaucratic system, where people are defined by paperwork, does the mid-level OFFICIAL become culpable?

While the abovementioned interventions/conversations are happening between individual spect-actors and actor-ACTIVISTs, the two groups of fighting spect-actors have settled down. There is only one GUARD outside the building's fence and the two groups are chanting slogans in a choreographed and intense way—both slogans are heard clearly; both slogans are created and performed as a piece of theater, hence the use of the term choreographed. When the ACTIVISTs speak to the spect-actors then, if the spect-actor member is participative and willing to engage more, they are invited to join the relevant group in slogan chanting. All spect-actors are given a chance to choose to join the protest.

Once all spect-actors have been given the chance to become ACTIVISTs, if spect-actor do join the protest, the slogan chanting continues for a while until the lights in the building are turned off and the actors playing the GUARDs and HEAD OFFICER leave. Noticing that there is only one GUARD left outside the building, the ACTIVISTs start to leave one by one.

If the spect-actors who join the activist groups are particularly engaged, there also might be a handful of actor-ACTIVISTs who decide to stage a "sleep-in" … where the protest continues into the night, when spect-actors fall asleep and are given sleeping bags and basic food/drink to sustain themselves. Maybe there's a portable washroom close by.

If possible, if spect-actors stay excited and engaged, there could also be a storytelling session of sorts. Where actor-ACTIVISTs, in torchlight, speak about how they came to become protesters for/against immigration. There would be two story-telling groups, of course—or one, if the other has no spect-actors left in it. In this story telling session, if it does occur, the ACTIVISTs use the stories that were created as part of their characterization process. Everyone goes to sleep after the storytelling session, when the last of the spect-actors seems to have fallen asleep, the actors quietly leave the space so that the spect-actors—when awake later that night or in the morning—have to decide for themselves what they will do.

The *Immigration* office can run the next morning for a different spect-actor group. And the morning after that. And the morning after that.

INTERLUDE

Immigration is similar to *War* and *Detention* in many ways and yet, the process of writing this piece highlighted different strategies that warrant consideration in this Interlude. As a result, in addition to the notes on context-specific adaptation that was focused following *Detention*, and the rehearsal strategies that were central to the Interlude following *War*, this chapter puts forth one more "global" strategy that I consider as being useful for anyone who is considering staging *War, Detention,* and/or *Immigration*: scale. While the experienced director reading this book might not need any clarification about scaling scripts differently based on the resources that are available, for someone who is relatively new to the world of Immersive and/or applied theater, it will be necessary to present concrete examples about how a piece like *Immigration* (and by extension, *War* and *Detention*) might be scaled based on the number of actors and spect-actors that can be recruited, and the financial/infrastructural resources that are available to the production team of the piece.

Framed as a thought exercise once again, I use the first part of this Interlude to ask how *Immigration* might be created with a team of fifty actors and/or fifty spect-actors; versus how the same experience might be crafted with as few as two actors and/or two spect-actors. What if, rather than having access to huge building in which *Immigration* could be staged, the director only has access to one small room in one small building? Clearly, I'm talking about extreme cases here, to make a point: that works like *War, Detention,* and *Immigration* are doable in multiple scales that are influenced by the budget, the number of actors and spect-actors, and any other logistical considerations that its production teams might be facing. This analysis of scale as a framing global strategy across the scripts in this book is then followed by the consideration of an aspect to "traditional," Realism-based playwriting that has had to shift in the scripting of the immersive aesthetics in *Immigration*: an aspect in addition to analyses about the positioning of text and the inclusion of pre/post-performance events that were highlighted in the preceding Interludes.

For an Immersive Theater Director

In many applied theater contexts, the process of recruiting performers and spect-actors can be difficult—more so when there are "less known" forms that are involved (like immersive theater); even more so when the use of these unfamiliar aesthetics requires a restriction on the number of actors/spect-actors based either on the demographic characteristics of the respective target groups, or the number of spect-actors who can be physically accommodated in the structure of the piece. And if these challenges were not enough, applied theater often encounters hurdles when the availability of resources is factored in. By this, I do not refer only to financial resources, though money is often an important and complex consideration for applied theater practitioners and researchers. Rather, when I speak of resources here, I also imply the availability or lack thereof of physical infrastructure, like rehearsal and performance spaces. I also use the term resources to refer to the positioning of "time": how much time can actors and spect-actors from that place give to the theatrical experience itself? The availability of resources, therefore—the quality, the quantity, and the nature of these resources—has an important impact on how applied theater projects are both conceptualized and executed. In this thought exercise, then, I consider how *Immigration* might be scaled up or down, based on the availability of/restrictions surrounding three kinds of resources: the number of spect-actors and actors that the production team is able to recruit, the kind of physical space that is available, and the quality/quantity of time that can be harnessed.

Scaling Numbers

What does a director of *Immigration* do when there are particular challenges that are faced vis-à-vis spect-actor and actor recruitment? As mentioned at the beginning the script, there are specific OFFICIAL profile types—five, specifically—that have been created for spect-actors to receive a few days before they arrive at the experience. These five archetypes have been crafted through material gleaned from various avenues: from my own lived experience, from archival research, and from informal conversations with individuals who are in similar positions of power as immigration officers. And in the presentation of the five OFFICIAL archetypes, the reader might recall my suggestion that these profiles be distributed equally across the number of spect-actors. So, if there are fifty spect-actors who have signed up for the performance, I suggest that ten spect-actors should get the same one of the five profiles (i.e., ten individuals get Profile 1; ten individuals get Profile 2; ten get Profile 3; ten get Profile 4; ten get Profile 5). Furthermore, the director could also choose to add additional archetypal profiles to the five that have been presented, and if a particular characterization relevant to the context is found to be missing from the list that I have suggested, there is room for directors to edit the existing list. For example, if it is the case that immigration officials in a specific context, where the piece is being staged, are often recruited from one particular racial/religious/ethnic group, could those identities be used to augment the existing profiles? Or could new profiles be created to add those markers into the mix? Consider the staging of *Immigration* in a context like the United States, where there is a climate of uncertainty around the country's openness to refugees from the Middle East. In this context, could it be that some of the spect-actor profiles are characterized as being of Middle Eastern descent; spect-actors who are asked to embody Others whose families became immigrants in the host country through processes of asylum seeking? By exploring such strategies of nuancing, editing, and/or adding profiles based on the particular locale in which the experience is being executed, the five archetypal profiles that have been provided for spect-actor-OFFICIALs could be scaled "up" to include many spect-actors as the production team is able to recruit.

What if there was the opposite issue, though, and if the production team was only able to recruit one or two spect-actors to attend the experience of *Immigration*? If this were to be the case, for instance, specific elements from each of the five existing spect-actor profiles could be combined to create nuanced characters for the handful of spect-actors who are in fact able to participate. So, for example, the profile that characterizes one spect-actor-OFFICIAL as someone who wants to be an artist and who is doing the job for the steady income, could be edited to also make that aspiring artist someone who needs to keep the job because of their financial obligations to a family that they have to support (combining Profiles 1 and 5). Or, perhaps the profile of the OFFICIAL who is currently characterized as being nationalistic and as having become an officer out of dedication to the idea of a nation-state, could be additionally crafted as being an individual who simply wants to be in a position of power over less powerful characters (a combination of Profiles 3 and 4). By combining the existing profiles to create a smaller number of archetypes, *Immigration* could be made viable for as few as two (or even one) spect-actor(s).

When applying similar considerations to the number of performers that might be needed/recruited, clearly, a piece like *Immigration* allows room for tens of actors to be involved: in addition to the HEAD OFFICER, there is room for multiple GUARDs, APPLICANTs, and ACTIVISTs. There is no "maximum" number that I see as being important to any of these character groups—what is important is that director be cognizant of proportions (the ratio of GUARDs to spect-actor-OFFICIALs, for example; or the ratio of APPLICANTs to OFFICERs). What is also important is that the director ensures that a diversity of profile types from the archetypes that have been scripted are shared across whatever number of performers might be available. There should be no worry about there being multiple actors who all have the same GUARD profile allocated to them, since the performers—through the use of the character questionnaires and other rehearsal strategies that have been spoken about in the Interlude following *War*—will have the opportunity to shape their characters in their own unique way. So, for instance, if two actor-APPLICANTs are given the same profile of being an applicant who is seeking to visit the country so as to attend the wedding of a sibling, one of these applicants might be a character who has a steady job in their home country and as a result, seen as presenting a lower risk. The other applicant with the same profile, while visiting the host country for the same reason, could be characterized as someone who is unemployed in their home country and as a result, especially because they have a sibling in the nation being visited, presents a more complex case of visa assessment. By using the same archetypes, therefore, while varying particular conditions in that profile, each of the ten potential profiles that have been scripted for the actor-APPLICANTs could be made applicable to multiple performers.

Conversely, if the production team for *Immigration* is only able to recruit, say, two actors for the entire performance, here are some adjustments and adaptations to make that possible. In terms of the roles that currently exist for performers (the HEAD OFFICER, GUARDs, APPLICANTs, and ACTIVISTs), the role of the HEAD OFFICER is the least expendable and even if there were only to be one performer available for *Immigration*, the HEAD OFFICER's role should be retained in as close a fashion to the original script as possible. The characters of the GUARDs, APPLICANTs, and ACTIVISTS on the other hand, are more expendable and based on the number of actors, there can be five GUARDs or there can be none—as long as, in the latter case, the HEAD OFFICER is able to maintain an atmosphere of surveillance and discipline on their own. With the actors who play the roles of APPLICANTs, there might be creative and interesting possibilities, even if there are only one or two actors available for these roles. For example, based on the skills of the performer in question, the same actor could keep returning as a different APPLICANT i.e., the same person could take on multiple roles and through the use of intelligent design choices and the casting of a multitalented actor, sufficient character transformation could be achieved. Furthermore, this one actor playing multiple APPLICANTs would not only be a solution to a logistical issue; they could also function as a metaphor for the problematic ways in which different and complex stories of emigration and immigration are often boiled down to the image of *one* body; one generic immigrant. Instead of the presence of one actor being a limitation then, this individual actor-APPLICANTs—by returning in multiple guises and by embodying multiple stories—could create the illusion of a multitude; of the specific, that is lost in the general. An additional option would be for the entirety of the applications to be paper-based; no APPLICANT comes in person. This, while primarily a logistical choice, would also add a different dimension to the experience: of underscoring the way in which increasing bureaucracy around immigration paperwork leads to the challenge of attempting to assess, from lifeless papers, the gravity, authenticity, and worth of the lives and experience that are being assessed. The HEAD OFFICER, in such a case, would double check a paper-based application that the spect-actor-OFFICIAL suggests for approval (instead of conducting an interview with the actor playing that APPLICANTs' role).

While these solutions would work for actors who are inside of the immigration space itself, a different kind of creativity would be needed if there were no actors available to take on the roles of the ACTIVISTs who are present outside the immigration building, i.e., the two groups of protestors that the spect-actors encounter when they are exiting the space at the end of their time in *Immigration*. While a larger number of actor-ACTIVISTs would allow for a more visible and crowded protest to occur and would create opportunities for spect-actors to channel their politics, should the context make it difficult for actors to be recruited as ACTIVISTs, the protest could also be framed as an "installation." In this installation, multiple posters and signs could be placed in significant and evocative ways outside the gates of the immigration building—symbolically representing the protest that took/is taking/will take place. Projections could be used on screen panels (if the resources are available) simulating the presence of groups of people—with the simultaneous use of voice recordings that ask spect-actors the same kinds of questions that actor-ACTIVISTs ask them in the script as it is. Furthermore, in addition to the posters with text and audio recordings, there could be blank poster boards and markers that spect-actors could choose to write on as they depart; there could be megaphones placed as part of the installation that exiting spect-actors could choose to pick up (or not). The installation, in this way, would recreate the same choice that spect-actors have to make when deciding whether or not to engage with the protesting actors—except that the choice they make would be about using objects, rather than people, to engage with a problematization of their previous complicity within the office.

If, in addition to issues recruiting actor-ACTIVISTs there were to be financial constraints on the production team, instead of projections and surround sound, the production team could use a "symbol" to represent the bodies of spect-actors. Let's consider the stone as a symbol; stones that have been used in protests in different parts of the world. So imagine this, if there are no actor-ACTIVISTs that can be recruited, but as the spect-actors exit the immigration office, they see rows upon rows of stones. Each stone has a little sign above it; a sign that includes the name of a person and says what they are protesting for/against: "Mr. Aybee Ceedee: he believes that we need stricter immigration laws." The stones are placed in rows with an aisle between them; the stones are thus on the two sides of the larger space, visually showcasing the opposition that exists between the two groups of stone-protestors. As the spect-actor walks through the passage between the two stone groups, a GUARD (or the HEAD OFFICER) could follow them; disrupting the stones as they walk through, and attempting to remove these stones from the spect-actors' sight. Perhaps the authority figure could ask the spect-actors to help them collect the stones and to put them into a sack? Symbolically, as the reader will have guessed, the authority figure in question will be asking spect-actors to perpetuate the silencing of protest; a further level of complicity that spect-actors could participate in or not. The stones could be balloons that are burst; balloons filled with paint. The stones or balloons could be sticks; sticks that are broken by the authority figure and the spect-actors. The stones or balloons or sticks could also be mirrors; mirrors symbolizing protest and activism; mirrors that are broken forcefully, till shards of glass cover the entirety of the space and till the breakers of the glass have to walk over them. Through the creative use of objects and installations, therefore, the concept of a protest and the spect-actors' decision to (dis) engage with that event could still be recreated.

Scaling Space

While the considerations and proposals above speak to how the numbers of people recruited—as spect-actors and performers—can be worked with to create a powerful experience with *Immigration*, let's move on to thinking about resources in terms of space. Since applied theater often occurs in settings and locales that might not have spaces for theater to take place, how can a director of any of the scripts in this book (*Immigration* being used as an example here) be creative in the face of spatial limitations? The physical environment that has been described for *Immigration* is defined as being a large building with a fence around it; a building that looks impressive and mysterious; a building that is, somehow, threatening in its "grayness" and fluorescent lighting. And while that approach of grandeur could create a heightened visual and experiential affect, I would suggest that powerful outcomes are possible even if the director is only able to acquire one small room in a non-descript location in order to conduct the experience of *Immigration*. If that is the case, for example, if only a single room will be available to the production team, I suggest that an effort be made to find a location that spect-actors are unfamiliar with; where spect-actors will still experience discomfort and surprise. And even if the only available space were to be one that that spect-actors are already familiar with, what could be done in terms of design to defamiliarize the space and to still enable spect-actor to feel uncomfortable and claustrophobic? Could paint be used creatively on the floor, walls, and/or ceilings to create optical illusions of space differentials within that room? Could a raked floor be built, so as to distort the spect-actors' experience of moving around the room? These "simple" adjustments and additions, therefore, could make the most basic, single room that spect-actors are familiar with, into a performance space that seems unfamiliar and distorted.

I say all of this about the notion of scale because the aspect that is ultimately important for the execution of *Immigration*, as I see it, is the orches-tration of an experience in which the spect-actor gets to "be" an OFFICIAL—within an immersive theatrical world that is framed to catalyze that spect-actor's critical self-reflections about their complicity within a larger, unjust structure. Creating the conditions for spect-actors to take away "something" and reflect upon that "something" as result of that embodiment of the Other, therefore, is the most important element of all the three scripts in this book. Unlike more mainstream, non-applied theater efforts, it is *not* important that there be "full house" or that there be a set design that astounds spect-actors with its technical brilliance; no. Rather, while I acknowledge that having a sold-out show, and using innovative design elements could make an immer-sive theater aesthetic that much more affective, given the pedagogical prin-ciples that guide all the three scripts in this book, what is most important to me is that that these experiences be scalable and adaptable: in terms of the context; in terms of the resources that are available to that particular group of performers and directors. The physical setting, therefore, like the number of spect-actors and actors, can be scaled based on what is present/absent in that applied theater practitioner/researcher's environment.

Scaling Time

Having considered the ways in which scale might be responded to—in terms of the numbers of actors and spect-actors and the physical location that is available—the final consideration with regard to this aspect of scaling is the notion of time. And in putting this forward, I must mention there are different temporal dimensions to consider. How do we deal with time in terms of what commitment actors can realistically make to the rehearsal process? How does the durationality of a performance like *Immigration* need to shift based on the time that spect-actors are willing to coming to a the-atrical experience? How does an understanding of time need to shift, since immersive theater often extends to processes that come before and after the central theatrical event itself? Let's look at these questions, and their inter-sections, briefly.

Sometimes, when working with non-professional, unpaid actors, as is often the case with applied theater initiatives, performers in a particular dra-matic piece are also students, community organizers, or otherwise employed.

And as a result of these individuals' embodiment of multiple personal and professional identities within that local context—each identity, which might be prioritized as being as important as the next—I have often had to adapt my schedule based on the time that these performers are able to commit to rehearsals; not to mention the extensive time that is needed for the durational nature of the work in pieces like *Detention, War,* and *Immigration.* This is not to say that the importance of the actors' multiple identities is a limitation; far from it, actually. The fact that participants in an applied theater project belong to various social networks is an element that I have found to be incredibly central both to the longevity of a project and the potential of its "impact." It is this interconnectedness between the performers and people in the communities around them that then becomes an essential component of the human infrastructure that is needed to facilitate the afterlife of an applied theater initiative.

While I have made some suggestions about adapting the rehearsal process to the project's time constraints in the Interlude that comes after *War,* I believe that it is important to consider the challenge that comes from creating durational performances—where both actors and spect-actors are also asked to commit to longer time periods within the performance event (and its pre/post-components); longer time periods that these individuals might not be able or willing to accommodate. As the reader might recall, *Detention* suggests a time frame between eight and twenty-nine hours for the experience; *War* includes multiple follow up sessions after the central performance event; *Immigration,* I suggest, continues as long as is needed for the quota of accepted applications to be reached, or for the duration a regular eight-hour workday. Each of these scripts therefore, asks for significant commitments from spect-actors and from performers—commitments that go beyond what is required of spect-actors and actors in more "conventional" approaches. So, how does the production team of an immersive theater script in an applied context scale the temporal dimension to the performances?

Unlike the other logistical adaptations that I encourage the executors of the scripts to make, with time, I would suggest that the creators be less accommodating; less flexible. Although I am still in the process of theorizing what exactly it is about longer durations in an immersive experience that might affect spect-actor outcomes—I'm in the midst of framing an experiment to explore this very aspect—there is, obviously, something different that happens the longer we stay in a particular situation. Is it that the odds become higher, with an increased duration, of a trace being left in spect-actors' minds and bodies? Does there emerge a potentially increased likelihood, with more time, for the spect-actor to internalize the experience? Time played an important role, for example, in the ways in which people behaved in the Stanford Prison Experiment (SPE; Zimbardo, 1971), where the outcomes might have been entirely different had the participants known that the experience would culminate in two hours (rather than two weeks). Time had an important role to play in the SPE having to be canceled a week before its original end date, because the participants' extended immersion in their roles as prisoners and guards seemed to become all-consuming.

It is because of such shared resonances, and because of the findings that have emerged from experiments like the SPE, that I insist for the production teams of *Detention, War* and *Immigration* to retain the durational options that have been suggested for each of the respective scripts. And to those who suggest that spect-actors cannot be expected to attend events that require so much time commitment, I would say the following: that given the pedagogical nature of this work, do we not want to engage with complexity—complexity that needs time to unravel and reveal itself? Given the goals that frame the scripts in this book, do we not want to focus on the spect-actor who is so keen to learn that they are willing to put in the time and the effort that might be needed to do so? Isn't the willingness to commit time the essence of most formal and informal educational settings, where any new knowledge is expected to be assimilated and integrated into existing knowledge systems? And if there emerges an immediate spect-actor bias in who comes to a performance, because of the time commitment that might be needed, can we not say that it is precisely such individuals who *should* be part of experiences like these—so that the immersive environments are seen (from the get go) as learning experiences, rather than vicarious and exoticising insights into an Other's way of being?

Scaling Actor and Spect-Actor Recruitment

All this being said, while I would suggest retaining the durations of *Detention, War,* and *Immigration* to be the same as what has been scripted in this book, I do not close the door to the need for creative, additional ways in which spect-actor and/or actor recruitment might be heightened. If it is the case that fewer performers and spect-actors are likely to commit to something that is less familiar in form, content, or both, I believe that very strategic pre-performance additions could be designed and executed by the production teams of *Detention, War,* and *Immigration*. What do I mean by this? First, it is important to state my starting point: that applied theater practitioners often work in contexts to which they are *not* complete strangers; contexts in which we have networks and connections to draw on. Therefore, I would recommend that, should spect-actor recruitment become a hurdle because of the duration of the experiences in conjunction with the unfamiliarity of both the content and the form, the production team might consider how to increase spect-actor and actor recruitment through the use of "primer" events. These primers could be designed in multiple ways; as short performances that are staged using more "conventional" strategies; short performances that will give potential actors and spect-actors a glimpse into what they might expect from their durational counterparts. Primer events could also involve the use of documented materials from other immersive experiences, which are sent to potential actors and spect-actors, to give them an idea of what the final experience might be like. The materials could include informal presentation sessions/readings/workshops where potential spect-actors could be led through interactive processes that show them what immersion might mean. Let me give you a few examples for such approaches.

First, let us consider the approach where a more contained preceding event is used to generate interest and enthusiasm both amongst potential actors and spect-actors. What would this look like? Consider this plan: a month or so preceding the final showcasing of *Immigration,* there is an event that is organized. In this scenario, we see an immigration official on a proscenium stage. The immigration official talks to the people in the spect-actor about why he does his particular job; what he enjoys about it; what he finds challenging. Then, we see a short scene where he interviews an a visa applicant: after the interview, the official turns to the spect-actor and presents another monologue that encapsulates the struggles he feels with making a decision about the status of the application. This process of interview/reflection continues for three or four iterations after which, there is a symbolic scene that shows the official's confusion at the job he must do. After the spect-actor group to this performance event has witnessed all the five monologues, the director could say something like this:

> Today, you saw one immigration officer deal with the task of interviewing and assessing applicants. Now, close your eyes, and imagine that you are an immigration official. You are in that chair, asking people questions, and trying to see who to let into your country, and who to keep out. What would you do if you were him? *(Pause)* This is what you will be asked to do in *Immigration.* You will become an immigration officer for a day and in this role, you will decide the fate of applicants who are trying to come into your country. The rest … the rest you'll experience when you come to the experience. We understand that we are asking for a lot of your time but I hope that all of you will find it to be worth your while.

Ultimately then, with this approach to a primer event, the spect-actor is given a "lead" through the use of a less novel theatrical experience. And in so doing, in facilitating more informed insights into what their final experience will actually be like, I wonder if spect-actors (even in less easy-to-recruit contexts) might be more persuaded to attend. This approach—of using a proscenium scenario interspersed with monologues performed by the actor playing the Other that spect-actors will eventually embody in the immersive experience—can be used in similarly structured primer events for *Detention* and

War as well. In *Detention*, for instance, the *scene-among-actors* <→> *reflection-monologue-with-spect-actor* approach could be used to show a detention center educator's attempts to teach a class of incarcerated youth on her first day in that context. In *War*, the *scene-among-actors* <→> *reflection-monologue-with-spect-actor* approach could put forward two or three different attempts of an outsider to interact with a particular situation in a conflict zone.

Now, while the abovementioned ideas seek to address how challenges with spect-actor recruitment might be addressed, how might these ideas need to change when seeking to recruit more actors rather than spect-actors? How can similar strategies be used with performers who might be hesitant to commit themselves both because of a hindered understanding of immersive theater, and because of the duration of the performances? To recruit actors, then, rather than self-contained performances I would suggest a "showcasing" of varied archival materials that might be sent to interested actors a few days/weeks before an audition. The director could send existing materials—in various media—about immersive theater in the work of a company like Punchdrunk or UHC Collective, about whom multiple archives are available. This sharing of archival material would ideally occur in a "live" session, where interested actors are invited to a screening or a talk that is hosted by the production team. In this session, after the audio-visual material is showcased, the director might expand on the connection between the showcased materials and the experience in which actors would participate—thus, hopefully stimulating more potential actors in wanting to participate.

Of course, in addition to using written or video archives, the production team could also invite potential performers to a panel discussion; a discussion with individuals who occupy various positions on the spectrum of characters in the script in question. For example, for *Detention*, the panel could include "real world" educators from a detention center, alongside former inmate-students, and/or prison administrators. For *War*, the panel could be composed of outsiders working in war zones, alongside the narratives of "real world" war zone residents who have had to interact with outsiders in different ways. Similarly, for *Immigration*, the panel could be made up of "real world" immigration officials, former authorities, immigration policy makers, and immigrants. The individuals on each of these panels could be given specific prompts to respond to; prompts that seek to draw out complexities of all those different voices from a particular socio-political realm. Through such an approach in which potential actors learn more, not only about the form, but also about the content it addresses, perhaps the attendees might be more likely to commit the time needed to rehearse and execute such works?

As a final example of a primer event, one that would work both with potential spect-actors and performers, I would suggest—for a piece like

Immigration—that a "publicity" or "recruitment" session is held with members in an organization that works around immigration rights. In this workshop, rather than explaining the form through the use of words, participants could be asked to go through a simple exercise (a version of which I used in Kashmir in 2015, with school students who were to come to a performance the next day). In this exercise each participant is first asked to list a maximum of five actions that define them: actions that could include a particular yoga pose; an action like cooking; an activity like cutting trees; a pursuit like mountain climbing; actions that these participants consider to be integral to who they are, as individuals. If I were the participant for example, I would probably list the following five activities as being ones that, somehow, define me: writing; working out; meditating. Then, each participant (individually) is asked to think about the following: if you wanted someone else (Person B) to do those actions you (Person A) just mentioned, but this time, with the added condition that Person B should have an embodied experience of what *you* (Person A) feel when performing those activities—and not what they (Person B) would feel themselves. If you wanted this to occur, what would you add to the list of your actions? Participants would probably suggest costumes, character profiles, set elements, and/or prop elements. They should be allowed to change the actions on their list if they can't think of a way in which Person B would be able to experience their initial ideas. Returning to my own example, then, here's what I might suggest:

- Writing: Person B could be told to sit alone, at a desk, with a cup of coffee and a laptop. They would be given a writing prompt, which could be the theme for a story. They could be given a word count goal that needs to be accomplished within a set amount of time; 1000 words in an hour, for example.
- Working out: Person B could have to watch a video of a vigorous cardiovascular workout regimen—between 45 minutes and an hour long—and complete it, however hard they might have to work.
- Meditating: Person B could be taken through a guided meditation exercise, in complete silence. The meditation is not religious but an exercise in independent thought, breathing, and reflection.

Upon creating such individual lists that outline potential actions that another person (Person B) could undertake so as to understand their peer's (Person A) life better, each participant shares their lists with the larger group. Then, based on proposals that resonate more with the immersive theater aesthetic in *Immigration,* the theater group that is facilitating the workshop picks two proposals from the group of participants—let's say they pick the actions put forward by Personal C and Person D. Then, the larger group of workshop participants is divided into two smaller teams: Team C and Team D. Team C works with one facilitator from the production team, aiming to create ways for Team D to experience Person C's actions (the originator of that idea should be in team that creates it: Person C should be in Team C). Team D, similarly, works with another facilitator to create Person D's action-based-experiences for members in Team C.

After the teams have had the time to develop the idea further, the facilitator helps bring those ideas to life and mentors the teams through a process of staging what they have been working on. Once both teams are ready, each one's work is experienced by the other group. The length of the devised works is not important though; rather, through creating these works for each other, and through a follow up discussion that comes after, participants will gain a little bit more of an informed opinion about what they can expect in the performance of *Immigration*, without giving away the exact premise of the experience. Through such a one- or two-hour long workshop—or through the use of other kinds of primer events that were described earlier—hesitant spect-actors from the target group, or hesitant performers from the target actor group, might be prepared for what to expect in a novel initiative; thus, possibly increasing the odds that these individuals might then be willing to commit to the entirety of *Detention, War,* or *Immigration* as performers and/or spect-actors. Ultimately, of course, no primer event is going to be useful to someone who just does not have the time available; however interested they might be. And that ... well, that is one of the challenges of making theater in applied theater contexts.

In light of the abovementioned considerations about the challenges that might emerge from an availability or scarcity of resources—resources as defined by the number of performers and spect-actors that can be recruited; the extent of space that might be available; constraints vis-à-vis time—I hope that potential directors of the scripts in this book will have gained more insights into the sheer multitude of ways in which *Detention, War,* and *Immigration* might be scaled in their execution. And having spent some time on this thought exercise vis-à-vis scaling and resource availability, it is time to turn the second component of this Interlude: what elements of more "traditional" playwriting have to change when scripting for an immersive theater?

For an Immersive Theater Playwright

In the Interludes that followed *War* and *Detention,* I have highlighted particular aspects to playwriting for an immersive theater that seem to differ from what is needed in more "conventional," Realism-inspired, dramatic scripts. As such, I have discussed the shifting importance of text in immersive theater—from being focused on the creation of dialogue, to being about the generation of scenarios. I have also considered the (sometimes extensive) inclusion of pre- and/or post-performance events in *Detention, War,* and *Immigration*; a characteristic that manifests differently in this book's immersive theater scripts than their less immersive counterparts. In addition to these two elements then, the process of writing *Immigration* has highlighted a third idea: the notion of "flexibility" and how particular writing strategies became useful in all three scripts, in scripting flexibility. While one of the writing strategies that helped with structuring flexibility—and no, that's not an oxymoron!—is the almost complete absence of dialogue that makes each of the scripts adaptable to different languages, actors, and situations quite easily, given that I have spoken about dialogue in an earlier Interlude, I shall not talk spend more time on it here. However, what I would like to do, is to spend time discussing two writing strategies that have been helpful in scripting flexibility into all the texts in this book: the concept of the archetype; the concept of fragmentation.

Before moving on to a discussion of these two concepts and their sub-categories though, I must underscore my acknowledgment that the use of archetypes and fragmentation are useful *for me*—for the particular ways in which I use immersive aesthetics in this book; for the specific pedagogical and socio-political objectives that I want *Detention, War,* and *Immigration* to put forth. Given the specificity, then, in the form and objectives of the pieces included here, the writing strategies that have come to be integral to my own scripting of flexibility, might certainly *not* be useful for *all* immersive theater. And yet, there still might be points of consideration in the discussion that follows, for practitioner-researches who use different aesthetic and pedagogical objectives but still seek to use a flexible, immersive aesthetic.

Rethinking Characterization

Because of the intensely improvisational and responsive quality to the scripts, where actors have to shift what they say and do based on spect-actors' responses and actions, the strategy that immediately became most useful was the creation of "archetypes" in the scripting of the characters who inhabited the worlds in *Detention, War,* and *Immigration*. The use of archetypes, in their *not* being stereotypes, became a way for me to allow for flexible characterization to be present, alongside concrete structural decisions surrounding the "kinds" of characters that I wanted to inhabit the worlds of these theatrical environments. This is to say that the archetypes that I propose in the character profiles, in all the three scripts, are not whims of my fancy alone; no. These archetypes are based on behavioral patterns that seem to occur in detention centers; in war zones; in immigration offices. And while the archetypes that I put forth do not present an exhaustive list, they do represent a mosaic of complex behaviors within a particular identity subgroup. A mosaic that draws from material encountered in archival research, in mainstream and non-mainstream representations in media, and via my own lived experience. This use of archetypes is quite different from the highly individualized portrayal of characters in the dramatic genre of Realism, for example, where a character is not an archetype—the character, in Realism, is an individual. The use of open-ended archetypes in the immersive theater scripts in this book, therefore, has become a strategy so as to ensure flexibility in the actors' characterization of their roles. So that each character's personalities, layers, and nuances can be shaped by the performers playing those roles—in conversation with the director, and in relation to the specificities of the context in which the script is being implemented.

I consider this attempt to frame a more flexible characterization process to be a strategy that is particularly important for applied theater interventions (rather than non-applied manifestations of immersive theater), where both the processes of creation and the performance products are as important as each other. In these applied initiatives that centralize learning at multiple levels, the goal is not to ask actors to stick to a script as a playwright has written it, without each performer's unique input in the development of their own characters. Rather, in the spirit of the devising and collaborative qualities that become important when theater is applied to non-traditional settings and toward social, political, and/or pedagogical objectives, the characters in these scripts hope to invite the expertise and the lived experience of the performers themselves. Since it is precisely these qualities of being devised and collaborative that make an applied theater intervention difficult to script— after all, how can you script a product that is hinged on the outcomes of an always unpredictable process—that the use of archetypes became a strategy that I came to find integral.

This use of archetypes, and this strategy's subsequent impact on an actor's ability to characterize their own contributions to the piece, was also integral to how profiles were designed for spect-actor-Others; to frame how these participants might enter into the world of the immersion. In addition, this particular decision was also based on trial and error in previous work. When I first started using immersive aesthetics, I would give spect-actors really ambiguous frames for which Other they would become for the duration of their experience. For example, Kashmiri male spect-actors were asked to become "a woman" in *Cages* (Dinesh, 2015a); they were asked to become "an asylum seeker" in my experiments in New Mexico (Dinesh, 2016b). This generic characterization worked for those particular initiatives, where part of pedagogical framework was to catalyze spect-actors to think about their own biases and prejudices; to get them to critique their own choices when characterizing those Others. So, for example, if Person M were to characterize

his asylum seeker as being someone from Somalia—with no geographic information stating that that should be the case—what does that choice say about
Person M's views toward Somalis? And as an extension, what might Person
M come to reflect upon as a result of encountering their own biases? With
this objective of self-critiquing one's implicit bias, therefore, choosing a
generic Other for spect-actor to embody seemed to be logical. However, this
use of the generic archetype came to cause an important (and contentious)
ripple effect. I came to realize through these experiences of asking spect-
actors to be "a woman" or "an asylum seeker"—without any more specificity
or context—became problematic. Problematic because, when being asked to
portray a large "category," if you will, in the absence of any more framing
information, spect-actors seemed to immediately fall back on preconceived
ideas and expectations surrounding what those general categories might
mean. For instance, "a woman" was often interpreted as "submissive"; "an
asylum seeker" was often interpreted as "desperate." Rather taking the opportunity to explore multifaceted narratives within that larger "category" of people, narratives that might have been more nuanced and astereotypical, spect-
actors seemed to choose what they already knew.

After a while, I came to think that a large part of this tendency amongst
the spect-actors to *Cages* and *Asylum*—of resorting to preexisting notions in
the embodiment of a generic Other—also had to do with the relative novelty
of the form of immersive theater. Since the form, in both cases, was mostly
unknown to a large number of the spect-actors, these individuals seemed to
immediately encounter some surprise/shock/discomfort in the face of the
expectations of interaction that were placed on them. The surprise/shock/dis-
comfort in understanding and stepping into an aesthetic that was unfamiliar,
seemed to lead to a reliance on latching onto the familiar (in characterization).

In order to address this issue, first, I began with the strategy of including
pre-performance workshops and preparatory sessions within my immersive
projects—to mitigate the novelty of the aesthetic, and as a result, the spect-
actors' reliance on stereotypes. In addition to this focus on how to frame the
work for spect-actors *before* an event, the idea about archetypes came about
organically. Having heard from spect-actors in the first iteration of *Asylum*
in 2016 that they did not understand who exactly they were supposed to
become, in a refurbished version of *Asylum* that was performed in 2017, I
created more clearly defined characters for the spect-actors. In these profiles,
I defined the circumstances of their character's fleeing into exile; their personal background; their name—and after the experience, spect-actors' comments suggested that the crutch of the profile prevented them from being
overly nervous about what they could/could not do within the world of the
performance. The additional layer of archetypal information that was given

to the spect-actors in the second version of *Asylum,* therefore, seemed to balance the immediate discomfort/confusion/surprise that came from the novelty of the aesthetic; from the jolt of processing what they were being asked to do within the immersive world. The creation of more rules then, through pre-performance work and through the use of character profile archetypes, seemed to assist spect-actors in their embodiment of an Other in immersive theatrical aesthetics. I am still exploring the limits of this approach, i.e., how much information about the character might be too much and leave no room for spect-actors' imagination, for example. However, even knowing that more exploration is needed, the observations from 2017's *Asylum* were convincing enough to make the case of the use of the strategy in all the scripts in this book.

In creating these archetypes then, and in using them to create flexibility, there was a particular process that I found to be useful: looking not for singular archetypes representative of a larger group (a larger group like "detention center educators," or "outsiders in war zones," or "immigration officials"). Instead, once I had decided on a particular gray zone that I wanted to focus on in each text, I began to look at archetypes that *within* a larger character sub-group. Archetypes *within* a larger group of detention center educators; archetypes *within* a larger group of outsiders in conflict zones. Archetypes *within* a larger group of immigration officials. In so doing, I hoped to create a more accurate representation of reality—where people take on particular jobs and particular roles because of a whole host of factors that make stories unique, despite the patterns and trends that nevertheless exist. This is to say, for example, that one detention center educator might take on the job for financial stability; another, for the idealism of working with young people; a third, because that's what everyone in their family has done. But just because a larger number of detention center educators might join the task for the financial stability, it doesn't make the idealists inconsequential; it doesn't make the "family lineage" workers inconsequential. In the creation of the archetypes then, the structure began with the formulation of a matrix: what are the factors that are likely to influence this "category"? Factors that, while not exhaustive, would provide a well-informed starting point from which to construct complex characters?

In addition to the use of character archetypes in creating a flexible process for actors in a devised and collaborative applied theater process; in addition to the use of character archetypes in creating a way of easing spect-actors into theatrical environments; these archetypes of spect-actor and actor roles allowed one more kind of flexibility that was important to me in the works in this book: the flexibility of the "message." It is not uncommon for applied theater projects to contain a specific message: a message where there is an oppressor and an oppressed; where the oppressor is usually in the wrong;

where the oppressed is usually romanticized as a blameless mass that is always victim to the perpetrations of the oppressor. Given my longstanding fascination with the gray zones then, it was important to maintain flexibility in what is perceived as being the "message" of *Detention, War,* and *Immigration.* A flexibility in what might be learned through these pieces. A flexibility of agendas. A flexibility of purposes. So, *Detention* can be about understanding the struggles of educators in juvenile detention contexts, yes. But it could just as well be about catalyzing discussion about the line between justice and rehabilitation. *War* could be about making more critically conscious outsider-citizenry who enter contexts of war. But it could just as well be about considering the ways in which we (on the insider end of the spectrum) might (mis) represent ourselves to different groups of outsiders for different purposes. *Immigration* could be about critiquing the complicity of the mid-level bureaucrat in an unjust immigration system. But it could just as well be about how stories of suffering can be "verified" and "authenticated" by one group of powerful people, based on factors that might lie completely outside those people's frames of reference.

The use of archetypal characterization, therefore, might also be seen as a way to intentionally promote a range of learning outcomes; outcomes that seek to complicate rather than simplify; to excavate rather than reinforce. By asking spect-actors and actors to take on particular archetypal roles within a particular character sub-group, there might be an increased likelihood for each person to take away something different from the piece. After all, if one educator is crafted as an idealist who loved their inmate-student, wouldn't they be likely to elicit different responses from the archetypal student characters than an educator who is crafted as authoritarian?

Rethinking Structure

In addition to the use of archetypes to incorporate flexibility in the spect-actor/actor experiences and in the theatrical environment's pedagogical objectives, another writing strategy that has enabled me to include flexibility at the core of the immersive theater scripts in this book is the notion of "fragmentation." Usually, when we look at a dramatic script in terms of its form on the page, we know what to expect: paragraphs that include descriptions of the set/costume/lighting/props; bullet point lists that name characters and sometimes provide brief summaries of their function within the larger text; scenes which are written as conversations—the name of a character, a colon as punctuation mark, and indented text that states what is to be said by the character in that moment in that scene (with the occasional stage director within the dialogue to tell the actor where to pause). In contrast, when we look at dramatic texts that inhabit another point on the formal spectrum—

texts that are intentionally Postmodern or Post-dramatic, for example—the form on the page showcases the aesthetics' fragmentation. The reader might encounter texts in irregular patterns and spatial alignment; texts that allows for an incredible amount of flexibility for the director and performers; texts that do not have any hint of a "narrative" or a "plot." These more "experimental," Postmodern texts are sometimes crafted without specific settings or characters or stage directions or dialogue. Instead, in these texts, the performative interpretation of the words on the page is entirely in the hands of the director in question. The director can choose to delineate characters or not; they can choose to perform (or not) what might, in more realistic texts, function as stage directions for the production team; they can choose to involve digital media and a collage of theater genres in the execution of the work.

The immersive scripts in this book are in no way as close to being Postmodern (or Postdramatic) in the way that Sarah Kane's (2000) *4.48 Psychosis* or Martin Crimp's (1997) *Attempts on her life* are—both texts that do not have specified characters or settings or dialogue or anything, really ... texts that have lots of fragments that are woven together with a linking thread that glimmers through, at the best of times. However, despite their relative Realism when compared to Kane and Crimp, *War, Detention,* and *Immigration* are still quite different (formally speaking) from the structure of scripts that follow a more realistic aesthetic: where characters speak to each other in intricately crafted dialogue within specifically contextualized or intentionally decontextualized settings, as in the case of texts belonging to the genre of the Theater of the Absurd. If I were to place the form of this book's texts between Realism on the one hand and Postmodernism on the other, then, I would say that the scripts here inhabit an in-between space: between structure and fragmentation; between the linearity of Realism and the (organized) chaos of Postmodernism. In so doing, in existing in this nebulous space that is hard to pin down, fragmentation in this book's immersive aesthetic has to do with having to the broad notion of "movement." Moving constantly back and forth between what actors do and what spect-actors are invited to do; moving, constantly, between the concrete actions that should be undertaken by the production team and the malleable elements within those actions that can be re-conceptualized and adapted in innumerable ways; moving, all the time, between scenarios that on one level are hyper-realistic and that, on another level, have nothing to do with Realism and might even cross over into the Absurd. Fragmentation in *Detention, War,* and *Immigration,* therefore functions as movements in the text: movements between addressing different constituents; different approaches; different realities. In summary then, it is the use of these fragmented textual shifts, in conjunction with the absence of dialogue, and the use of character archetypes, that were most highlighted through the process of writing *Immigration*.

Detention, War, and *Immigration* have each resulted in specific find-ings—findings that have led to the articulation of particular strategies for the production of immersive theater; findings that have led to the articulation of particular strategies for the writing of immersive theater. And it is the desire to create a conversation between the various findings that take me to the final, concluding, section of this book.

Conclusions

I went into this writing project with a lot of excitement and curiosity—after all, I have been on a search for immersive theater scripts ever since I began experimenting with the form more than five years ago! Scripting the works in this book, therefore, was a personal passion project; just as much it was to fill a void that exists within the realm of immersive theater; within the world of applied theater. There were different questions that I was asking myself as I took on this work: what would the gray zones of *Detention, War,* and *Immigration* manifest as, in each of the three texts? How would I make choices about the level of consequence, mirroring, social context, and freedom that needed to occur in each of the scripts? Furthermore, through the writing of each of the texts, would I be able to identify particular strategies that would be useful to both practitioners of immersive theater, when applied to an applied theater context?

In thinking about these questions, the Preludes in this book speak to the guiding frameworks and concepts that each text used as its point of departure. It was also in thinking about these questions that each of the Interludes focuses on two aspects. First, each Interlude speaks to specific "global" strategies that might be used by immersive theater directors across all the scripts in this book; also, potentially, strategies that might also be useful in different approaches to immersive aesthetics within and outside applied theater contexts. In addition, each Interlude also speaks to distinctions that might be drawn between writing strategies that are particular to immersive versus more "conventional" dramatic texts. This component to each Interlude has been included to assist the immersive theater playwright—whether they are crafting pieces using the same immersive aesthetic as in *Detention, War,* and *Immigration*; or whether they are looking to write scripts for other interpretations of immersive aesthetics.

In this concluding chapter, I begin by revisiting the reasons behind why I chose particular "gray zones" for *Detention, War,* and *Immigration*. Then, I move on to a summary of the material from each of the Interludes: the global strategies, and writing style comparisons, that seek to be useful to practitioners of immersive theater. Finally, underlying all parts of this chapter are ideas for next steps in my own research; next steps for what might be needed to further an individual and collective understanding of immersive theater as an applied theater aesthetic.

The Gray Zones

When beginning *Detention,* I knew from the outset that I did *not* want to make the spect-actor take on the role of the prisoner or the guard in the theatrical experience; not least of all because existing examples from social psychology experiments stand testament to the contentions problems that arise from giving people—even within a simulated context—power over each other. When approaching *Detention* in this book, therefore, I wanted to ensure that the final text would steer away from the better-known dynamics of the prison system: dynamics like complicity, authoritarian behavior, and abuses of power. Rather, I wanted the piece to work toward excavating intricacies that might go beyond a consideration of the most obvious binaries of power: this obvious binary in a youth detention center context being that between the inmate and their (prison) guard(s). As a result, I wanted to invite *Detention's* spect-actors to step into the shoes of a less considered Other within the juvenile justice system; an Other whose experiences are murky both because of that individual's particularly unique positioning in the juvenile justice context; an Other who occupies the shadows of prison walls, as it were, because of the relative silence that surrounds their narratives when compared to, say, the voices of detention center guards. Furthermore, this choice of intentionally *not* characterizing spect-actors as prisoners or guards was impacted by an ethical dilemma that came from my qualms of giving theatrical life to an experience that I did not have the lived experience of myself. As a result, therefore, when considering how I could give a respectful voice to perspectives that I do not have any lived experience of, when thinking about how I might frame the gray zones of juvenile detention centers, when trying not to fall prey to predictable modes of stereotyping, the Other chosen for the spect-actor to embody in the script of *Detention* became the role of an educator within a juvenile detention center's formal education system.

On a similar note, for *War,* I began by using Primo Levi's concept of the "gray zones" as a springboard and as a result, wanted the script to speak to the nebulous phenomena of violent conflict that are difficult to place on the victim/perpetrator spectrum. Thinking through this sentiment also involved becoming cognizant of the narratives that I might be ethically posed to tackle vis-à-vis my lived experience as someone who has never lived through war myself, but has intervened as an outsider in various contexts of conflict. With these considerations in mind I finally settled on the role that I wanted spect-actors of *War* to take on: the role of the outsider; a role that I have embodied, myself, in multiple conflicted contexts. This particular choice of gray zone in *War* seemed to be ideal for a couple of reasons. On the one hand, the outsider is someone who lies beyond the geographical and ideological boundaries of a specific conflict and, as a result, falls outside the spectrum of victimhood and perpetration in that context. And yet, in the outsider's positioning as someone who must decide how and when to intervene responsibly; in the outsider having to take on the responsibility of deciding whom to speak with; in the outsider having to choose how to act on their newfound knowledge about that conflict zone—doesn't the outsider become embroiled within the webs of that conflict? Not as victim or as perpetrator, but as someone in between?

This in-betweenness of a gray zone was slightly more complex to artic-ulate in the context of *Immigration,* given the biases that come with my per-sonal experiences of being/having been an immigrant in multiple contexts. In considering the personal dimension to this script then, I found it useful to go back to Hannah Arendt's (1963) *Eichmann in Jerusalem* and to ask myself: who are the Eichmanns in today's immigration systems? Who are the people that are part of (often unjust) immigration systems and who are so caught up in the banalities of their positions that they do not seem aware of the larger systems of injustice that they are perpetuating? Who are the Eich-manns in the world of immigration? Eventually, it seemed to me that this nebulous positioning within the immigration system (generally speaking) might be occupied by officials who do not influence policy, but rather, are the mid-ranking officials who accept or deny visa applications of aspiring visitors, immigrants, and/or asylum seekers. The officials are tasked with assessing visa and are asked, through these assessments, to validate the "authenticity" of individual's lives. I consider these mid-level officers to be the Eichmanns in the immigration world because, in their seemingly simple actions of "accepting" and "denying" a particular application, they have the power to tear a person's life asunder. Yes, these officers are simply imple-menting what they have been told to do; no, they have nothing to do with the creation of contentious immigration policies themselves. And yet, in doing what they do, without (it seems) a consciousness of how their individ-ual decisions might be part of a larger system that has the potential to dis-criminate, persecute, and oppresses. Even if/when there might exist a consciousness of complicity amongst some of these officers, don't these offi-cers become like Eichmann in their inability and/or unwillingness to take an individual stand? In their compliance with policies that can have life alter-ing consequences for those who must bear the consequences of the officers'

decisions? In the denial of their own power within the system? ... If all the
immigration officers at all ports of entry in the United States had refused to
implement the President's executive orders against refugees and asylum seekers, what might have happened?

In each of the abovementioned instances, of the gray zones that were
chosen for *Detention, War,* and *Immigration,* there were a variety of additional considerations that framed how those choices finally manifested in
the scripts themselves. The functioning of freedom, consequence, social
impact and mirroring in each of the scripts—to name the four concepts I
started off with—which were framing factors for effective interaction that I
came across in the crafting of Live Action Role Plays (LARPs). Beginning
with these concepts was extremely useful in thinking through initial ideas
for each of these texts. In execution, however, although social context and
freedom continued to be important in *Detention, War,* and *Immigration,* the
notions of consequence and mirroring were ones that I did not find to be
particularly useful to the aesthetics in this book. As a result of what did seem
to be useful in the writing process ultimately, if I were to put forward a particular series of points to consider in the scripting of immersive theater—in
the specific context of the form as used in this book—I would probably suggest the following:

Step 1

Role Creation: an identification of the particular Other that the playwright would like the spect-actor to embody in the immersive
world in question. In my case these choices were framed by the
notion of the "gray zones" vis-à-vis a particular socio-political conflict; but of course this does not always need to be the case.

Step 2

Social Context: the playwright's decisions surrounding the social context of the theatrical world, in terms of whether or not the environment that is being represented will be realistically specific to a
particular part of the world; or whether the theatrical world will be
intentionally allegorical or unspecified (lending to the work, like in
this book, being applicable to a variety of geographical contexts)

Step 3

Target Group Identification: the pedagogical objectives that the playwright has for the theatrical piece in question, and the subsequent
impact of those goals on spect-actor and actor recruitment. Who is
the ideal spect-actor group? Who is the ideal performer group?

Step 4

Pre- and Post-Performance Design: the pedagogical objectives that
the playwright has for the immersive piece in question, and the

impact of those goals on the need for—and design of—events that extend before and after the central theatrical experience.

STEP 5

Freedom: the extent of the actions that the playwright would like for spect-actors to be able to undertake in the immersive world, and the impact of that decision on the subsequent structuring of the script itself. How much liberty do spect-actors have in the creation and development of their character profiles? How much can spect-actors control the progression of the narrative within a particular scenario?

Ultimately, therefore, the process of writing this book has led me to conclude (for the moment) that the abovementioned conceptual ideas and their interactions with each other might be most applicable in the Prelude to writing for immersive theater, especially when the form is being used as an applied theater aesthetic. In future work then, what I would like to explore is the continuing relevance of the steps above, both to my own work and to the work of like-minded practitioner-researchers of immersive theater.

Strategies for an Immersive Theater Director

The process of writing each of the scripts in this book has also led to the articulation of three global strategies that might be useful across the board—both to the three texts in this book, and also to other immersive, dramatic texts that might seek to have applications to non-traditional contexts. This is not to say that there are only three global strategies that need to be considered across all immersive theatrical experiments. Simply that *Detention, War,* and *Immigration* have led me to focus on three particular overarching strategic realms that would be useful for an immersive theater practitioner to draw on.

Contextual Adaptation

The first global strategy, which emerged through the process of writing *Detention,* takes the form of a thought exercise that describes how the generic and unspecified location of the detention center in the piece might be contextually adapted for a very specific geographical setting (like India, as was the example used in that particular Interlude). Through this thought exercise, and using the example of *Detention,* I make proposals about particular tweaks that might be made to the characterization of actors and spect-actor profiles, to make the script more contextually relevant to a unique location. I also suggest that by making well-considered adaptations made to the overall schedule and design, the detention center school could be as intricately particular to a specific locale as a production team might desire. By suggesting ways in which such adaptations might be made, therefore, I hope to have presented a potential director of *Detention* with ways in which the framework presented in the original script might maintained in its entirety while also allowing for context specific adaptations to be made. This thought exercise vis-à-vis *Detention* enabled me to articulate the general steps below, which might be followed in adapting any (context unspecified) immersive text to a specific geographical location. While there is a suggested order below, directors are invited to reorder these ideas as best suits the specific nature of the production in question:

> *Step 1:* Find the local context's equivalent of the setting/scenario locations described in the immersive text i.e., the equivalent of the detention center school in *Detention;* the war zone and its dynamics in *War;* the particular type of immigration office in *Immigration.* Then, situate that local equivalent within the larger conversation surrounding its positioning within the context in question. For example: how does a particular village/town/city/country's approach to juvenile justice impact the composition of the school that is contained within it? What kinds of outsiders tend to create problematic interventions in a particular village/town/city/country's conditions of war? What demography do immigration officers tend to represent in that particular village/town/city/country? Ultimately therefore, every aspect of the unspecified context in the script should be localized and particularized to the specific village/town/city/country that the production team has chosen to based the work in.
>
> *Step 2:* Edit (if needed) the duration and/or overall schedule of the performance—including the pre- and post-performance events—so that the time frame is also applicable to the local context. For example: if the unspecified context is constructed as transpiring over the duration of twenty-four hours, but the chosen, specific, setting is more aligned to being contained within a twelve-hour duration, then the latter should be the timeframe that is chosen. With the use of the term "aligned," I do not mean to say that the production team should choose a duration that would make it easier to recruit spect-actors and actors. Rather, when I say "aligned," I mean that director should choose a duration that is factually relevant to the chosen context. For example: how may hours per day do young people go to school in the detention center in a chosen

context? What is the length of the working day for an average immigration officer in a particular village/town/city/country? When adapting *War* to a certain geographical setting, would it be more contextually relevant to extend the first common scenario (to be an hour long, for instance) to demonstrate local hospitality customs?

Step 3: Edit (if needed) the number of spect-actors and actors that might need to be recruited for an adapted version of the original script. For example, are the detention centers, war zones, and/or immigration offices in that context under/over populated in particular ways? And if so, how does the actor to spect-actor ratio need to change to demonstrate that dynamic?

Step 4: Adapt the design elements in the original script: the kind of space that would be more appropriate for a specific locate; the changes that might need to be made to the clothes that are worn; the smells that permeate the air; the tastes that spect-actors might encounter. Any design element that is part of the text, essentially. Does the average detention center school in a specific context have electricity all day? And if not, how might the lighting design in *Detention* reflect this reality? Is there a particular dance or song that is used as a welcoming ritual in a context, that might be appropriately used when the hosts invite spect-actor-outsiders into the world of *War*? Does the average immigration office in that local setting smell like disinfectant—or, if the only office in that context is next to a busy market, are smells of local food likely to waft in?

Step 5: Explore factors that would additionally influence the characterization matrix of spect-actors and actors. Since the character profiles for all participants, in all three scripts, have been created using a matrix of particular factors that might impact those "types" of people, attention should be paid to creating a holistic spectrum that might be representative of the demographic in that particular village/town/city/country. For example: is race a more relevant marker of identity to be used in the creation of prison inmate character profiles? Or would it be better to use a character's socioeconomic background in the matrix? Would intention be the relevant marker to be used in the creation of the outsider character profiles in *War*? Or would it make more contextual sense to define characters based on their national identities? Would immigration officers be better nuanced by considering their formal educational qualifications? Or would the number of family members that need to support, be a more accurate indicator of potential attitude toward visa applicants?

By following some or all of the steps above, in an order that best suits a particular theatrical initiative, an immersive theater director could take any of the three scripts in this book and adapt it to a very particular geographical area.

Designing the Rehearsal Process

Furthermore, just like the steps that I have suggested for contextual adaptation as result of *Detention,* the Interlude following *War* provides ideas for how an effective rehearsal process might be designed for immersive theater, given that these aesthetics require different tools that script-based, proscenium texts. As a result, I would postulate that the following sequence of techniques might be used for any training process that precedes the execution of an immersive piece—especially one that is intended to be applied to non-traditional contexts and as a result, involves particular pedagogical, social, and/or political ideals in addition to the aesthetic ones.

> *Step 1:* Introduce the performers who have been cast in/signed up for the production, to the concept of immersive theater—assuming that the actors in question do not have a pre-existing understanding of the form. For this introduction, I suggest breaking down the form into components that ask actors to focus on stimulating individual senses of their spect-actors. So, actors are facilitated through small-group exercises that lead to workshop participants devising short works over the course of three days—each of which focuses on the spect-actors' sense of sight (Day 1), sound (Day 2), taste, touch and smell (Day 3). These single-sense-focused explorations lead to sessions where the actors' are asked to devise original creations that invoke a multi-sensorial theatrical experience and ask spect-actors to walk around different spaces. Ultimately connections are made between these exercises and the form of immersive theater that will be used in the performance itself.
>
> *Step 2:* The actors are cast into specific roles and a first reading is conducted of the entire script.
>
> *Step 3:* Production Process
> - Actors work on their characterization through the use of character questionnaires
> - Actors work on their characterization through the use of physical exercises and hot seating
> - The script is broken down into scenarios for rehearsal purposes, so that actors can work on the piece in self-contained sections
> - Actors' script their characters' lines in conversation with their scene partners and the director

- The blocking begins and consultations occur between actors and directors about honing movement, dialogue, and characterization choices
- Once the blocking is complete, test spect-actors (who are performers in other scenarios in the same script) are invited to participate in their peers' work. These test spect-actors can also be given directions on what kind of spect-actors to be; so as to give the actors in that scenario practice on how different responses might affect the work
- Test spect-actors from outside the performance ensemble are invited to participate in the self-contained scenario rehearsals. For these test spect-actors, no directions or suggestions are given. Since they are completely unfamiliar with the scenario in question, they are encouraged to simply respond as they best see fit
- Based on the responses that are received from the two different levels of test spect-actors, the actors in each scenario are guided through the process of creating If/Then matrices as a way to prepare themselves for certain stock occurrences that might emerge (like spect-actors wanting to go to the toilet, for example)
- A final rehearsal that is put together with all the self-contained scenarios coming together. A group of test spect-actors is again invited for this session.
- Following this final full rehearsal, performers undertake a workshop/discussion that is framed around implicit bias training and around framing performers' unconscious expectations of what "good" and "bad" participation might be. Performers draw from their experiences with the different test spect-actors to critically reflect on their own problematic response in situ—responses that might be a result of predispositions that they are not even aware of.
- The final performances take place!

While I hope that the steps above will be of use to practitioners in different kinds of immersive environments, I do believe that they will be particularly useful to those performances that adopt an aesthetic that is closer to that which is included in this book. Since the three scripts are hinged on actors responding to spect-actors as authentically as possible—authenticity being understood, here, as the commitment to a character—the process above was what I have come to find to be useful through past trials and errors of different rehearsal designs. In an immersive piece that allows less autonomy for spect-actors and performers, however, significant changes would probably have to be made.

Considering Scale

After considering the questions of context-specific adaptation and general rehearsal strategies, the third global strategy that emerged as being relevant through the process of writing *Immigration* was the notion of scale. In writing the piece and in looking at the fact that there could be a large number of performers might need to be accommodated in the piece—especially given the challenges of recruitment that come with applied theater interventions—it seemed pertinent to speak to how the scripts in this book might be scaled based on the availability of human, capital, and temporal resources. In representing the considerations that resulted, the ideas have been articulated as an If/Then matrix below; acknowledging of course that more conditions of scale can certainly be added to the conditions that are currently included:

Table 11: Resource-based If/Then Matrix

If	*Then*
If there is a limit in the number of actors who can be recruited for the performance—	Then, the less essential roles in the script might be cut and/or some of the character profiles might be combined to create more complex profiles for the number of actors that are indeed available.
	In addition, alternatives presented by the use of multimedia (projections, audio, visual installations) could be explored—alternatives in which live performers might be replaced through symbolic/non-live representations of the particular perspective or narrative that needs to be replaced.
If there is a limit on the number of spect-actors who can be recruited for the performance—	Character profiles can be mixed and matched, so as to create more complex profiles for the spect-actors that are available.
	If particular profiles are irrelevant to a certain context, they might also be cut. As long as enough profiles, or combinations thereof, are maintained to present diverse, non-stereotypical characters.
If there are spatial constraints—	Then, the production team can make "smart" choices by considering other aspects. For example, the production team could look into choosing a site whose history (within the local

If	Then
	community) might make it more appropriate for the performance than another—despite that space potentially not having the number of rooms that are needed as per the script. Choices could be made to use familiar/unfamiliar sites, based on which resulting ambience might be more affective for a particular kind of setting. Outdoor spaces could be designed/adapted as spaces—locations under trees; locations near water; using desolate countryside.
If there are temporal constraints, in terms of how much time actors and spect-actors are willing to commit to the rehearsal/performance process—	Then, the production team might consider holding "primer events": events that are strategically designed to occur a few weeks/months before the auditions/rehearsal/performance. These events could either be a "show and tell" of sorts, where immersive works are explained through a demonstration of examples from existing practitioners and researchers of the form. These primer events could also be designed as more "conventional" performances through which spect-actors are eased into what the form and content that they might expect in the immersive world. Primer events could also take the form of panel discussions, where carefully curated personalities are brought together to generate interest in the form and content of the experiences.

All of the abovementioned global strategies that have been put forward, as mentioned earlier, are directed toward directors of immersive theater—so that each production team can make the scripts their own. These are particularly relevant global strategies that were also chosen as a result of my personal experiences as an immersive theater director who has often asked myself questions related to the points mentioned above. How can I adapt an existing immersive script—not that I could find one, of course!—to a very particular geographical context? How can I train actors for a theatrical aesthetic that functions so differently from its less immersive counterparts, so much so that other techniques that I have used in the past did not seem relevant or useful? How can I adapt an immersive piece for differing numbers of performers and spect-actors, given the difficulties of recruitment in applied theater contexts? Addressing the three global strategies through the Interludes this book then, has not only been about reflecting on this writing process in insolation from the rest of my repertoire. Rather, it has also been about creating the kind of resource that I wish I had had when I first made the choice of using immersive forms as part of applied theater initiatives in contexts of conflict. Of course, there might be many additional global strategies to be considered; strategies that emerge as a result of my ongoing work with immersive theater; other strategies that will no doubt come to the fore as my immersive experiments continue to evolve.

Strategies for an Immersive Theater Playwright

Just as the section above relates to what I wish I had guidance on as a director of immersive theater, the next part of these conclusions relates to ideas I wish I had been aware of as an interested writer of scripts for this form. Having written different kinds dramatic scripts leading up to this project—many of which were far more "conventional" in their realist aesthetics—I knew that the process of crafting *Detention, War,* and *Immigration* would be "something" different. But I had no idea what this "something" might be. When writing each of the scripts in this book, therefore, I attempted to consciously observe my own process, and to document the changes that I experienced in the writing strategies that I found myself adopting. I should say here that the points that emerged as warranting consideration, the points that are included in the Interludes, each arose through an inductive process. I had no preconceived ideas or decisions about what I thought I would discover. Rather, in the spirit of letting the practice lead my research, I hoped that the process of writing would—through its own mechanisms—allow me to identify points of convergence and divergence.

The Role of Text

The first observation I made, through the process of writing *Detention,* was the way in which the role of the text seemed to differ between the pieces in this book and the more Realism-influenced scripts that I have written and/or read in the past. In thinking through the different positioning of text further, I came to understand that while text—in more conventional pieces— might be mostly valued for its use as a tool to generate dialogue between characters, text in an immersive piece seems to be more significant as a tool that is used to sculpt scenarios and character profiles. As a result, one of the ideas that I propose for the immersive theater playwright, is the scale below: where the writer's goals vis-à-vis the degree of performers' co-creation in the script might allow them to have a firmer understanding, from the outset, about the role for text within their script.

Table 12: Scaling Performer Co-creation
Levels of Performers' Co-Creation

A performance that requires performers to execute a text that is *exactly how the playwright has written it.* In this particular approach, the text that is created by the writer pays attention to every line and action that is said and executed by the actor. Although the extent of detail on structural/staging elements might vary in such scripts—based on the genre being adhered to, and of course, based on the aesthetic interests of the writer in question— dialogue is one of the most important components in such works. Performers give voice to what the writers have to say.	A performance that invites actors/directors to *become co-creators of the piece.* In the scripts of such performances, like the scripts in this book, actors' personal contributions to dialogue and characterization are integral to every scenario within the text in question. As a result, therefore, the centrality of text in these scripts might tend to lie in its ability to craft scenario and character outlines. Consequently, these pieces are likely to minimally use text as dialogue.	A performance that is *completely devised by the performers,* where these actors are as much writers, as they are performers and directors. In such performances, the texts are rarely scripted. Even in the event that they are given written form, this script entirely depends on the piece's potential to be replicated. Since devised performances are often, intentionally, situated within a specific context, and as the product that emerges in the coming together of a specific group of performers, replication is not an issue that I have seen being paid much attention too. Hence, perhaps, the scarcity of written texts for such performances.

Related to the scale above, vis-à-vis performers' levels of co-creation and that choice's impact on how the role of text might manifest in an immersive theater script, the Interlude following *Detention* concludes that it also might be useful to consider a similar scale that correlates the spect-actors' co-creation levels with the positioning of text within the dramatic script itself. In order to visualize this, I use same format of a scale, where one end represents a more "conventional" production where the audience watches and listens; where dialogue is likely to be an integral part of the dramatic script. The other end of the scale might be representative of the kind of co-creation that is invited in the scripts in this book, where all the spoken material from actors is hinged on individual spect-actor responses in the moment of the experience. Wouldn't it be likely, as a result, that text has a different part to play in such work? And of course, in between these two extremes, there might be the kind of performance in which spectators have some agency but not as much as in the scripts in this book—the kinds of performances that are likely to be staged by professional theater companies; the performances that are classified broadly as immersive theater; that while sharing resonances with the work in this book, might be said to look at spectators as participants rather than "actors."

Table 13: Scaling Spect-Actor Co-Creation
Levels of Spect-Actor Co-Creation

A performance that requires *audience members to watch and listen* (and nothing else). The act of performing on stage, as it were, is only in the hands of the performers and the other members of the production team. The audience does not engage with any of their senses other than sight and sound. Given the objectives in the scripts of such performances, there is likely to be an emphasis on what is said/done/performed on the stage, by the actors—since that is the primary stimulus that the audiences are witnessing. The text in these dramatic works can speak to design elements too, of course (think of stage directions and design ideas that are often included in some scripts). However, a bulk	A performance that invites *spectators to engage* but *also has particular sections that occur only between the performers.* In scripting these performances there is an emphasis both on what is said/done between the actors *only*—in the sections that are structured to occur without audience interaction and that are intended to always stay the same. However, these works might very well contain other sections that use text to structure scenarios (rather than dialogue or movement of actors). In these sections, audience members' interactions become significant and as a result, text loses its footing as a dialogue generation tool. I am yet to encounter such scripts, which	A performance that invites *spect-actors to become co-creators at every stage* of the piece. In the scripts of such performances, like the scripts in this book, spect-actors' contributions are integral to every moment with the performance. As a result, all the focus is on the use of text to craft structure and characterization, with there being minimal emphasis on what is spoken—since what will be spoken is likely to change based on what happens in a particular interchange between a specific actor and each unique spect-actor.

of the text that is written focuses on what is shown by the actors, to the spect-actors.	publically call themselves immersive theater and put forth dramatic texts. The works that I am aware of, that fit this category, do not (to my knowledge) have written scripts.	

As I conclude my considerations around the positioning of text in the writing process, however, I must ask myself if there are other ways in which co-creation might be fostered amongst actors and spect-actors in an immersive theater piece (which also has a devised, collaborative pedagogy in place) without relegating dialogue to the backburner. I return here to one of the examples that I mentioned in the Introduction, where role-playing was used in the social science classroom, with dialogue cards being given to student participants in the game so as to frame exactly what could be said by them in the context of specific scenes—delineating, therefore, exactly what could also be said back to them. If I were to consider this strategy further, for example, what if the spect-actors playing detention center educators were actually given scripted lesson plans to follow in the roles within *Detention;* rather than creating their own? Would this choice enable more controlled and scripted dialogue to occur amongst the actors playing the inmate students in that teacher's classroom? What if the spect-actors in their roles as outsiders in war zones, in *War,* are given specific lines with which to respond, when specific cues are provided by the actors? Would this strategy give a structure to the piece's pedagogical outcomes? What if the spect-actor in *Immigration,* as the immigration official, is given a script to follow—a script that dictates both how they will conduct every stage of the interview and include a marking grid that will numerically assess the authenticity of the visa applications? In some ways, I can see these strategies as containing potential. I see this potential, yes; for scripted dialogue to be used far more widely within the immersive aesthetic that has been used in this book's scripts. And yet...

I have just returned from participating in an immersive performance that adopted precisely this strategy. Spectators were participants and it definitely was an immersive performance in its being multi-sensorial and integrating audience members into "in world" characters by "training" us to say certain lines and perform certain actions when performers in a subsequent scene would provide a particular cue. And sure, that choice not only remained aesthetically appropriate for a piece that called itself immersive theater; that choice also provoked spectators to consider how much/how little they wanted to follow the rules of the world and perform their rebellion and/or complicity within that theatrical environment. But ... that was a different kind of performance—a performance that was not classified or classifiable as applied theater; a performance that did not (seem to) have particular socio-political themes that it wanted everyone to think about; a performance that had more financial and human resources that I could dream of for one of my projects. Could it be, then, that in addition the spectator/actors' degree of co-creation impacting how text is positioned in the written form of immersive texts, that the role of text might also have to do with the objectives of that immersive theater effort? Could it be that my choice to leave dialogue com-pletely open to spect-actors' and actors' interpretations actually also links back to the political, social, and pedagogical objectives of each piece—sub-sequently allowing the specification of target demographic group as actors and spect-actors? It's hard to say with any certainty and yet, this is one par-ticular aspect to immersive theater scripting that I would like to explore fur-ther—the place for dialogue; the place for dialogue when seeking to foster a high-level of co-creation for both actors and spect-actors in applied theater usages of the form.

Extending the Theatrical Event

While *Detention* got me to think about the shifting role of text in the scripting of different dramatic aesthetics, *War* became a catalyst for me to consider the inclusion of pre- and post-performance events in the scripts themselves. Although it is not uncommon for dramatic works, especially in the applied theater realm, to include particular kinds of sessions that come before and/or after the central performance event, it is rare (I think) for these sessions to be included as part of a written script. And although pedagogical and ethical questions, about caring for my spect-actors, were central to the scripting decisions vis-à-vis the pre/post-performance sessions in *Detention*, *War*, and *Immigration*, the final decision to include these processes as part of the scripts as also made because of the aesthetic enhancement that they provided the texts. The choice to design the pre- and post-performance forums as being "in world," for instance, and the choice to see them as integral extensions of the central theatrical event rather than ornamental add-ons, made the inclusion of what comes before and after the central performance a part of each script's aesthetic core.

In one way, this scripting decision seemed aesthetic because it imme-diately changed the visual form that the written, dramatic text took on the page. The decision also seemed aesthetic because scripting these before and after forums as part of the dramatic event seemed to heighten their impor-tance to the larger project, making them components that need to be carefully rehearsed, designed, and performed—and not just added on at the end of the rehearsal or production process. The scripting of forums that precede and follow the central theatrical event, therefore, and the inclusion of these components within the dramatic text itself, might be important ideas for any immersive theater playwright to consider, especially when seeking to script works that have pedagogical and social applications. I stress the pedagogical and social applications since, if an immersive theater playwright were to be less concerned about the pedagogical/social trace of the piece and were more focused on the aesthetic experience that is contained with the central event itself, well, such a writer might not need to consider the pre/post-forums with as much attention. In summary therefore, the main points from the discussion above might be articulated as follows (see Table below):

Table 14: Impact of Focus on Pre/Post-Performance Events

Focus	Implications
Performances that focus on the *spectators' experience* only *during the central theatrical event.* This central event could either be a script-based performance that occurs in the proscenium; or an interactive performance that does not have different rules of engagement to the extent of the scripts here, but one in which audience members might speak from their seats in an auditorium; or a performance that uses immersive aesthetics that might be extremely novel to spectators, but where audience discomfort and/or vulnerability is actually an important part of the work's intentionality.	In such pieces, even if there are social and/or political themes/pedagogical objectives, the focus is on what is experienced *during* the contained theatrical performance itself. And as a result, there is no need for an event that comes before or after the event in question, to frame either the novelty of the form or the pedagogical outcomes of the experience. Therefore, the scripts of such performances—if/when they exist—are *not* likely to contain sections that explain what might take place for spectators, before and after the event in question. The written text is likely to begin and end within the temporal confines of a central event.
Performances that *focus on a project's outcomes*; this is to say that, these initiatives focus on what happens for spectators beyond the performance itself. However intangible these desired outcomes might be—outcomes like "awareness" or "learning" or "sensitization"—these kinds of performances focus on the creation of a particular kind of "impact" that occurs *after* the central performance event. As a result of such an emphasis, I propose that there will need to be	If the pre/post-performance forums happen "out of world" i.e., where the theatrical environment created in the central event does *not* need to be maintained, the subsequent scripting of these instances are either not present in the script, or they are likely to be less extensive and simply summarize what needs to happen during them. Consider here, as an example, a discussion that takes place after a play about malaria prevention—where audience members are taught how to use mosquito nets. Here, the actors will

Focus	Implications
some consideration (in these piece's script) about what precedes and follows the central event. The exact nature of the content/structure of these sessions will, of course, depend on the precise pedagogical outcomes desired by that piece of theater, and the details of the aesthetic that the performance will use. Immersive pieces like *War*, which assign characters to spect-actors, have very different needs, for example, from different kinds of interactive/non-interactive forms that still emphasize the notion of "impact."	most likely step off the stage and one or more facilitators will take over, to provide instructions on how to use the nets. In such cases, I am hard pressed to see the need for why this last instructional component will need to become a scripted part of the written text (assuming, of course, that a written text does exist).
Within performances that contain this focus, however, there is one more mode of demarcation that will decide whether/how the pre- and post-events are scripted: whether or not the events take place "in world" i.e., as part of the theatrical world in which the perform-ance is set. Or, if they take place "out of world" i.e., as events that are entirely different from the world of the theatrical piece.	If the pre/post-forums are to be "in world"—where they take place as an extension of the environment in the central theatrical event itself—then it is likely that these processes will also need to be extensively present during the script writing process. The play-wright, in the desire the ensure continuity, would benefit from scripting these sections as part of the dramatic text itself. Consider here an example like *Detention*, where the pre-performance preparation that takes place for spect-actors is framed in such a way that it actually becomes a "teacher training"—a teacher training in which spect-actors are prepared for *Detention* not as their "real world" personalities, but as teachers. Since the adherence of this space to the rest of the theatrical context of *Detention* is incredibly important, scripting it in as much detail as I could, became necessary to include within the script itself.
There are, of course, those performance events that place their *entire focus on a particular process that has nothing to do with a central performance event* (especially in the realm of applied theater). I consider, here, forms of theater—like Theater of the Oppressed; theater games; theater therapy—in which workshop-esque processes are conducted with groups of participants. Each of these types of sessions are not predicated on the	In such efforts, what is more extensively scripted is what happens during the process itself—since the process is the product, and in so being, changes the role of text in the writing process. Whereas more "conventional" works might centralize text as dialogue, and text in immersive aesthetics (as in this book) might centralize text as scenario creation, text in theater work that has a process-only focus might be said to centralize the written word as

Focus	Implications
execution of a final performance, however, there is some "impact" that is desired—hence the conduct of the workshop itself. This impact could be the promotion of collaboration between participants; or the dramatic exploration of a context's social or political issues; or the manifestation of therapeutic outcomes.	the documentation of activities. Where activities are described extensively, sometimes including the reasoning behind that game's inclusion in the process' particular repertoire. Activity in such process-only work is something I see as being different from the scenarios in immersive theater, in that there is no real distinction between "out of world" and "in world" settings within that central process. The spectators and workshop facilitators are all, consciously, in the "real world"—they are not asked to take on a different personality/character for the workshop itself (not including their own desires to self-present or self-display aspects of themselves to their peers on the workshop).

Characterization and Structure

Finally, after *Detention* catalyzing a consideration of text, and *War* stimulating a consideration of pre- and post-performance events' role within scripted dramatic texts, *Immigration* led me to consider two additional aspects that demarcate immersive theater scripts (as in this book) from its more "conventional" counterparts. And both of these writing strategies worked toward a similar end—of embedding flexibility within the written text of each script.

The first strategy involved the use of archetypes, i.e., particular kinds of profiles that exist among individuals *within* the particular identity group that is being represented by spect-actors or actors and the inclusions of these archetypes served to add different layers of flexibility to the scripts. First, the use of archetypes hopes to give performers in *Detention, War,* and *Immigration* the space to create their own characters, within a specified matrix of identity markers that have emerged as being important through archival research and/or lived experience. The complementing of the profile archetypes with the character questionnaires was an additional element that was then used to further the space for performers to use their own imaginations and their own lived experiences in fleshing out their roles. While the use of archetypes in the character profiles of actors was so as to enable their active inclusion within the devised process of an applied theater project, this strategy when applied for spect-actors was seen as manifesting in two ways.

First, the frame created by the archetypal roles given to spect-actors was seen as being a tool to address the otherwise extreme novelty that they might face in the immersive world. Furthermore, the use of the archetypes suggests that more experienced spect-actors to immersive theater might also be able to "play"—not simplifying the experience for these individuals in any way; but rather, allowing them the flexibility to scale the difficulty of the immersive experience based on their individual comfort levels. The second way in which the use of archetypal profiles for spect-actors manifests vis-à-vis flexibility is via this strategy's creation of avenues for more open-ended learning outcomes to occur. This is to say that each archetype that frames a particular spect-actor's profile—especially in light of that individual's co-creative freedom to engage with various dimensions of the experience—is likely to allow for that person to have an individualized takeaway from their theatrical immersion.

The second writing strategy that allows for the creation of flexibility in the scripts is the use of fragmentation. Fragmentation in these immersive scripts, however, functions differently from the scattered texts that have come more famously come to represent fragmentation in the context of Postmodernism. As a result, fragmentation here might be better understood through the concept of "movement" (rather than "fracture," which is likely to be used when speaking of its more mainstream, Postmodern counterparts). In this approach, fragmentation can be understood as movements in the text between what actors are asked to do and what spect-actors are invited take on; as movements between the concrete actions that need to be undertaken by the production team so as to achieve the particular goals of the experience and the many malleable elements within those actions that can be reconceptualized and adapted to fit a very specific geographical context; textual movements that occur between scenarios that are hyper-realistic in some places and scenarios that have nothing to do with Realism, containing hues of the Absurd, in others. Fragmented flow in the scripts of *Detention, War,* and *Immigration* therefore functions as movements in the text: movements between sections that seek to address different constituents; different approaches; different realities; all of these differences which then interweave in intricate ways to create a flexible formal structure for the scripts themselves.

The Building Blocks

Speaking of structure, the reader might recall that, in the Introduction, I described how I went into the process of writing this book—with a particular structure of script components in mind—components that I thought would be present in each of the three scripts; components that I thought might be present in the same order as proposed in the Introduction. But, the outcomes of course, were quite different, as the reader can see in the table below that compares and contrasts my expectations before the process and the developments that occurred during the process itself:

Table 15: Script Structure Comparisons

Introduction	Detention	War	Immigration
Pre-Performance Preparation & Spect-actor/Actor Recruitment	The Setting	The Setting	The Setting
	The Characters	The Spect-actors' Characters & their Introduction to War	Before the experience
	Audience		
	Actors		The Spect-actors
Overview of Context & Scenario	The Character Questionnaires	Common Scenario 1 *Characters*	*Character Profiles and Variations*
Design Elements (Set, Costume, Lighting, Props, Sound, and Make Up)	The Framework	Scenarios 1 through 8	The Actors *Character Profiles and Variations*
	The Design	*Characters in each scenario*	
	The Breakdown	*Description of the scenario itself*	*Character questionnaires*
	Section 1: Parts 1 to 6		
Character descriptions for spect-actors and performers	*Section 2* *Section 3*	*Evolution of that particular scenario*	During the experience
Script Part 1 *Individual scenes with dialogues, followed by a suggested timeline of events. This part to the script will wrap up with a flowchart that graphically maps possible actions/ responses for the performer.*		Common Scenario 2 *Characters*	
		Post-performance	
Script Part 2 *If/Then matrices for how commonly anticipated responses for the spect-actors*			

Introduction	Detention	War	Immigration
might be dealt with in the context of the performance. This If/Then matrix should make evident to the potential director how they might use the tool as part of their training process for the performers.			
Post-performance debrief			

The immediate difference between what was expected vis-à-vis the script sections, and what emerged during the writing process, is with regards to the order of the components. I initially anticipated a specific structure (in the Introduction) as a result of the multidisciplinary examples that I looked at in the initial research process for this writing project, drawing from the realms of nursing education, tabletop role playing games, Live Action Role Plays (LARPs), and other kinds of scripted immersive environments.

In practice, however, when writing *Detention, War,* and *Immigration,* while most of the script components in the introductory proposal were main-tained in some way, the order was different in each script. Furthermore, two components—"Script Parts 1 and 2"—emerged as being completely different in the three scripts than what was anticipated in the Introduction. Eventually, I came to see the two-part division as an artificial demarcation between script sections that was not appropriate for the final scripts and their structures. In the process of writing the pieces in this book, therefore, I realized that I had initially fallen into the "trap" of framing these scripts, as I would have done with Realism-inspired text and as a result, expected to see the same replicable structure across plays. However, the structure of immersive theater's written texts, I came to realize, embodies the philosophies that underwrite the form—where everything "depends" on something else. Where spect-actors' charac-ters' portrayal depends on an individual commitment to their profiles. Where the lines spoken by actors, however much the performer and director might have scripted them, ultimately depends on interactions with the spect-actor's responses in the moment. Where elements of the design and framework depend on the context and the scale of the production in question.

This "depends on" format is what, ultimately, frames the written structure of the scripts in this book: where how the script is written depends on what the reader needs to know first, in order to make sense of what follows. This need for a constant interplay between the reader's understanding of possible actions in the current scenario, while also being aware of those actions' repercussions on evolutions of those scenarios, results in the need for a script structure that is unique every time it is used. Ultimately, therefore, there is no "order" that I can propose for a script that uses an immersive aesthetic as those in this book. What I can propose though (as in the Table below), are the components that these scripts are likely to be composed of—the specific order being entirely dependent on the piece in question.

Table 16: Proposed Immersive Theater Script Components

Immersive Theater Script

Pre-performance	*The Setting*	*Character Profiles for Actors*	*Character Profiles for Spect-actors and an Introduction*	*The Framework*	*Design Elements*	*Scenario Breakdown*	*Post-performance*
Any information that needs to be communicated before the central theatrical event	An introductory summary of the premise: who the spect-actors become; who the actors become; what the overarching goal might be.	Descriptions of the different characters that are available for actors to play Potential variations of each character profile Character questionnaires, where needed, to help with actors' characterization	Descriptions of the roles that are assigned to spect-actors Potential variations of each spect-actor character profile Information about the pre-performance workshop or preparation that happens "in world"	Notes on the duration of the experience Descriptions of how the pre- and post-performance work integrates with the central performance's objectives	Descriptions of the set, lighting, sound, props, and costume design	Detailed outlines of each scenario within the larger environment of the immersive world The way in which the scenarios are sectioned will depend on what best fits that script's structure. The breakdown could have different parts that are based on a specific character's narrative	Anything "in world" that needs to happen after the central theatrical event

Pre-performance	The Setting	Character Profiles for Actors	Character Profiles for Spect-actors and an Introduction	The Framework	Design Elements	Scenario Breakdown	Post-performance
						arc; or different temporal sections that walk the reader through a minute-by-minute occurrence timeline; or something else.	

By mixing and matching the abovementioned elements, I believe that most immersive theater texts—with an applied theater focus—will have most of their bases covered.

Throughout this book, I have included the disclaimer that my thoughts and proposals are relevant to a particular type of immersive theater—one in which the spect-actor is asked to step into the shoes of an Other; one that is applied in non-traditional contexts toward specific socio-political themes, and with particular pedagogical objectives. In wrapping up this book, therefore, I would like to reiterate the same disclaimer but also include a caveat. That while my approaches in this book, and the subsequent strategies that have been put forward for immersive theater practitioners might be particularly relevant to those who share my aesthetic and pedagogical ideals, I also believe that the ideas contained here could be useful to any immersive theater researcher/practitioner, even if they use different aesthetic and pedagogical principles in their use of these forms. Ultimately, any piece that considers itself to be less "conventional" in how it uses audience interaction; any piece that hinges its final execution on the unique qualities of particular spect-actors' participation; any theatrical genre that involves an approach in which audience members are not watching and listening from seats in front of a stage, is likely to find some of the proposals in this book to be relevant. Perhaps as strategies that might be adopted. Perhaps, as approaches that might *not* work as they are, but could be reimagined.

When I went into this writing project, it was to address the scarcity of immersive scripts that are available to practitioners who are interested in the form. And in the process of writing *Detention, War,* and *Immigration* I am reminded why there is this particular scarcity; why immersive theater texts are so hard to craft and as a result, share and replicate. That said, I hope that this book will serve to fill the current void just a little bit; that this book will soon become one of many to put forward texts and strategies to help artists create theatrical environments that are immersive and pedagogical; aesthetically evocative and politically provocative; simple and complex.

Notes

Introduction

1. In terms of my use of terminology in this book, "spect-actor" is the term I use to refer to this particular mode of spectatorship—where an individual is asked to become an Other; a character. When other terms like "spectator" or "audience member" are used, the form being referred to is seen as being distinctive from this particular aesthetic approach.

2. When I say "traditional," I use the term to allude to scripts that might fall under the broad genre of "Realism"—scripts that have strongly influenced the way in which a dramatic script is generally imagined: stage directions that describe the setting and actors' actions to varying levels of detail, well-defined characters that performers will take on, and dialogue between these characters. I realize, of course, that definitions of "traditional," "conventional," and "Realism" are up for debate and that my usage of such terms in this book might, in many instances, be overly simplistic. However, since entering into a debate about the nuances of these concepts is beyond the scope of this book, I intentionally refrain from doing so.

3. Spectator-participants to *Chemins* are asked to embody asylum seekers in the European Union (EU) through character profiles that are given to them at the beginning of the immersive experience. These character profiles document the narratives of real-life asylum seekers in the EU and with colored stickers placed on foreheads as crude markers of their race, spectator-participants are asked to undertake activities—like clearing immigration lines, fold-

ing laundry for extended periods of time, being attacked along the passageways of the performance space—as the character allocated to them. For the duration of *Chemins* therefore, each spectator undertakes an individual journey as an asylum seeker to the EU (Haedicke, 2002:102).

4. For more extensive theoretical analyses surrounding particular examples, the interested reader is invited to consult the array of materials that have been included in the Bibliography.

5. Where I use the term "role-play," I employ a hyphen. However, where the hyphen does not appear (i.e., "role play") it is because of the use of the term as such in the original source.

6. Where "Realism" is used to refer to the broad theatrical genre as rooted in the work of Henrik Ibsen and the like, I capitalize the term. In other instances, where "realism" is not used as theatrical vocabulary but as an adjective, it is not capitalized. The same rule operates for the use of other terms as well; terms like "Absurd" and "Postmodern."

7. Everything except the Pre-LARP Preparation section has been adapted from Stark, Nilsen & Lindahl (n.d.)

8. The main facilitator of a LARP is called a Game Master.

Detention

1. The actor and director are at liberty to decide how best to articulate a character's "stability." Does it refer to the financial background? Does it refer to the STUDENT's family history, and/or whether there is a history of incarceration in the STUDENT's

family? Does the term refer to the STU-DENT's psychological "wellness"?

2. An identity group that is referred to differently as eunuchs, transvestites, transsexuals, or transgendered individuals—a choice of terminology that is based on the particular person being referred to; a choice that is also based on the particularities of the person doing the referring.

War

1. A dot in the middle of the forehead, usually a red circle, traditionally painted on with vermillion, serving as a marker of a marriage-ready or married Hindu woman (whose husband is alive). Nowadays, *bindis* are most often stickers in various colors, shapes, and sizes worn by women regardless of their religious affiliation or marital status.

2. A streak of purified ash, worn by Hindus, after a prayer.

3. Traditional tunic and pants.

Bibliography

Agamben, G. 1999. *Remnants of Auschwitz: The Witness and the Archive.* New York: Zone Books.

Alexander, M. 2012. *The New Jim Crow: Mass Incarceration in the Age of Colorblindness.* The New Press.

Alston, A. 2016. *Beyond Immersive Theatre: Aesthetics, Politics and Productive Participation.* Basingstoke: Palgrave Macmillan.

Arendt, H. 1963. *Eichmann in Jerusalem: A report on the banality of evil.* New York: The Viking Press Inc.

Asian Centre for Human Rights. 2013. *India's Hell Holes: Child Sexual Assault in Juvenile Justice Homes.* Available: http://www.achrweb.org/reports/india/IndiasHellHoles2013.pdf [2017, August 27].

Back, J. 2014. *The Cutting Edge of Nordic Larp.* Denmark: Knutpunkt.

Boal, A. 1985. *Theatre of the Oppressed.* New York: Theatre Communications Group.

Boal, A. 2002. *Games for Actors and Non-Actors.* London: Routledge.

Bowman, S.L. 2010. *The Functions of Role-Playing Games: How Participants Create Community, Solve Problems and Explore Identity.* Jefferson, NC: McFarland.

Bowman, S.L., & Vanek, A. 2012. *Wyrd Con Companion Book.* California: Wyrd Con.

Cover, J.G. 2010. *The Creation of Narrative in Tabletop Role-Playing Games.* Jefferson, NC: McFarland.

Crimp, M. 1997. *Attempts on her Life.* Faber & Faber.

CUNY. 2015. *John Jay College of Criminal Justice.* Available: https://jjcompare.org/2015/04/10/india/ [2017, August 27].

Dinesh, N. 2015a. Delusions of singularity: aesthetics, discomfort and bewilderment in Kashmir. *Research in Drama Education: The Journal of Applied Theatre and Performance.* 20(1):62–73.

Dinesh, N. 2015b. *Grey Zones: Performances, Perspectives, and Possibilities in Kashmir.* Ph.D. Thesis. University of Cape Town.

Dinesh, N. 2016a. *Theatre & War: Notes from the Field.* Cambridge: Open Book Publishers.

Dinesh, N. 2016b. *Memos from a Theatre Lab: Exploring What Immersive Theatre 'Does.'* London: Routledge.

Dinesh, N. 2016c. Information for Foreigners: Chronicles from Kashmir. *Journal for Artistic Research.* 11. http://doi.org/10.22501/jar.233777.

Dinesh, N. 2017. *Scripting Detention: A Project in Theater and Autoethnography with Incarcerated Teens.* Jefferson, NC: McFarland.

Dinesh, N. 2018. *Memos from a Theatre Lab: Spaces, Relationships, & Immersive Theatre.* Delaware: Vernon Press.

Epstein, R., & Ormiston, M. 2007. *Drills, Dialogues, and Role Plays: Tools and Tips for Using ELT Materials—Web Only.* Available: https://www.press.umich.edu/pdf/0472032038-web.pdf [2017, August 26].

Foster, D., Haupt, P. & De Beer, M. 2005. *The Theatre of Violence: Narratives of Protagonists in the South African Conflict*. Oxford: James Currey Limited.

Frieze, J. 2016. *Reframing Immersive Theatre: The Politics and Pragmatics of Participatory Performance*. Basingstoke: Palgrave Macmillan.

Grotowski, J. 2002. *Towards a Poor Theatre*. London: Routledge.

Haedicke, S.C. 2002. The Politics of Participation: Un Voyage Pas Comme Les Autres Sur Les Chemins De'L Exil. *Theatre Topics*. 12(2): 99–118.

Harpin, A., & Nicholson, H. 2016. *Performance and Participation: Practices, Audiences, Politics*. Basingstoke: Palgrave Macmillan.

Hartjen, C., & Kethineni, S.1996. *Comparative delinquency: India and the United States*. New York: Garland Publishing

Hill, L., & Paris, H. 2014. *Performing Proximity: Curious Intimacies*. Palgrave Macmillan.

Kane, S. 2000. *4.48 Psychosis*. London: Bloomsbury Methuen Drama.

Kangas, K., Loponen, M., & Särkijärvi, J. 2016. *Larp Politics: Systems, Theory, and Gender in Action*. Ropecon ry.

Krohn, M.D., & Lane, J. 2015. *The Handbook of Juvenile Delinquency and Juvenile Justice*. Chichester: Wiley Blackwell.

Kurz, J., & Balzer, M. 2015. *Learning by Playing—Larp As a Teaching Method*. Available: https://nordiclarp.org/2015/03/04/learning-by-playing-larp-as-a-teaching-method/ [2017, August 26].

Levi, P. 1988. *The Drowned and the Saved*. London: Abacus.

MacDonald, J. 2012. *From Performing Arts to LARP*. Available: https://www.youtube.com/watch?v=TeCJX-OeJz8 [2017, August 27].

Machon, J. 2013. *Immersive Theatres: Intimacy and Immediacy in Contemporary Performance*. Palgrave Macmillan.

Magelssen, S. 2009. Rehearsing the "Warrior Ethos": "Theatre Immersion" and the Simulation of Theatres of War. *The Drama Review*. 53(1): 47–72.

Massoodi, A. 2015. *Inside a juvenile home*. Available: http://www.livemint.com/Leisure/X4DChvj7KCXVjegtttegBI/Inside-a-juvenile-home.html [2017, August 27].

Milgram, S. 1963. Behavioral Study of Obedience. *The Journal of Abnormal and Social Psychology*. 67(4): 371–378.

Modak, S. 2015. *Children Housed at Borstals Meant for Prisoners Over 18*. Available: https://mumbaimirror.indiatimes.com/others/sunday-read/Children-housed-at-Borstals-meant-for-prisoners-over-18/articleshow/50249330.cms [2017, August 26].

Montgomery College. *Nursing Simulation Scenario Library*. Available: https://cms.montgomerycollege.edu/nursingsims/ [2017, August 26].

Perry, G. 2013. *Behind the Shock Machine: The Untold Story of the Notorious Milgram Psychology Experiments*. New York & London: The New Press.

Peters, W. 1987. *A Class Divided, Then and Now, Expanded Edition*. New Haven: Yale University Press.

Punchdrunk. 2011. *Sleep No More*. Performance. London, UK.

Red Cross. n.d. *In Exile for a While: A Refugee's Experience for Canadian Youth*. Canadian Red Cross.

Sabin, P. 2012. *Simulating War: Studying Conflict through Simulation Games*. New York: Continuum International Publishing Group.

Saitta, E., Holm-Andersen, M., & Back, J. 2014. *The Foundation Stone of Nordic Larp*. Denmark: Knutpunkt.

Shaughnessy, N. 2012. *Applying Performance: Live Art, Socially Engaged Theatre and Affective Practice*. London: Palgrave Macmillan.

Sherrin, D. 2016. *The Classes They Remember: Using Role-Plays to Bring Social Studies and English to Life*. New York: Routledge.

Simkins, D. 2015. *The Arts of Larp: Design, Literacy, Learning and Community in Live-Action Role Play*. North Carolina: McFarland.

Spolin, V. 1999. *Improvisation for the Theater: A Handbook of Teaching and Directing Techniques.* Northwestern University Press.

Srivastava, D. 2016. *Understaffed and overcrowded, juvenile homes are hell holes rather than reform centres.* Available: http://www.firstpost.com/living/understaffed-and-overcrowded-juvenile-homes-are-hell-holes-rather-than-reform-centres-2842894.html [2017, August 27].

Stark, L., Nilsen, E., & Lindahl, T.L. n.d. *Writing a larp script.* Available: http://larpfactory-bookproject.blogspot.com/p/writing-larp-script-how-to-describe.html [2017, August 26].

Stenros, J., & Montola, M. 2010. *Nordic LARP.* Stockholm: Fëa Livia.

Tresca, M.J. 2011. *The Evolution of Fantasy Role-Playing Games.* Jefferson, NC: McFarland.

UHC Collective. 2003. *This Is Camp X-Ray.* Performance. Manchester, UK.

Vermeal, M. n.d. *This Is Not Just a Drill* Available: https://www.nols.edu/media/filer_public/5c/8c/5c8c9b97–9fe1–42a8-ae02–73dd378f0bec/this_is_not_just_a_drill-handout.pdf [2017, August 26].

White, G. 2013. *Audience Participation in Theatre: Aesthetics of the Invitation.* Basingstoke: Palgrave Macmillan.

Zimbardo, P. 1971. *The Stanford Prison Experiment: A Simulation Study of the Psychology of Imprisonment.* Stanford University, Stanford Digital Repository.

Zimbardo, P. 2007. *The Lucifer Effect: Understanding How Good People Turn Evil.* New York: Random House.

Index